THE NEW SUPERIOR

D1602898

THE NEW
SUPERIOR

a better way to be the one in charge

JOHN M. COLLINS

Critical Victories, LLC

www.criticalvictories.com
(517) 803-4063

For information and permission requests, please contact Critical Victories, LLC at: office@criticalvictories.com or visit www.criticalvictories.com.

Minor revisions and updates are included in the soft-cover edition of this book, which will differ only slightly from the original hard-cover and ebook versions.

This book is also available in an unabridged audio format, narrated by Michael Chamberlain. Please visit www.thenewsuperior.com.

The author of this book is available for speaking engagements, interviews, and other public appearances. Please contact the author for information at: office@criticalvictories.com or (517) 803-4063.

Manufactured in the United States of America. Written by John M. Collins.

ISBN: 979-8-35091-424-5 (softcover)

ISBN: 978-1-66784-825-9 (hardcover)

ISBN: 978-1-66784-826-6 (ebook)

In loving memory of a superior man,

Kevin Collins

Contents

Author's Note

This book is a journey, a journey to understand what brings out the best and worst of a team. It is a book about leadership but not like others you may have read before. At times you will find that it takes on the feel of a memoir. This is intentional because the lessons of this book were drawn from unique experiences that taught me what effective leadership is really about, especially when the stakes are high. But these experiences also placed me face to face with what I know to be the devil that waits in the shadows to sabotage you and your efforts to be an effective leader. My goal is to help you sweep this devil away in a sustained and powerful gust of insights and strategies in which he is both ill-equipped and unprepared to keep his footing. When he is finally lost in the torrent of new possibilities and new ways of thinking about the relationships between leaders and their followers, you will find that you can more effectively and naturally optimize the conditions in which you and your team function each day. My task, however, is not an easy one because this devil has been around a very long time and, like an unruly seagull at the beach, he seems to show up whenever people are willing to feed him.

Our journey will begin thousands of miles away across oceans and deserts in a land I've never visited, beside a young girl I've never met. It is here that we will witness the devil inflict the worst of his evils. I want you to make his acquaintance during this darkest of moments so you can appreciate the range of atrocities that he is capable of inflicting. At first, you may be tempted to believe that this was an isolated incident having little or no relevance to you personally. But as I guide you through the pages of this book, I hope to convince you that this devil is a strangling presence in your life and mine, one with which teams, organizations, families, and communities in every corner of the world must contend if they are to function at their best. Yet experience seems to confirm that a shocking number of people have neither the will nor the interest to put forth a resistance of even marginal strength. As a result, the devil seems always to have a place where he can practice his malevolent craft in safety and solitude.

The most challenging aspect of writing this book was the inclusion of my own personal memories in a way that both complements and emphasizes the greater messages I seek to convey. As an author, it is quite tempting to sell my own professional soul to the aforementioned devil by making my own story a prominent feature of this book. I've done my best not to fall into this trap and I hope that you, my reader, will view me not as your teacher but as a fellow student and trusted partner on this journey of ours toward greater personal and professional success.

Every aspect of this book is based solely on my own recollections, interpretations, and research and should therefore be construed as my opinion. Having written two textbooks prior to beginning this current work, I remain aware of the important differences between scholarly and conversational writing. I'm under no illusions that this work meets the literary standards of the former, but I also know that few scholarly works can match the impact of a well-told story, especially when that story helps to bring the reader's own priorities into sharper focus.

As you will discover and probably expect, it was necessary for me to mention certain people such as clients and former associates whose identities I disguised because protecting their privacy is a moral and ethical necessity. At other times I've mentioned people whose names and affiliations are a matter of public record. Either way, I ask you to refrain from passing judgement on these individuals, whether positive or negative, and instead learn from them as I've described them. They are human beings like you and me, and like you and me they are on their own personal journeys that will hopefully lead them toward greater clarity, achievement, and peace-of-mind in this life. This is what I want for you, too.

PART 1

NATURE OF THE THREAT

"Somebodies who can't get down off their pedestals turn into statues."

Robert W. Fuller
Somebodies and Nobodies: Overcoming the Abuse of Rank
New Society Publishers, 2003

INTRODUCTION

A Choice to Be Made

Malala was only fifteen years old. After boarding the bus that would bring her home from school, she took her seat and bantered with classmates about the exam they had just taken and perhaps the homework to be completed before the day's end. Education was more than just important to Malala; it was in her blood. Her father was an executive administrator for a learning institution in the city while her grandfather was a high school theology teacher. When Malala was but a mere toddler her father would bring her to his school where she would pretend to teach, waving her arms and babbling incoherent baby noises because she hadn't learned to talk yet. Even now as a teenager, Malala still cared deeply about school and enjoyed the company of other kids who appreciated the liberating power of learning as much as she did.

Malala, however, was not an ordinary teenager, and the 9th of October 2012 would not be an ordinary day. She was the primary target of an armed gunman who stopped her bus as it proceeded along its route. Boarding the bus, a menacing bearded man scanned the faces of the children. Malala knew exactly who the man was and why he was there. As he barked out her name, she looked up and stared him directly in the eyes. He recognized her and Malala knew it. Crippled by fear, she gripped her friend's hand so tight that her friend would later report that it still hurt days later. The man found what he was looking for. Time stood still.

The bullet that penetrated Malala's skull arrived before the sound of the gunshot, ripping a hole in her left temple, grazing her eye, lacerating her facial nerve, collapsing her left eardrum, and breaking her jaw before exiting the back of her head and lodging into her shoulder. Unconscious, she slumped into her friend's lap. High-velocity blood-spatter stained the white walls of the bus as the shooter fled the scene.

According to a report by *The Guardian*, the motive for killing Malala Yousafzai was recounted by a spokesman for the Taliban who complained that "the teenager's work had been an 'obscenity' that needed to be stopped."

The so-called obscenity for which Malala was targeted was her demand that her right to an education be respected. Living in the beautiful Swat Valley of northwest Pakistan, her community was overrun by a Taliban insurgency that, among its many atrocities, banned girls from attending school with promises of killing them if they disobeyed. A campaign by the Pakistani army to drive the Taliban out of the valley was underway and young Malala sought to support the campaign by attracting attention to what the Taliban were doing to her people.

So, she began writing a blog hosted by the British Broadcasting Company that attracted an international following. She told the story of how the Taliban burned down schools for girls and sought to bolster its own power and twisted ideology by accelerating the socioeconomic wasting of women who might otherwise pose an intellectual threat if permitted access to an education. Malala stood in their way and even had the audacity to express her intent to create her own political party and a school for marginalized girls in the valley. For both her courage and her efforts, 14-year-old Malala was nominated for the International Children's Peace Prize in 2011. When she did not win, Pakistan's Prime

Minister awarded her with what would become the country's first National Peace Award.

Sitting on the bus on that fateful day, Malala knew the Taliban had found her and that her days of political activism and her life were probably over. Fortunately, they were not. Malala survived the attack and went on to become an international advocate for those she described as "the forgotten children who want an education." At the age of 17, still recovering from the lasting effects of her wounds, Malala was awarded the 2014 Nobel Peace Prize, becoming the youngest recipient in the award's history.

A Reason to Lead

The story of Malala Yousafzai is more than just a story about political will or the courage to stare down a barbarian. Her story is one about leadership and it began long before a psychopath boarded her bus and barked out her name. As the greatest of leaders do, she cared about something so much that it recalibrated her sense of self. In her own mind she was far more than just a young girl from the Swat Valley. She was a champion for the right of young girls to become educated, and she was a formidable enemy to anyone who might attempt to violate this right. One who sees herself as just a young girl will have neither the strength nor courage to take on a foe as intimidating as the Taliban. On the other hand, one who sees herself as an international champion of girls' rights will, in fact, have the necessary strength and courage. When the moment requires it, she will find herself empowered by the primordial inspirations that are reserved exclusively for people having a purpose. Leadership is the act of protecting a purpose. In the absence of purpose, there can be no leadership.

Purpose, therefore, is the distinguishing trait of effective leadership, and this purpose must be sufficiently compelling to inspire individuals to set aside personal ambitions in the service of a greater cause. Too often, however, leadership is misunderstood. It is mistaken for a symbol of status when in fact it is a symbol of being trusted with the execution of purposeful action. As we learn from the story of Malala, true leadership emerges naturally when purpose is threatened by circumstance in the presence of a champion. Purpose is the treasure and leadership its guardian. For you to be known or perceived as an effective leader, you must be willing and able to champion a compelling purpose in the presence of a significant threat. If the purpose or threat are not clear to people, they will lack the inspiration needed to fully engage. It then becomes your responsibility to create clarity where clarity is needed. That's what leaders do.

A Matter of Intention

Leadership is challenging because the blending of these ingredients does not come naturally. If it did, everyone would do it and everyone would be good at it. We wouldn't need the countless leadership books that have been written, leadership podcasts that are hosted, leadership videos on YouTube, and leadership workshops being taught. And I would go so far as to say that leadership is not even something you can consciously create; it can only be perceived. When it *is* perceived, it tends to originate from rather imperfect, flawed human beings who made the right decisions, said the right things, and executed the right strategies at the right time. They are not trying to be great leaders; they are trying to be great people faced with a great opportunity to handle a situation of great importance.

Opportunities to perceive competent leadership, unfortunately, are quite rare. And there seems to be two fundamental reasons why. The first is because so few people can pull it off. They are eager to hold the titles of leadership but can't seem to meet its responsibilities. The second is because leadership does not occur naturally in the human species. Quite the opposite, leadership is an *unnatural* phenomenon the defies the predictions of how animals, including humans, should behave when living, playing, or working together in groups.

That leadership is both rare and unnatural may or may not ring true to you personally. After all, you may know or observe people in your life you would describe as having natural leadership abilities. You get the feeling there's something they are born with – something special that equips them to be confident, assertive, and influential. They motivate people. They inspire people. They get things done.

That which you so appreciate, however, is *not* natural, it's intentional. What does, in fact, come naturally to human beings and other species is the sorting of themselves into hierarchies. Within these hierarchies, some individuals are naturally wired to assume roles of dominance while others naturally subordinate themselves. Dominance and subordination are like two sides of a biological coin; you can't have just one. Dominators, like the Taliban, have a sharp instinct for asserting control over others in a group. Subordinators, on the other hand, accommodate this dominance by signaling their willingness to conform. Once the relationships among dominators and subordinators have stabilized and all know their place, we have a hierarchy. When these relationships are not stable or when individuals are competing for control or prominence in a group, there is conflict.

So, while dominance occurs naturally among human beings, dominance is not the same as leadership. And just as hierarchies arise naturally among people who've assembled themselves into groups, a hierarchy is not necessarily a team. In a professional environment such as a private business or government agency, creating a hierarchy is rather easy because it comes so naturally. We're pretty good at that. We can identify decision-makers and contributors and create clear lines of reporting that govern how information is communicated and in what order people are permitted to make consequential decisions. But functioning as a *team* does not come so easily because the leadership necessary to unite and energize its members does not come naturally either. There are many hierarchies in today's workforce who think they are a team, just as there are many dominators who think they are leaders. But the goals, aspirations, and expectations placed on today's hierarchies by their many clients, customers, and stakeholders require degrees of effectiveness and competitiveness that only *teams* can produce and that only *leaders* can inspire.

Entitled Management

In my own professional experience, most would-be leaders do not fail because of a lack of ability or knowledge. They fail because they confuse dominance with leadership and hierarchies with teams. In doing so, they fall prey to the dominator's delusion, mistaking fundamental truths about successful leadership as being threats to the fundamental truths they wish to believe about themselves. This is to say that, as dominators, they want to believe their roles as managers make them special, anointing them with magical powers worthy of worship. Dominators need to feel dominant, and when they use their power to self-medicate in this way, they can display a troubling pattern of behaviors that cause their followers to lose trust and confidence in them. The result is a cascading series of foibles that strip teams of those characteristics that distinguish them from mere hierarchies. They become ineffective. Worse, there are very talented and ambitious people out there – in all walks of life and career – who want the power of leadership but have no desire to use it in the service of others. When they are promoted into positions of management, they advance an outdated, out-of-style, and corrosive approach to leadership that will eventually tear apart even the most cohesive teams.

Old School. This entitled approach to influencing others is alive and well mainly because it's so natural and because its advocates believe they've somehow earned the right to use it. They also feel like it works, and it often does. When they ask for something to be done it usually gets done. If it doesn't, they can exact consequences on the offending subordinates. These consequences may be active or passive, subtle or obvious, immediate or delayed, mild or severe. Whatever they are, avoiding those consequences becomes a central source of motivation for subordinate employees. They do what they're told by their managers to keep their managers happy – to steer clear of trouble. They perform because they're afraid not to, so they allow themselves to be controlled and compelled, to be dominated. If they behave or perform in such a way that deprives their managers of their pathological need to feel dominant, the professional lives of these employees will become painful and frustrating. They learn to find solace in playing the role of the dutiful *inferior*, clearing the way for each dysfunctional manager to assume what he believes is his rightful place as the *superior*.

In the role of the superior, some managers are vulnerable to the onset of a genuine superiority complex. Such is the belief that one's power to control and compel others is a right to which she is entitled. In the worst instances, she will view her span of control as a sort of kingdom in which she demands that her superiority be honored and celebrated. But eventually something interesting happens. *Entitled* managers are so distracted by their need to preserve their feelings of superiority that they neglect their teams and stakeholders. As a result, there is a measurable and noticeable decline in team performance which is usually preceded by very subtle declines that are quite *im*measurable and *un*noticeable to those dysfunctional managers who are blinded by the fog of their own entitlement. When it comes time to be held accountable for their teams' underperformance, managers with a superiority complex cannot bring themselves to believe or admit that it's their fault. So, they pass blame onto their people or onto circumstances they argue are out of their control, and they can be remarkably convincing in their efforts to do so.

One might hope that the upper authorities to whom these entitled heads-of-hierarchy report would recognize who's actually to blame – that it's the fault of the entitled and their inability to manage their teams effectively. But here's what often happens in scenarios such as this. Those same authorities are distracted by their own superiority complexes and their own sense of entitlement. They see within the failing managers that which lives within themselves, and they are unwilling to punish attitudes and ways of managing people to which they are accustomed. Consequently, those responsible for acting decisively to correct the dysfunction are quick to excuse it. With enough time, the internal dysfunction will reach a point where an egregious error is made that destroys the reputation of a once-respected team or where a catastrophic failure paralyzes an entire business. Even still, the entitled managers may never be exposed for the damage they caused. Good people will step forward to fix the problem, a new normal will somehow arise, life will carry on, and a new team with new talent will rise to prominence – that is, of course, until another entitled manager with a superiority complex finds his way to the top.

Rooted in History. Entitled management and the superiority complexes that arise from it have deep roots in the history of professional hierarchies, especially in the days when access to information and the ability to gather and analyze business data were far less sophisticated than they are now. It doesn't take a particularly gifted administrator, for example, to keep machines running on the floor of a manufacturing plant. Nor is the performance of the machines' operators likely to decline significantly just because their manager has a superiority complex. But in a contemporary, high-stakes, high-pressure professional environment, employees rely on communication, collaboration, and an impressive wealth of knowledge, skill, and expertise to do their jobs. Their performance, therefore, is far more sensitive to fluctuations in leadership styles. In these environments, entitled managers with a superiority complex have devastating effects on how people perform. And because today's employees have options for where to take their talents and loyalty, they will exercise these options when they feel that entitled managers are eroding the quality of their professional lives.

Back in the day, it was reasonable to feel and act superior if you were the person who was in control or could compel people to do what you wanted them to do. It was also reasonable to think of yourself as being better than everyone else because *you* were the one rewarded with a position that gave you more responsibility and higher compensation – a position that bestowed upon you the power to control and compel others. Nobody really cared if you used your authority to inspire or motivate people. You were simply expected to use your authority to make sure people did what they were being paid to do. That's how leadership was defined. As a result, it was also reasonable for employees to feel inferior because they had so few options available to them.

During the Great Depression and the years that followed, work was so hard to come by, workers were willing to take on very dangerous jobs despite a stunning lack of safety precautions, at least by today's standards. During the 13 months of construction on the Empire State Building, five workers died – although some unofficial reports estimate a higher toll. During construction of the Golden Gate Bridge, eleven workers lost their lives. The construction of the Hoover Dam claimed the lives of 96 workers. But these risks were tolerable when compared to the prospect of hunger and homelessness.

And speaking of having no options, World War II reinforced the rigidity of military command structures in which soldiers were not free to quit their jobs. They were compelled to serve regardless of who was leading them. When the war ended and the world's major economies began to recover and eventually grow, the command-and-control mentality of military leadership endured in the many new businesses that were born and matured in the decades following the war. Organizational structures were created to look like those of the military, positioning certain people with decision-making authority so they could maintain control of subordinates beneath them while being controlled by the superiors above them. If for some reason a person working within this structure did not adhere to its standing procedures or failed to follow a clear direction given by a superior, that person was accused of being *insubordinate*, which was punishable by any number of disciplinary options available to the superiors. And the superiors certainly took advantage of the pull they had on these organizational levers, allowing them to preserve and strengthen their existing power even as their organizations grew.

The *old superior*, a term to which I will refer often in this book, is a perception of leadership power as being a sort of blessing, a blessing granted to a presumably deserving recipient who then demands that his power be respected and that his directions be followed, or else. This way of thinking is alive and well in many organizations throughout the world and on many teams having customers and stakeholders whose well-being depends on a better approach. But there's an underlying fatal flaw in those styles of leadership that rely on the old superior as a model with which to control and compel people. This is to say that the old superior has clear and identifiable limits to how much it's able to accomplish, how many opportunities it's able to leverage, and the complexity of the threats it's able to mitigate. The old superior derives its strength from fear and manipulation, and people motivated by fear and manipulation are unable to sustain high levels of performance and competitiveness over long periods of time. Teams that rely on the old superior as their fuel for motivation will eventually succumb to the various forms of decay, both personal and cultural, that entitled leaders are doomed to accelerate.

Entrusted Leadership

There comes a magical point in time when it's realized that the success of a team, a community, and even a society depends on the contributions of people who are inspired. It is then that the old superior becomes as outdated and awkward as a thinning hair comb-over. When it's clearly understood that people function with greater ease, effectiveness, and commitment when empowered by *entrusted* leaders – leaders who feel a strong sense of responsibility for the well-being of their teams – then entitled management collapses under the weight of its own inefficiencies. It evaporates in the team's heightened awareness of the opportunities to which entitled leaders are chronically blind.

Two endearing qualities of entrusted leaders are worth mentioning because it's not always easy to explain or understand what entrusted leadership means and how it's executed. First, entrusted leaders have the confidence and sense of purpose needed to shun the old superior and the empty promises it likes to heap on those who conform to its rules. In doing so, entrusted leaders expose themselves to considerable risk. Second, entrusted leaders don't try to manage people because they know it's an illusion to think they can. They chuckle at the notions of entitled managers who believe that things are only done when they demand that they be done. As entrusted leaders appreciate, people manage *themselves*.

Even when given a direct order by an entitled manager, an employee will follow the order by her own choice once she's decided the consequences of following the order are more favorable than not. The entrusted leader knows the employee was never being managed by the leader; she was managing herself. Giving orders is the cheater's way of influencing people.

The implications of this are quite significant. An entrusted approach to leadership focuses not on the management of *people* but on the optimization of *conditions,* such that people can manage themselves with more effectiveness. This, of course, requires the exercise of some actual managerial talent and leadership capability. Entrusted leadership requires more expertise, more effort, and more vigilance, which is why entitled management has such allure. When leaders make the time and effort to focus on the conditions in which their people are working, their people will feel entrusted with their own sense of responsibility for taking advantage of these optimized conditions in a way that manifests their best efforts.

An employee who is being managed by someone else is an employee who has less incentive to manage himself. The employee who feels controlled by her manager is an employee with less incentive to control herself. The only way to bring the best out of the members of a team is to first ensure that trustworthy, qualified individuals are recruited to join the team. Then, these team members must be trusted to develop and demonstrate their capabilities. The result is being afforded the opportunities they will need to build their own confidence. It becomes the responsibility of their managers to continuously monitor workplace conditions and make improvements when opportunities to do so present themselves. To be an entrusted leader is to care about all the factors influencing how people perform, understanding that people decide for themselves what they will do, how they will do it, and when they will do it. To be an entrusted leader is to be dissatisfied with functioning as a hierarchy. An entrusted leader empowers people to function as a team, and in doing so, willingly accepts stewardship of the greater purpose for which the team exists.

There are dire consequences to *entitled* management and significant benefits to *entrusted* leadership. All that remains, then, is a choice between the two – the choice to be the champion who protects a compelling purpose from its natural threats, or an impediment standing in the way of people striving to function as a team. To choose the latter is to breathe life into the beast that destroys a team faster than anything else: the *old superior*.

Chapter 1

They All Looked So Impressive

It was the morning of September 19, 2013, as I stood at the front of a long, narrow room within the Rayburn House Office Building in Washington, DC. Flanking the south grounds of the United States Capitol, the Rayburn Building accommodates the working congressional offices of the U.S. House of Representatives. At its main point of entry on Independence Avenue, our invited guests made their way through the building's security checkpoint before navigating the tunnel-like corridors leading to our meeting room. Another 400 attendees prepared to watch from their remote locations, connected through a live video feed being managed and monitored by our technical support staff. A contingent of international viewers joined us from Cambodia, Canada, the Cayman Islands, the Czech Republic, Italy, Nigeria, Pakistan, Sudan, and the United Kingdom.

Behind me, a small but influential panel of experts took their seats as they exchanged pleasantries and prepared themselves for the sensitive and potentially controversial discussions to unfold in just a few moments. As thought-leaders on the subject of criminal sexual violence, they represented law enforcement, victim-advocacy groups, academia, research, healthcare, and forensic science. If all went well, a vigorous but informative conversation would be had about a public emergency now gripping authorities at the federal, state, and local levels of government. But if things went sideways, the proceedings might devolve into a bitter shouting match that would overtake our agenda and prevent our experts from sharing their wealth of knowledge. As the event's moderator, I could only do so much if ideological grandstanding or strong personal reactions boiled out of control.

Like the panelists behind me, my own expertise in the investigation of criminal sexual violence came from experience. As the Director of the Forensic Science Division of the Michigan State Police, I once led a team that conceptualized, designed, and implemented a special laboratory unit near Detroit aimed at streamlining the analysis of sexual assault evidence. The decision to create this unit, a unit that later won a prestigious award from the International Association of Chiefs of Police, was a bold but necessary step toward cleaning up a historic mess that, just a few years earlier, brought national embarrassment to the city of Detroit and the entire state of Michigan.

The Rape Kit Stockpile

The crisis erupted in 2009 when authorities discovered approximately 11,000 sexual-assault evidence kits languishing in a makeshift storage area managed by the Detroit Police Department. Known as *rape kits*, these packages contained forensic evidence collected directly from rape victims by specially trained medical personnel. Of the kits discovered in Detroit, most were never tested by a forensic science laboratory, inflaming public perceptions that dismissive police investigators tossed the kits aside with little interest in seeking justice for the victims.

Shortly after being hired by the Michigan State Police, I began working closely with other officials within my agency, as well as officials within the office of the Wayne County Prosecutor, the Detroit Police Department, and Michigan State University. It was our job to review and inventory each rape kit to determine both its significance and what should be done with it.

Before long, we learned that over many years detectives made an alarming habit of making snap judgements about complaints brought forward by women reporting to have been sexually assaulted. In too many instances, victims were treated with disrespect, not taken seriously, or prematurely judged to be lying or exaggerating their stories. As a result, investigators often failed to initiate reasonable investigative inquiries thereby reducing the chance that perpetrators could be brought to justice.

It was not only the stockpile of rape kits that enraged survivors of sexual assault and their advocates across the country. It was also the appearance that police officers harbored troubling attitudes of apathy and cynicism when it came to survivors of sexual violence and their families. The rape kit stockpile was a prominent symptom of an underlying disease in need of treatment.

A National Problem. Unfortunately, Detroit was but one of several major cities afflicted by the same crisis. Writing for the Washington Post on the 20th of February 2018 in a retrospective article titled, *A Wrenching Dilemma*, Jessica Contrera reported on the scale and scope of the problem. "In New York City, an estimated 17,000 kits went untested. In Houston, there were 6,000. In Detroit, Los Angeles, and Memphis, there were more than 11,000 each." A true national crisis had emerged, prompting sweeping demands for reform in how authorities responded to complaints of sexual violence.

Now gathered in such hallowed halls of American government, it was the perfect opportunity to shed light on why these problems occurred and how they could be prevented. Assembling an elite panel of experts and asking them the right questions in the right way could elicit insights that might help us to improve how sexual assaults are investigated in the United States and, hopefully, prevent them from happening in the first place.

The Boys on Base. Glancing casually at my watch, I could feel the nervous tension building in my belly. Now less than five minutes from our scheduled start time, I turned back to the panelists to confirm they were in place and ready. My technical team flashed me a confident thumbs-up, letting me know the online video feed was live and streaming without interruption. A quick audio-check confirmed my microphone was operational and pushing my audio signal to those watching and listening through the webcast. Those still mingling about the room would be asked to take their seats, after which I would make some opening statements and introduce our panelists.

Taking my position behind the lectern, I smiled at the audience to signal my intent to get started. My smile, however, quickly gave way to a look of surprise when I noticed that a contingent of high-level, fully uniformed military officials had joined us for the event. In the hubbub of my anxious preparation, I entirely missed their arrival.

Decorated with what seemed like more ornaments than a Christmas tree, they sat rigidly but attentively in their seats with their arms resting on their legs and their eyes gazing at me with a look of impatient demand. Their formality did not intimidate me – at least I don't think it did – but I was struck by the optics of it all. They looked special. They acted special. And, in many respects, they *were* special. These were the defenders of our freedom, disciplined and proud. Yeah, that seemed pretty special to me. But I also knew why they were there; they were not special enough to prevent a dangerous and embarrassing situation of their own, one playing out at military bases at home and around the world.

Looming on the horizon was a bombshell to be released by the U.S. Commission on Civil Rights titled, *Sexual Assault in the Military*, a comprehensive report measuring the number of official complaints of sexual assault within the ranks. When finally made public, it would reveal that reports of sexual assault rose from 1,700 in 2004 to over 3,000 in 2012. By the end of 2013, the total number of complaints would rise to over 5,000.

The significant increase in victim complaints enraged members of Congress and advocacy groups who blamed the previous under-reporting by victims on a lack of trust in the military's leadership and its apparent unwillingness to administer justice to perpetrators. So just as the rape kit crisis exploded in the faces of police commanders in major cities across the United States, their counterparts in the U.S. military were now under fire for the shocking rise in predatory sexual behaviors and failing to address the problem with due diligence.

So, what the hell was going on? Certainly, this was not the question with which I wanted to open our discussion at the Rayburn Building, but I really wanted to know just the same. I could only presume that everyone in attendance, including the military commanders who joined us that day, knew that the current state of affairs was unacceptable and wanted to be part of the solution. I could feel it, and I could see it. My job was to help them.

The Successful Disappointment

As it turned out, the event lived up to its billing, celebrated for its engaging conversation, the formulation of new ideas and recommendations, the sharing of emerging best-practices, and a heightened resolve to rethink our understanding of sexual violence and how it can be prevented and investigated more competently. Our panelists were masterful in how they engaged the issues, able to assert their professional authority with both warmth and compassion. Even attendees representing groups fighting for women's and victim's rights were pleased with the depth and quality of the conversation. Their validation gave me a much-appreciated feeling of relief.

As daytime folded into night, I flew back to Detroit and made the 90-minute drive back to my home near Lansing. I threw on a pair of jeans, plopped down in my favorite chair, and reflected on what took place that day. I was beyond grateful and relieved that those in attendance felt more informed about the serious issues surrounding sexual violence and its many horrific consequences. For some reason, however, a nagging sense of disappointment washed over me – a feeling that something important and relevant to our conversation had somehow been ignored. I couldn't put my finger on it, but it bothered me to my core and would continue to bother me for years to come. The more I contemplated the matter the more I resigned myself to a painful reality. We had identified ways to respond more effectively when a sexual assault occurs. *How nice for the victims.* But we failed to expose the root cause of this public crisis that was gripping the Department of Defense, the Detroit Police Department, and so many other law enforcement agencies confronted by their past ineffectiveness in responding to sexual violence. But what was it? What did we miss? What did *I* miss?

In the years since our gathering at the Rayburn Building, I've often recalled those military commanders who sat before me. With the benefit of hindsight, I've come to realize that those commanders had something remarkable in common with the police chiefs and sheriffs who were struggling to right their agencies' past wrongs in how victims of sexual violence had been treated. That *remarkable something* is that all of them worked and operated in rigid organizational cultures where rank means everything and tends to regulate how people are treated.

Rank and Abuse

In strict rank-and-file organizational cultures, rank is held in ceremonious regard mainly because it establishes the perks and benefits to which people are entitled, the basic respect and courtesies they are afforded, and the degree to which their opinions and suggestions are given serious consideration. Said another way, in these kinds of cultures, respectful treatment is often distributed not as a basic human courtesy, but as a benefit that must be earned. When the eventual toxicity becomes too much, an organization's obsession with rank can give rise to a chronic dehumanization of people that eventually destroys the integrity and effectiveness of its workforce.

Having worked for 20 years as either a non-sworn, civilian scientist or executive administrator in forensic science laboratories, all of which were operated by and within law enforcement agencies, I frequently observed and experienced this phenomenon first-hand. Now as an executive coach working in private practice, I've spent many years working directly with clients in a variety of occupations and organizations, some with very intense rank-and-file cultures and some with more collaborative, accountability-based cultures. What I know from direct experience is this: My clients who work in cultures where a person's rank is celebrated as a prized possession are far more likely to have witnessed or suffered some form of abuse, mistreatment, or marginalization.

During one recent engagement in which I facilitated a leadership development workshop on the subject of ethics, I learned of a major-city police department whose sworn officers habitually referred to their agency's non-sworn, civilian employees as *FCs*. The *C* stands for civilian. I'll let you guess what the *F* stands for.

In such cultures, the degree of mutual courtesy and respect that individuals experience in their interpersonal exchanges may depend heavily on their rank when compared to the ranks of others with whom they are communicating. For example, a police captain may be treated with far more respect and courtesy than a lieutenant. A university professor with a doctorate degree may expect greater deference than would be paid to a part-time adjunct instructor who boasts only a master's degree. A hospital neurosurgeon may feel justified in being rude to nurses because, after all, *they're just nurses*.

Hopefully it's not a stretch to see how these poisonous cultural dynamics relate to the controversies surrounding the investigation of sexual violence. The true problem plaguing the police and military was not a lack of knowledge or ability in how they investigated sexual violence. It was a problem of *rank*. In those stubbornly rigid rank-and-file cultures where people have to earn their honorable treatment by achieving the requisite rank, it stands to reason that women will be vulnerable to being *outranked* by men. Police investigators and military commanders who failed in their responsibilities were, in my opinion, incapacitated by their careless and discriminating organizational cultures. Whether consciously or subconsciously, they were conditioned to discount the value of women and therefore failed to acknowledge the legitimacy of victim complaints. Then, the physical evidence collected in association with their respective crimes was neglected with shocking frequency. To make matters worse, many of these female victims were black and poor, sometimes prostitutes, pushing them even further down the social ranks where their credibility and perceived worth were at risk of being discounted even more. At military bases around the world, in much the same way, commanders were accused of tolerating the sexual abuse and assault of female soldiers at the hands of male soldiers who probably saw themselves as superior and therefore justified in their actions. *Boys will be boys.*

Those of us who reflexively perpetuate the institutionalized ordering of human affairs that we call rank do so for three important reasons. First, we've been conditioned by our environments to equate rank with personal worth. Second, we regard the rank we've attained as something earned, therefore we want it recognized and celebrated – a ring to be kissed, so to speak. Third, we crave a structured system, whether formal or informal, in which we can follow the rules, play the game, and carve out for ourselves specific roles that make us feel needed and secure – in other words, a rank.

A Basis for Comparison. Without such a structure, many grow frustrated by a culture in which people seem to be chronically equal, a fate worse than hell for those who derive a false sense of identity from where they fall in the pecking order. Like a ship sailing the ocean without instruments, they feel lost and directionless if they don't know where they stand in comparison to others – or how to progress upward in the ranks. They make the mistake of seeing their rank as confirmation of their worth, their purpose, and their progress. They see their rank as the score of the career game they play in competition with others. With this confirmation comes validation and peace of mind, that is until they become victims of their own delusions. If they go on to be promoted to positions of management, it is almost certain they will work to preserve the game they won to achieve the rank they got, even if it comes at the expense of an organization's productivity, innovativeness, and competitiveness. Given enough time, leaders preoccupied with rank eventually fail because they are seen as massaging the system to their continued advantage. By doing so, they sacrifice the trust and engagement of their followers.

Where a captain is treated with more respect and courtesy than a lieutenant, or where a doctor is treated with more respect and courtesy than a nurse, the conditions are set for men to be treated with more respect and courtesy than women, or for any other person to be treated with more respect and courtesy because they are seen as having a preferred race, color, ethnicity, age, religion, or sexual orientation, to name a few. God only knows how a rigid rank-and-file culture will prioritize the needs of an emotional and confused rape victim armed only with her story and the trauma that came with it.

Organizations that permit and nurture a culture in which a person's rank or level of authority either limits or elevates the basic human dignities to which she is entitled will eventually produce chronic behaviors among its members that are abusive, hostile, or inhumane.

The Legitimacy of Rank

If you believe that rank has its place in organizational life, you are correct. Rank establishes the authority to make consequential decisions and execute action. Higher rank in an organization is associated with higher levels of knowledge, experience, skill, and professional judgement. Rank matters to organizations. It aligns decision-making authority with the capacity to make those decisions effectively. But the amount of time a leader actually spends making decisions or executing actions that require the exercise of rank is but a small fraction of all the time spent on the job. Furthermore, when rank is leveraged with legitimate intentions, it will never unfairly demoralize or condescend others. Rank exists to influence decision-making and execution. It does not exist to justify the mistreatment of those who don't have as much of it. In the healthiest organizational cultures, the custodian who cleans the toilets is treated with the same degree of basic respect and courtesy as the CEO.

Rank is powerful because it is sufficient in itself to move people to action, even when the ranking leader has yet to demonstrate any character or competence. This may be why rank is so intoxicating to those who have it. If you have rank in an organization, people will follow your orders and directives simply because of your rank. You don't need anything else.

To be an entrusted leader, however, the objective must be nobler than this. Entrusted leaders don't aspire to simply have and exercise rank. They don't see value in the tendency to lead and influence others by leveraging their rank without any remarkable effort or willingness to actually be *effective*. Perhaps in our days as newly promoted leaders, we might rely on rank in the short term to legitimize our decisions and actions until such time that our people follow us because of our *effectiveness*, which is when real leadership begins.

A Better Way

The purpose of this book is to explain some strategies, solutions, and ways of thinking that will enable you to attain and retain the power of influence in the right way. In doing so, you will cultivate the respect and appreciation that all leaders need to fully engage their people and get the results their teams and stakeholders want. Entrusted leaders are effective leaders. They lead by encouraging others to contribute their very best as often as possible. As their teams become more effective, their styles and methods are validated as a matter of course. In other words, entrusted leaders thrive by helping their teams thrive.

Over the years, I've thought a lot about that morning in the Rayburn Building and the topic we were there to discuss. Although the event was billed as a policy summit on the investigation of sexual violence, the real issue was and remains something else entirely. In both my opinion and my experience, catastrophe befalls people, teams, and organizations who chronically and insufferably leverage rank as a counterfeit substitute for the exercise of competent leadership. It is a worthy and honorable goal, therefore, to help current and future leaders deepen their understanding of what it *really* means to lead and how to sustain leadership success over long periods of time.

Of all the themes and topics we'll explore together in this book, there is one foundational principle I hope all current and future leaders will absorb into the deepest recesses of their professional awareness:

True leadership is not a position or title that can be ranked; true leadership is a life lived as an example for others, done so with confidence, class, and character.

If this is the life *you* want to live, I have good news for you. You can. You *can* be a highly effective leader, a leader who earns trust, respect, and admiration. You *can* be the one people look to for guidance, motivation, and inspiration. You *can* be the mentor about whom your people speak with gratitude and fondness long after your time with them is over. But first, you will have to confront some culturally reinforced myths about what competent leadership actually is. You will have to reach beyond the pages of this book into the turbulent waters of personal transformation where toxic attitudes are neutralized, bad habits are broken, and more constructive ways of thinking are established. Indeed, you will have to reach beyond learning. You will have to change.

So, if you're willing to reach beyond learning in search of the leadership presence you seek to create for yourself and your team, then I want to reach beyond teaching and coaching to help you confront truths about leadership that are too often ignored. I will share personal insights and experiences drawn from a high-stakes, high-pressure career in which leadership decisions had life and death consequences. By the time you finish this book, you will have done much more than simply *learned* about the many nuances of leadership. You will have experienced them.

Chapter 2

The Urgency Reflex

Lauren Kiefer was a beautiful 24-year-old fashion model who was bludgeoned to death in the foyer of her Oakbrook Terrace, Illinois home on Christmas Eve, 2006. She returned home to what she thought was an empty house after enjoying an evening of holiday festivities with family and friends. The house was not empty. Later that evening, Lauren's mother would discover Lauren's battered body lying partially unclothed just inside the front door of the split-level home.

It was uncommon for me and my colleagues at the DuPage County Crime Laboratory to assist in the processing of crime scenes. We were based in Wheaton, about 30 miles due west of Chicago, and it was our job to scientifically analyze evidence in the laboratory after it was collected from a crime scene and transported to our facility by properly trained officers. It was there that our team of about fifteen scientists and support personnel worked feverishly each day to keep up with the flow of incoming evidence. We didn't have time to make runs into the field and it wasn't necessary. Our crime scene guys were good at their jobs and we trusted them as much as they trusted us. But the Kiefer murder was different from most investigations with which I'd been involved during my 20-year career in forensic science. Despite the amount of blood staining the front foyer, there were no suspect shoe impressions, no fingerprints, and no traces of hairs or fibers deposited by the suspect. If a crazy witness had come forward to tell us that Lauren beat *herself* to death, we had no evidence to refute the claim. It was a cold winter evening – the night before Christmas. Even perpetrators of murder don't sweat very much in those conditions, so their skin is dry – poor conditions for leaving fingerprints. Once Lauren's mom was ruled out, we had no viable suspects and little hope the case would be solved anytime soon.

A Team in Sync

Now, you'll have to forgive me for any suggestion that some murders are worse than others or that *any* murder should be even remotely construed as having some positive aspects to it. But the Kiefer murder was, without question, one of those singular cases that triggered what I can only describe as an *urgency reflex* among the members of our team, both individually and collectively. We had experienced it in other cases as well, especially during those difficult years of 2004 and 2005 with the brutal killing of a 16-year-old high school girl by her stepfather in Aurora, as well as the quadruple murders of a mother, father, sister, and son-in-law in Naperville. In each case, as in the death of Lauren Kiefer, the perpetrator was on the loose for some time, raising fears that more victims might die if we couldn't identify a killer in short order.

When you feel the urgency reflex kick in, you know it. It is that moment in which you feel the unmistakable sense that you've just become part of something bigger and more important than you. Intense feelings of responsibility and purpose wash over you, and you find yourself searching inside of yourself for whatever talents, skills, knowledge, or insights you can bring to bear on the problem at hand. Little sources of irritation that used to bother you don't anymore. People you once found annoying now become your close ally. The alarm clock you needed to wake yourself up in the morning is no longer necessary as the purposeful energy within you grows restless. As the urgency reflex takes full command of your individual faculties and those of your colleagues, you find yourself at the threshold of the ultimate professional bliss, which is to be part of a relevant team whose full, undivided attention is focused entirely on its mission.

For those not familiar with DuPage County, it is a relatively safe and affluent community of just under a million people. The major crime load that comes to bear on its citizens is a combination of drug and property crimes with some sexual offenses and other types of violent crimes among the mix. Murders are infrequent as compared to its neighbor to the east, Cook County, but when they happen they can be quite horrific and challenging to solve. The crime laboratory, which falls under the authority of the sheriff, had been in existence since the early 1970s. In years past, crime laboratories in the United States sometimes served as a good place to reassign wayward police officers who couldn't make it on the street. The DuPage County Crime Laboratory fit that bill to some extent. But in August of 2000 when Sheriff John Zaruba gave me the opportunity to serve as its director, the expectations were justifiably higher. By the time I left the laboratory in 2010, it had become only the second county-based forensic science laboratory in the United States to earn international accreditation. Some of our innovative methods attracted the attention of our peers around the country. We had become one of the best in the business and it felt really good.

Here Comes the Sheriff. Growing impatient with the lack of scientific evidence in the Kiefer case, I decided to meet our crime scene commander at the Kiefer home to see if some fresh eyes and a different perspective might do any good. As it turned out, I was no help at all. By then the body had been collected and transported to the DuPage County

Coroner's Office where Coroner Peter Seikmann had already arranged for the post-mortem autopsy. Alone in the house, I walked carefully to the foyer where the murder occurred. Hung on the walls were pictures of a smiling Lauren in a variety of personal and professional poses, a disconcerting reminder of the life that was lost. Happy pictures of people who are now lying dead on a stainless-steel table create an existential contrast that's hard to deal with emotionally, especially when the victim is young. But for me, the pictures of Lauren were not nearly as startling as the festive Christmas carol that rang suddenly from a clock above the kitchen sink upon the arrival of the noon hour – a hollow attempt to spread holiday cheer through a dark, quiet house marked by tragedy. Both me and the hairs on the back of my neck were ready to get back to the lab where we belonged.

As I was preparing to leave, a large black SUV rolled up the Kiefer driveway. It was Sheriff John Zaruba, and stocky, salt-and-pepper haired man of middle-age and extensive experience in law enforcement administration. Dressed in blue jeans and a jacket, he jumped out of his vehicle with a battery-powered spotlight. If it was unusual for *me* to be at a crime scene, it was even more unusual for our sheriff to be there. He too was hoping to discover something that might have been missed.

We exchanged greetings after which I accompanied him to the backyard where a broken window was thought to be a possible point of entry. We didn't discover anything new, but I remember feeling impressed that our elected Sheriff, with no cameras or constituents watching, had rolled up his sleeves to lend a hand. It was one of the very few moments I would ever spend quality time with him. Zaruba always struck me as being rather uncomfortable with socializing. To be candid, I think he found me annoying. I was energetic, confident, and willing to say what was on my mind. And although I respected rank and its role in law enforcement organizations, I was never one to subordinate myself or my energy to it. As far as I could tell, we all had the same mission which was to keep the public safe. I had a job to do, and I expected even those having higher rank than me to respect my responsibilities as much as I respected theirs. I guess it's how I'm wired, for better or worse. But for Zaruba and me, our leadership styles and personalities were very different, and I suspect he interpreted my self-confidence as a sign that I was difficult to control, a common error among those loyal to the old superior, which I believe he was. But he was also the boss, and I was mindful of the many expectations that his constituents had of him as their sheriff. There at the Kiefer home, I was happy to collaborate with him, even if only for a short time.

Perpetrator Identified. As luck would have it, DNA would eventually solve the murder of Lauren Kiefer. Scientists in my laboratory brainstormed with investigators to estimate where the killer might have touched Lauren's body with his bare skin – assuming the perpetrator was a male. Although there was no evidence that Lauren had been raped prior to her death, her pants were found pulled down to her feet. We suspected the killer likely grasped Lauren's pants with his bare hands in two locations near Lauren's belt line. So it was from those locations that small samples of fabric were cut and removed for testing. To our delight, they revealed the DNA profile of a male suspect. The profile, which is nothing more than several pairs of numbers that can be easily typed into a spreadsheet, was immediately uploaded into the Illinois State DNA databank for searching. A short time later, the system returned the name of a suspect, Robert Rejda, a local electrician who reportedly made a habit of wandering aimlessly around his otherwise quiet neighborhood of suburban Chicago. Records showed that Rejda was previously arrested for rape in the city of Aurora, a few miles to the west. Rejda and Kiefer, as it turned out, were essentially neighbors. They were also childhood acquaintances, which we came to find out later.

Robert Rejda was arrested but his case never went to trial. In December 2007, almost a year after the Kiefer murder, Rejda committed suicide in the DuPage County jail by ingesting a large quantity of psychiatric medication he hoarded from unsuspecting medical staff responsible for treating his apparent psychosis.

Looking back now, I suspect that Rejda intended to rape Lauren on that tragic evening in 2006 but not kill her. The baseball bat he used was probably one she attempted to use for self-defense only to have it pulled from her grasp and used against her. No one can be sure. Fortunately, forensic science was able to deliver answers in the Kiefer murder that not even the most talented detective could have produced with such certainty. That's the value of forensic science; it gives a voice to evidence that cannot speak for itself. The DNA-packed human skin cells resting patiently on Lauren Kiefer's pants were given a voice by a collaborative team of professionals at the DuPage County Crime Laboratory who were acting under the influence of the urgency reflex. As a result, Lauren's family could begin healing with the knowledge that her killer had been identified and brought to justice.

I also believe that Sheriff Zaruba's participation in the case and his willingness to position himself as a *collaborator* rather than a *superior* helped to energize the many meetings and conversations that took place in our efforts to establish and execute a viable investigative strategy. We had to take some risks in the case – relying on a rather new and novel form of DNA testing to produce a break in the stalled investigation. Waiting another year or two for the technology to advance might have given us more hope for success. But Zaruba listened, commented, and listened some more before finally giving us his approval to take a chance on the less-proven forensic method. It was a decision that may have saved other would-be victims from the attacks of a serial predator.

Coping and Thriving

Among the many problems with superiority complexes is that they require attention and praise even at the most sensitive times when more pressing urgencies should be the center of attention. I can imagine exactly how the Kiefer investigation would have turned out if Zaruba's ego had sucked the air out of the room in which our investigative team met frequently to discuss ideas and strategies. Our attention would have been diverted from Lauren to Zaruba. Energy that should have been spent on the solving of Lauren's murder would have been sapped by our Sheriff's delicate ego. Instead of a team *thriving* on its commitment to solving the case, we'd have been a team *coping* with its leader's insecurities. Zaruba, thankfully, was gripped by the urgency reflex as much as the rest of us, perhaps inspiring him to focus on solving Lauren's murder as his main priority. He didn't demand our praise and gush. He only demanded our commitment to Lauren and her family, which is exactly what he got.

The old superior was kept in check by the intensity of the Kiefer investigation and the responsibility we felt to identify Lauren's killer. But make no mistake, the old superior finds safe harbor in many of today's law enforcement agencies where impulsive commanders distracted by their own insecurities threaten many high-stakes investigations or other sensitive police activities. I believe it is why the policing profession has struggled to earn and keep the trust of the public in recent years. But there is good news. Leaders in all occupations will find themselves behaving with more character and competence when they subordinate themselves to the urgency of a situation rather than exploiting the situation for their own self-gratification. Perhaps this is the lesson to be learned in high-stakes investigations such as the one that solved Lauren Kiefer's murder.

Facilitated Excellence

As the urgency of a professional situation grows, so does its need for a collaborative and inspiring style of leadership that elevates the energy of a team rather than bolster the emotional needs of its leader. And, as you might expect, the more urgency that surrounds a criminal investigation, the more likely it is that forensic evidence will be needed to solve it.

One of the skills I learned during the 13 years I served as a forensic laboratory administrator is the art of facilitating conversations and decision-making when everything is on the line – especially during investigations in which a diversity of knowledge and skill is needed to figure out what happened and who was responsible. Investigations requiring a wide range of forensic expertise, by necessity, also require a competent team of forensic scientists having those same areas of expertise. These scientists were *my* people, the members of *my* team whose job it was to scientifically analyze crime scene evidence and report their conclusions in a prompt, trustworthy manner.

Like many technically minded professionals, however, scientists don't always have the most impressive social skills and are vulnerable to speaking in ways that can sometimes be perceived as aloof or arrogant if they aren't careful. So, sitting at the end of more major-case conference room tables than I can remember, I found myself to be most effective when I tried to create an environment in which scientists, police investigators, and prosecutors – all with their own unique ways of thinking and expressing themselves – felt safe and comfortable making their own contributions in their own way. I was an experienced forensic expert myself and I carefully positioned myself not only as everyone's advocate but also as their facilitator – insistent that we keep moving forward together, making thoughtful decisions as an investigative team – *together*.

For me, this role came very naturally because I value the bliss that is the making of difficult choices while being buoyed by multidisciplinary collaboration. The executive coach and facilitator I am today was born and bred from the pressures of those many investigations in which I participated during my forensic science career. To this day, many of my clients are leaders and decision-makers in forensic science located throughout the United States and overseas. Just as I got to experience how powerful a collaborative style of leadership can be in the most difficult cases, I've also witnessed the devastation caused by the old superior as it wraps its jealous hands around the throats of investigators being pushed to their limits. One instance, in particular, became the subject of a motion picture directed by Clint Eastwood in 2019. It happened ten years before the death of Lauren Kiefer and may help to explain how a guy like me goes from being a forensic scientist to an executive leadership coach.

Chapter 3

A Forensic Life

My interest in forensic science ignited when I was 13 years old. It was 1983, marking the 20th anniversary of President John F. Kennedy's assassination in Dallas. Leading up to the anniversary, the few television channels we had back then devoted an increasing amount of time to recalling the events that unfolded on that horrible day in 1963. What caught my attention were claims that President Kennedy's assassination was the result of a conspiracy that likely required the involvement of high-level officials in the U.S. government. Many of these claims were reinforced with fascinating applications of science and technology. These resulted in theories that sometimes conflicted sharply with the explanations given by the now-famous Warren Commission after its review of the assassination and all of the forensic evidence associated with it.

As often happens with the commemoration of major historical events, opportunistic attention-seekers will come forward with new "explosive" and controversial claims about what *really* happened. In 1983, one such perspective gained more attention than the others. It was a book titled, *Best Evidence – Disguise and Deception in the Assassination of John F. Kennedy* by David S. Lifton. Claims made by Lifton have since been disproven, but in 1983 his crafty interconnection of historical events with the available forensic evidence seemed to expose what could be described as the most evil and complex governmental conspiracy in history.

After seeing Lifton's book discussed during a television news program, I jumped on my bicycle and rode 3 miles to a local bookstore with money I earned from my weekly newspaper route, purchasing a copy of *Best Evidence,* and with it, my own personal piece of history. When I got home, I immersed myself in the book's shocking accusations and supporting evidence. Within a few days, I had read the book cover-to-cover, something my parents noted as being unusual because it *was* unusual for me to read anything with that kind of urgency. It was all so fascinating and yet so tragic – the headwound, the bullet trajectories, the autopsy, the fingerprints, the theories. Oh my, the theories!

Seven years later, it was time for me to declare my college major. Like many students, I was uncertain what I wanted to do or what I wanted to study. My parents, however, reminded me of the interest I had taken in the Kennedy assassination and suggested I consider forensic science as a possible career choice. It just so happened that Michigan State University had one of the largest and oldest forensic science programs in the world, headed by Dr. Jay Siegel who would become a close, personal friend and mentor to me until his death in 2017. When I first met him, Siegel was gaining attention by being retained as an expert witness for the defense in the highly publicized rape trial of William Kennedy Smith. Smith was the nephew of the late Senator Ted Kennedy, accused of raping a woman with whom he was romantically involved. The alleged crime took place on a beach at the Kennedy family compound in Florida. Siegel compared soil samples collected from the scene with stains on the alleged-victim's clothing. The results of his analysis disproved the accusations against Smith, who was eventually acquitted.

By the time I was appointed Director of the DuPage County Crime Laboratory in August of 2000, only 8 years had passed since I graduated from Jay Siegel's program. Much to Jay's delight, I went on to have an active and rewarding career in forensic science. Even more to his delight was the fact that I developed a professional reputation for being somewhat outspoken about a variety of occupational issues and controversies related to the practice of forensic science. When you spend enough time saying what many others are thinking but aren't willing to say themselves, your reputation for being outspoken becomes a reputation for being a leader.

Although I was emerging as a leader, I had yet to be the leader of a team, which is another matter entirely. I was only 30 years old when I became a laboratory director. Unlike many new managers who base their styles of leadership on things they were taught by people who were willing to mentor them, the extent of my own management knowledge was a complicated mix of professional accomplishments that blended awkwardly with some horrible personal experiences of being exposed to abusive, incompetent management. I'd rather not dwell on what happened, but I will say that doing the opposite of what others had done to me became the foundation upon which I would build my career as an organizational leader. To this day, I feel fortunate to have gotten through it with my sanity and career intact.

An Explosion at the Park

The experience that forever changed the trajectory of my career, as well as my philosophies about leadership and teamwork, began on a fateful day when a bomb exploded in downtown Atlanta. I was working as a forensic scientist in the city chosen to host the 1996 Olympics, which were now underway and meeting even the highest expectations of guests, athletes, viewers, and Olympic officials. Television ratings for the opening ceremonies were at record levels. Security was tight thanks to the team of law enforcement officials who surveyed previous Olympic venues in an effort to formulate a set of safety and security strategies that could be implemented and followed during the Games. Security, of course, is always a priority for the Olympics, but in 1996 there were deep concerns about the potential for violence. In 1993 a car-bomb exploded in the basement of the World Trade Center in New York City. In 1995 a deranged Timothy McVeigh perpetrated the bombing of the Murrah Federal Building in Oklahoma City.

By the time the opening ceremonies for the 1996 Olympics were about to begin, authorities in Atlanta were keenly aware of the social instabilities that could potentially erupt in an act of violence during the games. When that act of violence *did* erupt, many of those same authorities were eager to showcase their investigative skills and demonstrate before an international audience that the United States was ready and able to respond effectively to acts of terrorism, to include the delivery of swift and certain justice to the perpetrators. It wasn't pretty.

A Nail in the Bag. The bomb at Centennial Olympic Park in downtown Atlanta exploded at one o'clock in the morning on July 27, 1996. Hundreds of people were injured from the force of the blast which sprayed nails in all directions. Tragically, one woman died from her injuries. The victim was a 44-year-old mother named Alice Hawthorne who was there at the park with her only daughter participating in the revelry and wonder of the Olympic Games. Alice's body would soon be lying in the morgue of the Fulton County Medical Examiner's Office.

At the time of the bombing, I was working as a forensic scientist in the forensic laboratory headquarters of the Georgia Bureau of Investigation (GBI) in nearby Decatur. My colleagues and I were paying close attention to news reports and hearing stories about what was happening at the blast scene, but we knew that a bombing such as this was a federal crime that would be investigated by federal authorities. Besides, we had our hands full with all of the forensic evidence from the murders, rapes, and burglaries happening throughout the state each and every day. But for me personally, the bombing investigation was of particular interest mainly because I'd recently been offered and accepted a position with the federal forensic laboratory in Atlanta where the Olympic bombing evidence was being analyzed. I was scheduled to begin work at the U.S. Bureau of Alcohol, Tobacco, and Firearms laboratory later that summer.

One of the routine forensic tests we performed at the GBI lab was called *Determine Type of Weapon*, or *DTW*. A DTW involved the analysis of bullets recovered from the living or dead bodies of victims to determine what make and model of gun most likely fired them. One morning, as a matter of routine practice, our laboratory received a paper bag full of individually sealed bullets from the Fulton County Medical Examiner's Office. Each bullet was contained in its own small clear plastic envelope with an affixed label bearing the name of the victim. It was my job that day to go through each of the bullets, measure the grooves imparted to each bullet by the gun that fired it, then refer to a reference database that would allow the most likely gun types to be reported to investigators. One by one, I selected an envelope from the bag and conducted my analysis, as I had done countless times before.

One envelope, however, stopped me in my tracks. It didn't contain a bullet; it contained a nail. Written on the envelope was the name, Alice Hawthorne. I knew in that moment that I was about to become one of the very first forensic scientists to examine evidence from the bombing of the 1996 Olympics. As a heavy feeling of gravity washed over me, I conducted a rudimentary analysis of the nail, recording its weight, its size, and other basic features. Being familiar with construction products,

I knew it was a masonry nail. Unlike common nails cut from wire, masonry nails are cut from steel plate with toolmarks from the manufacturing process clearly visible on the sides of the nails. When my analysis was over, the nail was transported to the ATF laboratory where forensic experts – experts with whom I'd soon be working – would subject the nail to more extensive tests.

The Wallpaper. Witnessing the bombing investigation from the inside was a sight to behold and nothing short of a comprehensive study of *what to do* and *what not to do* as a leader in a high-stakes, life-and-death situation. From the moment the bomb exploded, federal law enforcement agents began to clash in their efforts to seize control of the investigation. Disagreements erupted, tempers flared, and dominance behaviors began to erode the collaboration and communication needed to make a fast start of solving the case.

Although the FBI was considered to have procedural authority in terrorism cases, the ATF was responsible for the investigation of explosions. Both agencies desperately wanted the opportunity to showcase their talents in a high-profile incident of international significance, and they scraped and clawed at each other until a collaborative agreement on how to proceed was reached. Although I wasn't privy to those discussions, the way things played out in practical terms was for the FBI to lead the investigation in the field while the forensic experts in the ATF's Atlanta laboratory would lead the scientific investigation of the crime scene evidence.

My first day of work at the ATF laboratory came in September of 1996, about two months after the close of the Games. It felt like jumping onto a moving train. Initially, I would only play a minor role in the investigation, providing some basic technical assistance when necessary. Those first days at the ATF laboratory are a bit of blur for me when I think back on what was going on. What I do remember was sensing the frustration of our laboratory personnel with the shenanigans taking place among the investigators in the field. It seemed like they were more interested in protecting their own relevance than solving the case. I often heard our more senior laboratory scientists mock what they called *the wallpaper* when describing the field portion of the investigation. The wallpaper, as I came to find out, was the line of federal agents and local law enforcement officers in dark blue jackets standing with their backs facing the television cameras. On their backs, printed in large yellow type, were the letters FBI, ATF, or GBI, clearly displayed for all to see. I'm sure that at some point you've seen the wallpaper for yourself when watching the evening news, its purpose being to advertise the services of the respective agencies to any legislators who might be watching – legislators who might be responsible for approving and appropriating those agencies' annual budgets.

The Wrong Guy. The behaviors we witnessed at the start of the investigation were far more than a mere annoyance. They destroyed lives. A young man named Richard Jewell became the prime suspect in the investigation. He was also the security guard who found the bomb under a bench at Centennial Olympic Park, clearing away hundreds of people before it exploded. He was hailed in the national news as a guardian angel, that is until his naiveté and awkwardness led him to make strange statements that were as incriminating as they were foolish. He had a history of being the quintessential police-wanna-be who loved to have authority and use it to boss people around. Investigators were suspicious and came to believe that Jewell planted the bomb to give himself the opportunity to save lives and be worshipped as an international hero.

Richard Jewell was and *is* a hero. He likely saved dozens of lives as the result of his fast response. But his life and the life of his mother were nearly ruined by the predatory actions of investigators and news reporters who zealously manufactured a narrative for which he could be convicted in the court of public opinion. This is not to suggest that Jewell was intentionally railroaded. The belief that he was guilty was genuine, in my judgement. But under the intense pressures of the investigation and a worldwide audience curious to see if Americans had the grit to solve a crime of this magnitude, *wanting* Richard Jewell to be guilty outweighed any desire to question *if* he was guilty.

To be fair, it was entirely reasonable that Jewell became a suspect. That he remained a suspect as long as he did was the result of misplaced investigative priorities. My colleagues working in the ATF laboratory watched the saga play out with alarm. The construction of the Olympic bomb was sophisticated, with three individual pipe bombs wired to an alarm clock. It was more likely the bomber had formal military training. Richard Jewell, however, was neither sophisticated nor trained in the use of explosives – and he had no military service to his credit. Chances were good that Richard Jewell had been wrongly accused, so his ongoing excoriation in the press did nothing to slow the intensity of our laboratory work being conducted behind the scenes. The longer Jewell distracted investigators from their search for the actual perpetrator, the less likely the case would ever be solved.

Case Closed. The identity of the bomber became known in January of 1998 when a bomb detonated outside a medical clinic in Birmingham, Alabama. Far deadlier than the Olympic bomb, it was constructed with dynamite, nails, and an alarm clock. Off-duty police officer, Robert Sanderson, was working a part-time detail as a security guard at the clinic. As he approached the suspicious bag, it exploded, killing him immediately. That the bomb exploded just as Sanderson approached it was a clue that the bomber was likely nearby and elected to manually override the timing device before Sanderson disturbed it.

A witness drinking coffee at a McDonalds saw a strange and suspicious figure pass in front of him. He instinctively wrote down the license plate number of the man's Nissan pickup truck on his coffee cup: KND1117. Armed with the information, investigators began their search from Alabama, through Georgia, into North Carolina. But because of the most devastating of investigative miscues, the Nissan pick-up truck owned by a Mr. Eric Rudolph was found abandoned near the side of a North Carolina road. Rudolph knew he was being chased thanks to overzealous law enforcement officials who took to the airwaves after the Birmingham explosion to boast of this newest and most dramatic of developments. A local sheriff in North Carolina later complained that if everyone had kept their mouths shut, Rudolph would likely have gone home where he would have been arrested without incident. Instead, Rudolph would not be seen by authorities for another five years.

I suspect that Rudolph only intended to bomb the Olympics but became enraged by the public attention directed at Richard Jewell, as if Jewell took credit for Rudolph's own handiwork. So, he went on to detonate four more bombs over the next several months, all in the Atlanta area, including the bomb in Birmingham. All were constructed with dynamite, nails, and steel plate. It was a miracle that nobody else died in these attacks.

Upon the realization that a serial bomber was at work, and with so many resources being exhausted on the investigation of the Olympic bomb, I became entirely immersed in the investigation, having been assigned to the forensic analysis of the nails and steel plate used to construct all four of the dynamite bombs. Fortunately, it wouldn't be long before one of my colleagues at the ATF laboratory made the first forensic confirmation associating Eric Rudolph to the Olympic bomb. He did so by identifying nails used in the Olympic bomb as having the same pattern of microscopic manufacturing marks as nails found at Rudolph's property.

A Lesson of History. My involvement in the Olympic bombing investigation had a deep and lasting impact on me, and it continues to inform how I conduct myself as an executive leadership coach, especially when working with leaders and professionals in positions of public trust, which is my area of specialization. While my colleagues from the investigative team may remember the bombings for their forensic and criminal significance, I remember them most for their *leadership* significance. The initial law enforcement response to the Olympic bombing was clearly unimpressive. Discord among investigators and agency heads, turf battles, grandstanding, and spotlight-seeking took precedence over collaboration, conversation, and strategically competent decision-making. The urgency reflex that overtook me and my colleagues in the forensic laboratory wasn't enough to squelch the egos causing problems at the scene. If anything, we witnessed the urgency reflex in reverse, whereby the intensity of the situation exposed deeply rooted shortcomings among those entrusted to make key investigative decisions immediately after the blast. Those who embraced the power of the urgency reflex found themselves humbled by the enormity of the situation and focused sharply on their responsibilities. Those who didn't found themselves incapacitated by the pressure, acting out their panic in a variety of strange and confusing ways. It was a contrast of stunning proportions and one I'll never forget.

It's fair to wonder why a bombing of international significance would fail to trigger the urgency reflex among those authorities who ended up compromising the quality and speed of the investigation. Even if they were loyal disciples of the old superior, why wouldn't such a serious and threatening situation wake them up?

To answer this question, we must confront an alarming truth. To the old superior, the urgency reflex is a clear and compelling danger because it inspires people within a hierarchy to come together as a team. When this happens, domination tendencies and tactics are quickly exposed for what they are – a threat to the team's performance. Gripped by the urgency reflex, inspired professionals confronted by a challenge of existential significance are unwilling to subordinate themselves to dominators who don't know what the hell they're doing. All the while, the dominators scurry in a panic to hold onto whatever control they can, often doing significant damage in the process.

During those early hours and days after the explosion of the Olympic bomb, there were too many high-level leaders who didn't know what the hell they were doing. They were jealous of each other and each other's agencies, trying to preserve their power and control over the investigation. They wanted to win the turf war. They wanted to draw attention to themselves. They wanted to draw attention to their own agencies. They wanted to bask in the spotlight of international attention. They wanted to leverage the bombing investigation as a platform from which to flaunt their *superiority*. What they should have wanted was to solve the case as quickly and as competently as possible, regardless of who gets the credit. But with so many distracting motives, the old superior was slow out of the gate, on a collision course with an unsuspecting mama's boy named Richard Jewell.

Chapter 4

Institutional Power

In the previous chapters, I emphasized how superiority complexes can compromise police investigations of all kinds. Although law enforcement agencies are among the most notorious abusers of rank, the problem can exist in any place of work or business. In the introduction, I shared my experience with police and military commanders trying to solve very difficult social and organizational problems related to sexual abuse or assault. Police and military are called *guardian* professions in that they exist to protect the public. Fire departments are also considered part of the guardian workforce and, like police and military, are among the most obvious examples of organizational structures where the distribution of decision-making power is based on a strict adherence to rank. In both police and fire departments, ranks are often identified using naming designations common to the military, such as *sergeant, lieutenant, major,* or *colonel* – a traditional practice that emerged after the civil war to maintain discipline and prevent corruption during the reconstruction.

Rank

Rank is one of the three primary sources of institutional power that people can leverage in their efforts to influence others in a hierarchy. It is generally understood that a person having lower rank is compelled to follow the orders of someone who has higher rank, and that a person of higher rank must be given the opportunity to make the more complex decisions within an organization before someone of lower rank attempts to do so. When this doesn't happen, the person of lower rank is said to have been *out of order* and may be held accountable for it. One can appreciate the value and legitimacy of rank because it ensures that the most reliable decision-makers are making the most consequential decisions. When we ignore the importance of rank within an organization, or if we fail to respect how decision-making power is distributed, we can unknowingly expose ourselves and others to danger. The establishing of rank is something to be respected as a natural tendency of human beings who are trying to remain calm, safe, and organized in a chaotic world full of risks, threats, and uncertainties.

When an experienced professional is promoted for the first time to a certain level of managerial responsibility, among the more difficult challenges he will face is learning how to leverage the power of his new rank. Some people handle this better than others. For some, rank is a toy with which they feel compelled to play, or like a new lawnmower that makes a homeowner eager for the grass to grow. When someone is given a new level of rank, there is a strange urge to use it, one that I have felt myself. This can result in impulsive actions or decisions that make little sense and cause members of a team to lose trust and confidence in their new leader.

Rank, of course, is not a toy. It's more like a chainsaw. It can empower an individual to be remarkably effective but can also be extremely dangerous when not used properly. Of course, how managers utilize their rank is heavily influenced by culture. When professionals are exposed during the early years of their careers to the entitled management styles of the old superior, they are more likely to mimic those styles when they become managers later.

Appreciating the temptations of rank is a first step toward leveraging its power with more skill. But our respect for organizational rank is not sufficient to further our understanding of how institutional power is exercised *outside* the formal confines of an organization. What happens then? How do people influence each other when there's no organizational structure to govern it? Well, we first have to relax our notion of what it means to be an organization, something we'll be discussing in more depth later. Yes, an organization might be a corporation or government agency. But it can also be a less formally structured group of people who share a common interest or common goals. Although rank is a useful method of power distribution, it is not a requirement.

There are two other forms of institutional power commonly relied upon to influence people and their behaviors: *stature* and *authority*. Both are prevalent in many situations and contexts in which people function in groups. Similar to rank, they are relevant because they empower their holders with the ability to exercise influence without necessarily having any remarkable leadership skill or talent. Simply having access to these sources of power provides the leverage needed to influence people.

Stature

In the absence of a formally structured organization, groups or networks of people will be held together by common interests. These interests may include:

- Participation in the same favorite activity
- Fascination with the same subject matter
- Living in the same community or neighborhood
- Being part of the same profession
- Belonging to the same club, church, or social group

• Having the same hobby

Within each group or network, there will be certain individuals whose experience and knowledge have earned them the reputation of being especially relevant. These individuals are said to have *stature*, which means that their opinions, ideas, and desires carry more weight. With stature, they are leaders and can assert heavy influence over people within the same group or network. This is not to suggest that such influencing of people is always a bad thing. In fact, it often has great value because it moves people to do things that are in everyone's best interest, inspired by a perspective that is more developed and nuanced than what others have. But again, it is a form of power than can be leveraged with or without any evidence of leadership skill or talent.

A-Listers. One of my favorite examples of the power of stature is reported to have come during the production of the 1992 blockbuster movie, *A Few Good Men,* in which Jack Nicholson played opposite Tom Cruise in the role of Colonel Nathan R. Jessup, an irritable, narcissistic military commander eventually found responsible for the death of a soldier under his command.

During an interview with talk show host, Rich Eisen, fellow cast member, Kevin Pollak, recalled how Nicholson was paid $5 million for ten days of work. But only five days were scheduled for the shooting of the famous courtroom scenes in which Nicholson spars with Cruise to create what has become one of the most enduring moments in cinematic history. With his reverence for Nicholson unmistakable, Pollak explains how director Rob Reiner seemed to panic at the end of Nicholson's fifth and final day on the set when Reiner realized he needed Nicholson to return for a sixth day to complete the courtroom scene. As Pollak explained:

"He only had five days in the courtroom to shoot everything. And at the end of the five days.... *Rob had to go to Jack and say 'I can't afford to pay you to come back another day, but if you, out of the goodness of your heart, come back for a couple more shots, I'll get you out by noon, wherever we are – I promise.'* [Nicholson responded:] *'Whatever you need Robbie, I'm here.'"*

Pollak's description of this exchange captures the powerful but beloved presence that Nicholson had on the set. He energized the other actors and their director, Rob Reiner. The list of actors that would have to be begged for a few additional scenes by their directors is a very short one, especially actors who can command a half a million dollars per day.

Rank Outranked. What makes this story such an impactful example of stature in action is that Rob Reiner outranked Jack Nicholson. Strictly from an organizational standpoint, Nicholson was the subordinate. Reiner was the superior. Nicholson worked for him. But Nicholson's stature was, and continues to be, such a tremendous source of power on the sets of his movies that he gets what he wants. His stature, even in the absence of rank, has the power to impact the overall movie-making experience for all of the other actors, directors, and supporting personnel. This makes Nicholson a leader on the set, whether he sees himself in that light or not. And the good news, according to Kevin Pollak, is that Nicholson is among the kindest, most approachable, and most generous superstars he's ever worked with.

In your own life and career, there may be individuals with great influence over you, even though they don't have any formal rank. Perhaps *you* have influence over others because of your stature. Like rank, stature can be used *con*structively or *de*structively, usually depending on how entrusted or entitled the person with stature seems to be. To have stature is to have amassed a set of credentials within a particular group or network that gives you influence over them. When stature exists among people who feel entrusted with the responsibilities their stature gives them, they tend to be more effective, inspiring leaders who can influence people in a positive way for long periods of time. But when stature is a manifestation of the *old superior*, it seeks to control and compel people in a way that makes them feel small and irrelevant. And guess what? They eventually act like it.

Stature is something that all professionals or members of professional teams should strive to build for themselves. But the power of this stature should prioritize the well-being and effectiveness of others, rather than the promotion of self-interests. *Whatever you need Robbie, I'm here.*

Authority

There's a third source of institutional power that's available to people who may have neither organizational rank nor any personal or professional stature. We call it *authority*. Authority is a form of influence assigned to an individual who represents a governmental agency or other kind of organization having the power to enforce legal, professional, or constitutional requirements. Authority, of course, is sometimes used interchangeably with stature – as in *Rebecca is considered an authority on oil paintings from the Victorian era* – although, what is really being said is that Rebecca has stature among people interested in Victorian-era oil paintings.

My own appreciation for the power of authority became clear during a business trip in which I flew from Detroit to San Diego to attend a professional retreat for coaches. Arriving at the TSA checkpoint, I placed my duffle bag on the belt, emptied my pockets, and walked through the metal-detection vestibule, after which I turned towards the TSA agent who was screening the bags. As my bag passed through the detector, the agent's eyebrows furrowed in an expression of concerned curiosity. The belt shifted into reverse, and my bag was removed by the agent and brought to an inspection table. At that point, I was asked if this was my bag, which I agreed it was.

The TSA agent reached into a small side pocket with a gloved hand and removed a single Winchester 357 magnum caliber cartridge, a piece of ammunition that I inadvertently left in the bag after a weekend trip to my cousin's cabin in the woods of northern Michigan. The agent lifted the cartridge up to eye-level and looked directly at me. "Anything you can tell me about this, sir?"

A strong feeling of anxious tension filled my stomach as I felt the blood drain from what must have been my expressionless face. "Oh my God," I chimed, before explaining what happened. I had no idea what would happen next or if I'd be taken away for interrogation.

Thankfully, the agent smiled and said "We see these all the time. People forget about them until we find them during screening." At that point, the agent performed a full inspection of my bag, closed it up, then handed it to me as he wished me a good day.

This TSA agent had no rank over me and no relevant professional stature to speak of – at least not as far as I was concerned. But if he had any reason to believe that I was a threat to my fellow travelers, he had sufficient authority to detain me. In positions of authority, considerable power can be asserted on others in a wide variety of contexts and situations. In this instance, I was fortunate not to have had the authority of the TSA asserted upon me. Had I accidentally left a firearm in my bag, it might have been another story.

The Power to Lead

If you have *rank* in an organization, you have the power to control and compel people. If you have *stature* in a professional community, your recommendations and opinions are more likely to shape policy or standards of practice. If you have *authority*, such as that held by TSA agents at the airport, people are compelled to heed your warnings and instructions. With rank, stature, or authority – or any combination thereof – you have considerable power over others even if you've never earned their *respect*.

Over the long term, your objective should be to harness the beneficial power that comes from having rank, stature, or authority while *also* earning the respect and appreciation of those you lead or influence. In my own professional life, I've always found (and continue to find) that my influence over other people is amplified when I prioritize empathy over rank, service over stature, and generosity over authority.

If you have rank, stature, or authority, there is a perpetually unanswered question that is deserving of your consideration. Will you utilize these sources of institutional power to enable people, or will you use them to make you feel better about yourself? Rank, stature, and authority are not, in themselves, forms of leadership. Instead, it is the special characteristics and attributes of highly effective human beings that allow rank, stature, and authority to become the mere ingredients of a larger, more important way of influencing and motivating people, one that consistently produces positive results.

Chapter 5

Equals in the Moment

The problem with using rank as the foundation of leadership power in an organization is that it requires the positioning of a superior over an inferior. Of course, there are times when this is necessary and acceptable, especially when critical decisions are being made. But during the normal flow and routines of everyday life, the contrast between superiority and inferiority creates a tension that interferes with the kinds of communication and interpersonal connectivity that collaborative relationships need. It also sets up conditions whereby dominant behaviors can be mistaken for leadership behaviors.

A Very Special Thing

One thing we can say about effective leadership is that it's self-evident; we know it when we see it. We know how it looks and how it sounds. We know how it feels and how it fills us with an unmistakable sense of purpose. It surprises us when we accomplish goals we thought were beyond our reach. It finds us when we feel lost. It picks us up when we fall. It listens to us when we speak. It encourages us when we feel down. It charts a course, sets a destination, warns us of obstacles, and challenges us to press on with our journey even when we feel intimidated by the adversities encountered along the way. On this journey, effective leadership instills within us a burning desire to be the best we can be with the tools and resources we have. And if we fall short, effective leadership directs our attention to the lessons we must learn to have success the next time around. While effective leadership doesn't always make us feel happy in the moment, it fills us with confidence *between* the moments, preparing us to act more decisively and reliably when opportunities come knocking.

If we're lucky enough to experience what it's like to be led by an effective leader, we discover something rather interesting. Effective leadership does not make us feel big and mighty, as much as we might wish that for ourselves. Quite the opposite, effective leadership makes us feel small by inspiring our commitment to a mission or cause that's much bigger than our individual selves. Effective leadership is born of humility, so it shrinks our egos; but in doing so it grows our sense of purpose and commitment. Like a magnifying glass that gathers and constricts sunlight into a beam hot enough to start a fire, effective leadership enables us to focus our strengths and talents on a mission that matters.

A Rare Find. A 2015 Gallup study reported that organizations fail to promote managers with the right set of leadership talents 82% of the time. And only about 1 in every 10 people have the natural talent to be highly effective leaders. This isn't to say that the other 90% don't have *any* leadership talents. What it means is that the overwhelming majority of us don't have the requisite combination of skills, attributes, and character needed to lead successfully. So, it strikes me as being no wonder that organizations muck it up 82 times out of a 100. It's probably because so many of the individuals selecting new leaders for promotion don't understand what it takes to be an effective leader.

Individual Effectiveness at Level

As an executive coach, I deal a lot with clients who want to improve their leadership skills, and many of them can be rather vocal about it. When they decide to engage the services of an executive coach, it's often because they're trying to fix some problems that have emerged on their teams or in their professional lives, or it's because there's some new opportunities on the horizon for which they want to be better prepared. But I've also come to appreciate how easy it is for me as a coach, and for my clients, to become distracted from what's most important – forgetting what are the true origins of what we might describe as effective leadership, consummate professionalism, and healthy organizational cultures – and that is individual effectiveness *at level*.

Effective leadership, we find, is simply the byproduct of individual effectiveness demonstrated by someone in a leadership position. Similarly, what we might describe as consummate professionalism is the byproduct of individual effectiveness demonstrated by someone who works in a professional capacity, applying their expertise in the interest of certain stakeholders. And what we envision as being a healthy organizational culture is really nothing more than teams of people, with varying degrees of knowledge and experience, demonstrating individual effectiveness as collaborators and communicators. When individuals are effective at level – when they infuse excellence into the meeting of their own individual responsibilities, they produce all of the good things and sources of satisfaction that all of us hope for in our personal and professional lives.

So, let's pause for a second and reflect on what we're *really* trying to accomplish here and what it *really* means to be effective at level. It means we're able to influence the many people with whom our responsibilities and priorities allow us to interact on a regular basis. And the result of that influence is the uplifting and energizing of those people.

Effective people are motivated to use whatever influence they have to bring value to as many people as humanly possible. And, not surprisingly, every person they help becomes more influential, too.

The Power of Influence

Influence is the muscle of life, that which distinguishes the spectators of the world from the players. To be influential is to weave your intentions into the fabric of human affairs, affording you the opportunity to negotiate more effectively with circumstance. With influence, the grip that luck and chance conspire to keep on the direction of your life can be eased.

Almost everything you accomplish in life precipitates from your ability to influence others. We may call it *personal effectiveness* when it helps you live a more joyful and impactful life. We call it *professionalism* when it enhances the quality of your workplace contributions. We call it *leadership* when it inspires others around you to volunteer the best of themselves. If, therefore, you aspire to become more successful in your professional capacities or more effective in your approach to leadership, then you must first endeavor to become more *influential*.

Back in 1936, influence was the focus of Dale Carnegie in one of the most celebrated self-help books ever published. *How to Win Friends and Influence People* explored the nature of human interactions and what factors produce more cordial, constructive, and lasting relationships. Similar to Stephen Covey's *The 7 Habits of Highly Effective People*, published in 1989, *How to Win Friends and Influence People* was not written as a book about leadership. It was a book about how to create and maintain the relationships necessary to make good things happen in our lives and in the lives of others.

Despite the books written by Carnegie and Covey, not to mention the countless other leadership books and resources available in today's marketplace, people have a remarkable capacity to shoot themselves in the foot just when they find themselves with a legitimate opportunity to influence others. This might include the respected employee promoted into a managerial position within his company only to find that he makes his team miserable and unproductive thanks to his erratic behavior and irrationality. Or it might describe the team of geologists who observe alarming signals coming from instruments anchored to the slopes of an active volcano but can't seem to convince local authorities to issue a public warning. A distinguished college professor is awarded grant funding to conduct an important research project but fails to motivate a team of graduate students to complete the work on time. In these examples, we see very capable people with rank, stature, and authority who are unable to influence others in a meaningful way. Somehow, they lack the ability to assert their intentions adequately or constructively. As a result, they cannot motivate or persuade others to take action.

To influence others in a positive way, we must meet them where they are – not just face-to-face or eye-to-eye, but side by side. We must be *equals in the moment*. As equals, we are more likely to earn trust and inspire agreement on important topics or necessary courses of action. As equals, leaders and followers can work synergistically toward common goals and objectives. When disagreements arise that cannot be resolved, it might be necessary for leaders to *pull rank*, as they say, and give specific directions or instructions. This, of course, is why we have rank. Rank provides its holders with the authority to make certain decisions when such decisions must be made *now*. But when leaders become addicted to dominance, their bad habits are funded at the expense of their credibility and worthiness to be followed. For one person to influence another in a meaningful way requires that both feel and act like they are in it together. Side by side. Equals in the moment.

Fury from the Sidelines. If you ever watch a college football or basketball game on television, you might find yourself surprised by the verbal outbursts that so many coaches direct at their players. Head coaches, especially, hold the highest rank on a team, using their power to build and sustain winning performances in every contest.

During the 2019 March Madness campaign for the NCAA men's national basketball championship, Michigan State University's legendary head coach, Tom Izzo, was excoriated by the press and public for the apparent rage he leveled at one of his freshman players, Aaron Henry, during a timeout. Henry seemed to lose his focus at a crucial moment in the game and Izzo let him know it. But when Henry made the mistake of returning Izzo's volley, Izzo's anger exploded into a fury fit for a winter storm on Lake Superior. Although Izzo never made physical contact with Henry, his appearance of being out of control raised questions about the effectiveness of his coaching style.

Those questions, of course, came to an abrupt halt in the very next game when Henry had a career night, leading the Spartans to a historic win against Duke to reach the Final Four. Izzo was vindicated; but left out of the discussion was *why* Tom Izzo is able to motivate players in a way that would leave mere mortals like us quaking in our shoes.

It's because Tom Izzo is a master of positioning himself as an equal in the moment. Yes, he is the boss and what he says goes – and everybody knows it. But the reason Izzo's outbursts motivate players is because his players know that Izzo is fighting alongside them. Izzo does not berate players to make himself feel good, nor is his yelling intended to demoralize, condescend, or humiliate. Izzo is a fellow soldier in battle and his players feed off his energy. Does Izzo's style work in every situation? Probably not. But his players trust him, they admire him, and they follow him. Izzo is their leader because he influences them as an equal in the moment. He's in it *with* them. And guess what? As an equal, Izzo allows himself to be influenced by his players, a responsibility his more experienced athletes take very seriously. It's a recipe for success that's made basketball at Michigan State University a perennial powerhouse.

Earned Impact. The idea that leaders can be more influential as equals in the moment is, admittedly, difficult to comprehend if your natural instincts compel you to seek dominance in your interactions with others. A police chief, for example, may balk, arguing that dominance in the exercise of command is critical to maintaining a tactical advantage in the most dangerous situations. So too might a chemistry professor recoil at the thought of relaxing her grip on distraction-prone students who are exposed to dangerous materials in the laboratory. The truth is, however, that the degree of influence one has over others is proportionate to the quality of the relationships involved. People are resistant to the influence of leaders and managers they perceive as being poor stewards of their rank, stature, and authority. To enthusiastically follow a leader we know to be ineffective or destructive is nearly impossible because it fills our hearts with feelings of resentment, shame, and guilt over the role we play in enabling their dysfunction. The pain we feel can become so overwhelming that it exhausts every bit of energy we might need to be even remotely mistaken as a loyal follower. Nothing good comes from this. And, as I'll explain later, there is strong science behind why dominators have such a detrimental impact on collaboration.

Self-Reflection. As one seeking to improve your leadership and managerial competencies, you may find yourself confronted by your own inadequacies. Perhaps you see tendencies or habits in yourself that signal some counterproductive attitudes. Maybe you like to dominate people. Maybe you hunger to be celebrated or praised by those in your charge. Maybe you genuinely think you're better than everyone else. Perhaps you are a bit of a manipulator and like playing games to keep people off balance and confused, eager to neutralize any threats to your sense of power and security. Maybe you're just a bully. If you recognize these in yourself, they are probably hurting you more than you realize. Commit yourself to replacing them with more constructive approaches to engaging people. Until you do, you simply cannot meet your potential as a leader and you are more likely to inflict harm upon others than you are to spark their imagination or inspire their best contributions.

Later in this book, I will share strategies for effecting personal change. In the meantime, as you look for opportunities to make transformations in how you interact with people, make sure you cut yourself some slack. The human experience is challenging for everyone, especially when trying to modify lifelong habits. Nobody is without flaws and most of us harbor some counterproductive tendencies to one degree or another. Your first goal is to become aware of them. Your second goal is to recognize what you are trying to protect. As human beings we are hardwired to protect ourselves and defend our territory. We're conditioned for self-preservation through the eradication of threats to our well-being and the well-being of those we love. Indeed, this has allowed the human species to survive as long as it has – by staying safe. But defensiveness is an especially powerful and destructive response in professional settings, so it's important to recognize those moments when it seems to get between you and your team.

Missing in Action

In April of 2016, I embarked on a professional journey that would take me to Hanoi, Vietnam. There, the U.S. Departments of State and Justice collaborated in a project to support local and national authorities in their efforts to use forensic DNA technology to identify the remains of over 400,000 Vietnamese soldiers killed in battle. As Vietnam gained increased access to forensic DNA technology, its politicians saw an opportunity to ease the emotional burdens of fellow citizens whose loved ones had never come home and whose remains had never been identified. *Over 400,000 of them.* It's hard to comprehend. Not only did Vietnamese officials want the remains identified, they wanted it done quickly and were willing to pay a handsome price for it.

As often happens when demand and dollars find each other, there's no shortage of people wanting in on the game. Government agencies and private organizations shoved themselves into position to participate in what became known as Project 150, a noble undertaking by Vietnam to honor its dead and bring closure to families still grieving their losses. It didn't take long, however, for the reality of the situation to outpace the political rhetoric. There simply was not enough money to complete the work in the timeframe being quoted by authorities. This realization precipitated a palatable tension that only worsened the prospects for Project 150.

About 8,000 miles away in Washington, DC, American officials were paying close attention to the situation. Since the attacks of September 11, 2001, American policy has focused on regional stabilization and competent criminal justice practices as key deterrents to international terrorism. With Southeast Asia being of great importance to global stability, cultivating goodwill in Vietnam, while supporting the proliferation of forensic DNA technology in the region, made sense.

The United States committed to assisting Vietnam in Project 150, but it was clear that a lack of funding was only a part of the problem. The agencies and businesses in Vietnam seeking to participate in the project were not collaborating or communicating to the degree necessary for the project's success. All would have to work together, requiring approaches to leadership that could unite these disparate entities in a wave of solidarity. My job was to facilitate a weeklong gathering of about 30 leaders whose agencies and businesses would determine the fate of Project 150.

I departed Detroit and made a connection in Seoul, South Korea on my way to Hanoi. The 20-plus hours of flying gave me a chance to review my presentations and reflect on what I was expected to do. I'd been heavily briefed by my point of contact in DC and concluded that the challenges of Project 150 were probably the result of some big egos that weren't willing to get along. But I wasn't sure.

When I arrived, I was treated like a celebrity. A large banner standing about 10 feet tall and about 16 feet wide was hanging in the front of the room, printed with my name and the name of my workshop. It was probably the warmest welcome I'd ever received for a facilitation. But within one hour, I felt confident that something else – something far more poisonous – was threatening the future of Project 150.

The Threat of Tradition. As I always do in my events, I pick a person in the front corner of the room and have her or him make a quick personal introduction. I then go around the room until all have had the chance to say hello and be greeted by their fellow attendees. Normally, this process doesn't take long, but with translators involved, it doubles the time.

"Good morning," I said to a lady seated to my far left in the front row. "Would you please tell me your name, where you work, and what you do in your current position? We can then go around the room until we've heard from everybody."

Upon being addressed by me, she seemed startled and glanced toward three other ladies and a gentleman seated immediately to her left in the same row. The three ladies shook their heads in a sort of embarrassed compliance, then deferred to the gentleman who now stood up to introduce himself and them. I was startled by what was a clear cultural phenomenon that I had neither witnessed before nor prepared myself to witness. *Do men need to introduce women here*, I wondered? *Or do bosses need to introduce their subordinates? Maybe a bit of both?* As we went around the room, this awkward deference to rank, seniority, and male dominance played out again and again. And, over the course of the week, we found our conversations repeatedly compromised by the unwillingness of some participants to share their individual views.

I became 100% convinced that Project 150 would fail if the leaders in the room could not collaborate. And I was equally convinced this collaboration would never happen if their intense cultural addiction to rank, stature, and authority continued to erode the quality of the conversations that needed to take place. So, after Monday's session, I went back to my hotel and completely redesigned my plan for the remainder of the week. I certainly didn't want to create an international incident, but our group needed to confront what was an obvious impediment to the interagency communication needed for Project 150 to survive. There was a choice to be made. The leaders in the room could choose to prioritize teamwork or they could choose to prioritize their place in a hierarchy. Project 150, of course, was not a customary undertaking devised to solve a customary problem. Therefore, custom had little of value to offer, a point I went out of my way to emphasize with as much tactfulness and diplomacy as I could.

To my delight, what I feared might be a heavy and onerous conversation seemed to brighten the room, and there was a noticeable release of tension, like air being let out of a balloon. The attendees seemed to almost get a chuckle out of admitting how customs and traditions get in the way of progress. As equals in the moment, the rest of our conversations were more productive, insightful, and enjoyable. When the week came to a close, several attendees personally thanked me for helping them get unstuck, and for giving them *permission* to think about themselves and their challenges in a different light.

Letting Go

Permission is a powerful force in any campaign to effect change. I've witnessed this truth play out for so many clients seeking to improve as professionals or as managers. I've also witnessed it on teams trying to create healthier cultures. Resistance to change and progress do not come most often from the *unwilling* or the *unable*; it comes from those who've not given themselves *permission*. To become a willing agent of progress requires the letting go of the past and a relaxing of one's grip on the way things used to be. Change is like jumping out of an airplane with a parachute. Walking through an open door doesn't require any special skill or ability. What it requires is permission granted to self – permission to say goodbye to the comfort and safety of the airplane, a necessary step toward enjoying what will be a singularly thrilling and inspiring few moments of freedom in the sky. But first you have to jump out of the damn plane.

To be an equal in the moment is to let go of the comfort and safety that your rank, stature, and authority seem to afford you. You may have high rank in your organization. You may have great stature among your professional peers or within your community. You may have considerable authority that gives you power over others in certain situations. To be an equal in the moment, therefore, is to subject yourself, as a leader, to the uncertainty that comes from having to consider a variety of viewpoints, answer difficult questions, open yourself up to criticism, engage in debate, or have your decisions second-guessed. The result, however, is the thrill and inspiration that comes from leveraging a more powerful style of influence that creates more engagement. Don't worry, your rank, stature, and authority are there for you when you really need them, but that won't be very often. Why, you ask? Because, as you continue to grow and mature in your leadership role, you'll find yourself becoming increasingly effective at influencing people through quality relationships. Effective leaders don't need rank, stature, and authority to be effective. People willingly follow them because they're sincere, engaging, inspiring, motivating, and encouraging.

Give yourself permission to be the kind of leader that influences people the right way. Let go of any outdated or destructive attitudes about rank, stature, and authority and instead leverage the power of your character and competence. There is little satisfaction to be enjoyed by leading people who follow you because they have no other choice, or because you manipulated or bullied them into doing so. Leading from the low branches, you might say, requires no talent and therefore earns no respect or admiration. There is, on the other hand, great satisfaction that comes from watching people follow your lead because they want to, because they respect you, and because they have confidence in you. This is the kind of talent you want to develop as a leader. But, as you may discover, the hardest part of doing so may be giving yourself permission to do it.

Chapter 6

Vulnerable by Choice

His name was John, and the young man was visibly frustrated. His dark gray necktie hung dutifully over his light gray, short-sleeved shirt, adorned with a NASA identification badge clipped to his left breast pocket. He stood up and pushed his way to the front of the room, confronting NASA's legendary director of flight operations, Gene Kranz. The room went silent. Having listened to the bickering and posturing of his colleagues over the last several minutes, he'd had enough. With vintage browline glasses framing his resolute eyes, he made his opinion known, and everyone listened.

"Whoa, whoa, guys! Power is everything. Without it, they don't talk to us, they don't correct their trajectory, they don't turn the heat shield around. We've gotta turn everything off – NOW! They aren't gonna make it to reentry."

It's among the most dramatic scenes from the 1995 blockbuster film, *Apollo 13*, and a vivid portrayal of how effective leaders enable excellence from the members of their teams, even those who may be young or less experienced.

After learning that an onboard explosion has placed the lives of the astronauts in danger, the NASA team in Houston is now desperate to come up with a solution. The Lunar Excursion Module, or LEM, is being used by the astronauts as a sort of celestial life raft while NASA figures out how to get them home. Every minute that goes by drains valuable power from the batteries of the spacecraft. And the idea that the flight crew should confine themselves to the freezing temperatures of an intentionally disabled ship while zipping through space without control or propulsion, disturbs many of the experts in the room.

We've gotta turn everything off – NOW!

Gene Kranz, played by one of the more intimidating screen-actors in Hollywood, Ed Harris, listens attentively to what his young engineer has to say. "What do you mean, everything?" Kranz asks.

"With everything on, the LEM draws 60 amps," John explains. "At that rate, in 16 hours the batteries are dead, and so is the crew. We've gotta get them down to 12 amps."

"You can't run a vacuum cleaner on 12 amps, John!" barks another voice from the room.

John is undeterred. "We have to turn off the radars, cabin heater, instrument display, guidance computer, the whole smack!"

"Whoa, wait! Guidance computer?" Another colleague intervenes. "What if they need to do another burn? Gene, they won't even know which way they're pointed."

"The more time we talk down here the more juice they waste up there," John continues. "I've been looking at the data for the last hour."

Kranz stares into the eyes of his young but confident colleague, perhaps afraid of what he already knows is true. "That's the deal?"

"That's the deal," John responds.

Kranz pauses, looks around the room, then returns his gaze to John. "Ok John." Kranz's voice is almost broken from the gravity of the decision he's about to make. "The minute we finish the burn, we'll shut down the LEM."

What's more instructive than what Kranz said and did during this exchange is what he didn't say and didn't do. He didn't puff up his chest and tell John to *sit-the-hell down, I'm in charge here. I've been directing flight operations since you were in diapers. When I want your opinion, I'll ask for it, son!* Instead, Kranz does what effective leaders do. He gives John the space and safety to say what he needs to say, and he extends the same courtesy to others in the room who may disagree. Eventually, Kranz has to make a decision because only he has the authority to make it, not to mention that lives are on the line. At no time, however, does it become personal. And at no time does Kranz compromise the effectiveness of his team by making it about him or demanding that his own personal need for respect and deference take higher priority than the problem confronting all of them. He was an equal in the moment. Had he not been, I venture a guess that the bodies of the Apollo crew would still be floating somewhere in space right now. But they aren't. They came home alive. *Equals in the moment.*

Creating Space for Contribution

As a leader, there's some risk in giving people the floor to speak their minds. Things might get out of hand. Something might be said that makes you look or feel ignorant. You might feel threatened by the competence of others. You might get caught not being as well-informed as you thought you were – or as you want people to think you are. A disagreement may arise, even a conflict. You might get angry and lose your temper. A member of your team may appear to be smarter and more capable than you. Or – God forbid – you may have to make a difficult decision.

These dangers, of course, are illusory. They're nothing more than self-inflicted anxieties suffered by would-be leaders who insist on being superior to everyone else – or, at least, everyone else they believe is inferior. This sets up a vicious emotional cycle that plagues influential people with superiority complexes. Their efforts, behaviors, and priorities become focused on creating opportunities for their own superiority to be on display. At the same time, they avoid or derail situations that may threaten the perceptions that others have of them – perceptions that they are, in fact, superior and deserving of it. In doing so, their self-aggrandizing behaviors are deflating to those they are supposed to be leading. But why?

Because people don't like to be treated like inferiors. It's offensive and tiring. And they're usually smart enough to know that competent leadership is about building everyone up, making everyone as relevant as possible and affording everyone an opportunity to shine as often as possible. Superiority-based leaders don't do these things. The result, therefore, are teams of people who quickly lose confidence in their leaders, and their leaders know it and feel threatened by it. This leaves them few other options but to do what they do best – to micromanage, to control, or to even abuse or harass their inferiors as reminders of who's superior and who's not.

This incompetence and overall lack of professionalism come to bear heavily on those members of a team who are creative, loyal, committed, and engaged. These are the people that organizations need to remain energized. But these high performers will not tolerate condescending treatment for long. They may leave to go find other work or they may stick around and hope for a change in leadership. But what often happens is a sort of quiet revolt of the mistreated. Effective people *want* to be effective. Effective people *will* be effective. And if they can use their creativity, knowledge, and professional skills to work around the many barriers put up by their incompetent leaders, they will do so even when it exposes them to unpleasant consequences, including the possibility of malicious retaliation – something to be expected from the wounded egos of leaders who are hypersensitive to their superiority being challenged.

A Gut-Wrenching Decision

On August 16, 2012, Mike Martindale of the Detroit News reported that I had submitted my resignation from the Michigan State Police:

"The head of the Michigan State Police forensic crimes division said Wednesday he's resigning less than a month after helping to win a coveted international accreditation for the department's seven crime labs. When he took the state police labs job two years ago, John M. Collins inherited a backlog of thousands of cases across Michigan awaiting analysis. He also became responsible for labs that needed changes and attention to pass accreditation, plus the entire caseload of the shuttered Detroit police crime lab, including thousands of untested rape kits."

My resignation came as a surprise to everyone, and it ended what was a remarkably satisfying and accomplished career as a forensic laboratory scientist and administrator. The fact that I had a wife and two teenaged children added to the enormous stress I felt over leaving such a prestigious and well-paying job. But I had to do it. I'd exhausted every ounce of patience I could muster to cope with the egos, entitlement, and superiority complexes of so many police commanders to whom I'd reported over two decades of public service. For a variety of reasons, some explained in this book and others not, I didn't trust my superiors and I didn't trust the culture they were perpetuating. So, I decided to quit while I was on top. It was the most difficult decision I ever made.

Don't get me wrong, I appreciate law enforcement and the profession of uniformed policing. I really do. And I'm proud to have served in a capacity that allowed me to assist police investigators in the solving of crimes. There are many amazing police officers out there, officers who really care about the communities they're serving. But the organizational cultures of many police agencies are highly toxic. Worse, the higher you go in the ranks, the more you'll witness erratic behavior and inconsistent decision-making that seems unguided by any thoughtful strategy or the consideration of organizational values. In my opinion, it's because police culture encourages the selection of uniformed leadership candidates based more on their demonstrated history of loyalty than actual talent. Said another way, the level of superiority you are allowed to achieve is proportionate to your willingness to preserve the system as it is. Things like continued learning and disruptive innovation may be acceptable if you're talking about holsters, patrol cars, and ammunition. But it's not acceptable when you're talking about organizational culture and leadership practices.

The result of this dysfunction, where it exists, is the stacking of the executive ranks with individuals having few leadership skills of value. And it's likely they were selected for their positions by upper-level commanders who'd be scared to death to promote an individual who might challenge the status quo.

A Chance to Come Home. When the Director position opened up in early 2010, a representative of the Michigan State Police contacted me to ask if I'd be willing to apply and sit for an interview. At the time, I was ready to make a change. Both of my parents who lived in the Detroit area were recently afflicted with terminal diseases. My mother was losing her decade-long battle with breast cancer while my father had been diagnosed with ALS, also known as Lou Gehrig's Disease. The chance to return home to Michigan, be hired into one of the most prestigious forensic science positions in the United States, while making myself available to assist my parents felt like the universe had stacked the deck in my favor. When the position was offered to me, I enthusiastically accepted.

I can't begin to tell you the excitement and pride I felt to be entrusted with this new position and this new set of responsibilities. As a youngster, I idolized the police. I wanted to be a police officer and probably would have been had I not had such a strong interest in science. I was sure this would be the last position I would ever have. I had landed my dream job.

Over time, I realized something was wrong. Very wrong. As I explained in the introduction, 11,000 untested rape kits were found by state and local authorities in Detroit almost two years prior to my hiring. Governor Jennifer Granholm, who I learned had a reputation of being disrespectful to the State Police, responded by ordering the layoff of over 40 newly trained state troopers who'd recently graduated from the State Police Training Academy. With the resulting savings, she instructed the State Police against its wishes to hire civilian forensic scientists who could subject the rape kits to DNA testing and potentially identify perpetrators who could be brought to justice.

Words cannot express the rage that erupted within the trooper ranks of the State Police, nor the subtle forms of retaliation that were directed toward the leadership and staff of the Forensic Science Division. What Governor Granholm did was a slap in the face to the Michigan State Police and its troopers and their firmly held cultural belief that troopers are superior to civilians. After a short time on the job, I could sense the anger and tension in the dealings I had with the upper command. I felt like an enemy, even though I'd gained a reputation as a pretty effective administrator within the agency. As explained by the Detroit News, among my key priorities was the reduction of the case backlog plaguing our laboratories, which exploded to over 20,000 cases after the City of

Detroit shuttered its crime laboratory after 80 years of service. The discovery of shoddy work and erroneous results triggered the closure, prompting all of Detroit's crime scene evidence to be redirected to the labs of the State Police, which had neither the staff nor the facilities to handle the new influx of cases. Again, all of this happened before I ever arrived for my first day on the job. But it was my mess to clean up and I knew it.

Although my time with the Michigan State Police was brief – about two and half years – it was a time when I did some of my best work. My team and I cut the backlog by over 50% while reducing overtime expenditures by 27%. We earned international accreditation for the first time. But the greatest compliment I ever received in my career came right after I tendered my resignation. The resident psychologist employed by the Michigan State Police was a thoughtful and caring man. We enjoyed each other's company and used to meet for coffee to discuss leadership issues, stress management strategies, or whatever else was on our minds. During what would be our last coffee chat, he told me that I should be proud of what I'd accomplished under some of the worst circumstances imaginable. He went on to explain that since my hiring, he'd seen a remarkable decline in the number of forensic science employees coming to his office for counseling. Of course, I had no idea, but it continues to be one of the professional achievements that I'm most grateful for. To this day, I think about that conversation back in 2012 quite often. It fills me with a sense of satisfaction knowing that my team and I made a positive difference in people's lives. We took very seriously the responsibilities we'd been entrusted with, and it made a big difference for lots of people.

Quitter's Remorse. Looking back on my departure from what I thought would be the greatest job I'd ever have, I sometimes wonder if I made the right decision to resign. I chuckle at the memory of being summoned to the office of the Director of State Police, there with her dutiful legal counsel by her side, as they did their best to butter me up. I had power. I was leaving, and they knew I was in a position to head straight to the press where I'd likely be welcomed and given a platform from which to air my dirty laundry. Of course, I didn't and wouldn't. But how I would have enjoyed doing so. Twenty years of coping with egotistical police commanders had worn me out and seemed only to be getting worse. The eventual deaths of my parents, who passed away exactly 60 days apart, flooded me with grief that would take me years to get over. I had simply run out of gas and I didn't want to hurt the Michigan State Police. It was a proud agency trying to recover from some very hurtful political wounds that were outside of its control. I just wanted to step away and start the next chapter of my life.

Over time, I reflected on my tenure at the Michigan State Police, what I'd accomplished, the mistakes I made, and what I'd learned. Most of the challenging personalities I had to deal with are probably gone now, but I still find myself recounting and processing the experiences I had with them. Finally, it dawned on me. My hiring was, in itself, a form of retaliation against the forensic laboratories by the command of the State Police who were bitter about the firing of the troopers. In that regard, I was the perfect candidate. Yes, my resume was strong and so was my reputation within the forensic science community. But I also knew nothing about the inner workings of the Michigan State Police. I would be easy to confuse and manipulate, unlikely to threaten the budget priorities of those intent on preserving the more traditional policing functions, which does not include forensic science. Perhaps I would be weak in negotiating resource allocations to the forensic science laboratories. And I'd be largely unknown to the criminal justice community of Michigan, affording me no network of supporters with whom I could build a consensus on how forensic laboratories should be funded and operated. Yes indeed, I was the perfect candidate for the superiors who were looking to fill the forensic director position with an inferior, someone who wasn't a threat to them.

If this was the mindset of those who hired me, which I believe it was, they didn't count on the fact that I'm pretty quick to learn and even quicker to develop strategic relationships. I do not draw my influence from the wells of the *old superior*, so the speed at which I'm able to make the connections I need to be successful is much faster than what they might've been used to. It didn't take me long to learn the game. And the more effective I became in advocating for my division, the more I was perceived as a threat – something that still puzzles me because I'm a pretty approachable and agreeable guy. I don't like getting my way at the expense of others' peace of mind. I thrive on being an equal in the moment, no matter how much rank or authority I may have. But I had found myself in a position of having become *good* at my job, which made it almost impossible for me to *stay* in my job.

No Holding Back. In the following years, making the transition to private practice and becoming a business owner were challenging but liberating because, for the first time in my career, I felt entirely unrestrained by dysfunctional superiors. I was my own boss and could trust that whatever skills and abilities I had would be put to good use and not wasted within an organizational culture that didn't value them. I was free to succeed and free to fail. And the experience was, and still is, nothing short of invigorating. But I had a lot of healing to do when I retired my forensic laboratory career. The grief I felt over the deaths of my parents and the way they died – so close together but so isolated from each other due to the nature of their own individual illnesses – took a heavy emotional toll on me. I wasn't able to fully grieve the loss of my mom in November 2011 because we had to turn our attention immediately to my dad, whose condition was worsening by the day. After he passed the following January, he was buried next to my mom, whose grave site was still soft and unsettled from her burial 60 days earlier. Her headstone had not even been placed yet.

Grief and Empathy. People who are grieving have a strong need to feel a connection to the people in their lives who are most important to them, both personally and professionally. These connections help draw the grieving person back into the activities of life and away from the compulsive dwelling on the intense sadness he feels. The sadness, in many ways, feels like a tribute to those who were lost, so it can become almost addictive. Having people in your life who empathize with what you're experiencing and who understand that you won't be your normal self for the foreseeable future, gives you the feeling of being carried in a lifeboat from a sinking ship to shore.

The best description of empathy I've ever encountered was written by Brené Brown in her 2018 bestselling book, *Dare to Lead*. If you haven't read it, you should. I think it's among the best leadership books available – and I've read a lot of them. Brené explains that empathy is about sharing – not observing or commenting on – an experience with another human being. Sympathy is the expression of *it sucks to be you*. Empathy is the expression of *I feel what you're feeling*. To sincerely empathize with another human being requires that you be an equal in the moment, that you feel what he or she is feeling. It doesn't require you to say anything or do anything. It just requires you to be present and to experience what someone else is experiencing.

Looking back on those challenging years at the Michigan State Police, I came to realize that I had become overwhelmed with grief, and it was affecting my performance. And the source of that grief was not simply the result of losing my parents, but also of having coped with their diagnoses, treatments, and steady declines for a number of years. Their deaths certainly punctuated the grieving cycle, but the pain had been with me for a long time. As I've learned from so many years of working in and with law enforcement agencies, the superiority complexes that dominate police culture make it difficult for the hurting to heal and for their colleagues to empathize.

Comfort and Closure. During my time at the Michigan State Police, I had the opportunity to report to a gentleman who I consider the most effective administrator to whom I ever had the pleasure to report – even if it was only for a very short time. His name is Shawn Sible and he was the Director of the Administrative and Support Services Bureau under which the Forensic Science Division was arranged. Shawn was the only civilian (nonsworn) member of the executive council, the cohort of top-level administrators reporting to the Director of State Police, who in-turn reports to the Governor. When you look at group-photographs of newly minted troopers after graduating from the academy, standing proudly behind the members of the executive council, Shawn is the only one wearing a suit. All the others are in uniform.

What struck me about Shawn was that he exhibited personal qualities that made him a professional force to be reckoned with. And in working with him for the short time I did, I began to realize that he had professional attributes that I did not – attributes that I wished I'd had. He was not an arousing motivational speaker or a guy from whom you'd expect to hear inspirational words of wisdom. Instead, I perceived him to be a consummate professional – steadfast, consistent, and direct.

As the only civilian member of the executive council, Shawn was remarkably effective at navigating the egos and attitudes of the sworn command staff, but without taking it personally or losing his own sense of self in the process. In watching Shawn, I could directly observe what I needed to develop within myself, that being an unwavering foundation of self-confidence and purpose that stands immune to the chaotic approaches to leadership that are endemic in police culture. I was a leader who was visionary, innovative, and entrepreneurial, vulnerable to being perceived as undisciplined and inconsistent if I wasn't careful. But I also took things too personally, especially considering the political and operational challenges that our laboratories were facing. And as my parents' lives were coming to an end, and with the stresses of caring for their needs mounting, I took it more personally than I should have. Simply put, I needed more than what I had in my gas tank, which is why my resignation became necessary. The environment in which I was operating was not conducive for me to elevate my executive leadership skills in the way I knew would be best for me and my team. So, as disappointing as it was for me to give up my position and leave the team that I'd assembled, it started me on a journey of personal and professional growth that might otherwise have not happened.

I share my experience of working with Shawn so that I can tell you what happened when I ran into him several years later at an annual meeting of the International Association of Chiefs of Police. I had been doing some consulting work with Franklin Covey and agreed to work the Franklin Covey exhibit booth at the IACP meeting to drum up interest among police administrators for the company's training and consulting services. While at the booth, I saw Shawn approach but could tell he didn't see me. When he stopped to check out our materials, I greeted him warmly. Surprised, he smiled and asked how I was doing. We chatted for several minutes before I paused and told him how much I appreciated him and the opportunity to work with him. I went on to explain how difficult my departure from the State Police was for me, but that the challenging circumstances in my life had made it difficult for me to function at my best. His response was both gracious and therapeutic.

"You know, John, I really appreciate your honesty," he began. "Our agency sometimes does a lousy job of paying attention to what's going on in the lives of our employees, and we don't stop to find out if there are ways we can help and support them during difficult times. It's a part of our culture that needs work."

I'm paraphrasing Shawn's comments, but that's the gist of it. It made me feel good to close that loop and to briefly explain my decision to resign from an organization I idolized with a man who may be remembered as one of the State Police's most prominent and effective executives. When we said our goodbyes, I felt like a weight had been lifted off my shoulders.

But I'm also realistic. To achieve the vision that Shawn described would require a dramatic shift in how police organizations think about their people. Empathy for others is difficult to nurture across a team when the members of that team are preoccupied with how they compare to each other. If I see my fellow team members as obstacles to my own attainment of rank, stature, or authority – or if I judge my own sense of organizational worth by where I fall within the ranks – then it limits my willingness and ability to see myself in other people's shoes because, after all, I'm perpetually focused on making sure my shoes are better than theirs.

The Risk of Reaching Deeper

For a leader to make a deep personal connection with a subordinate member of the team requires the personal fortitude to withstand the vulnerability that comes with it. To be an equal in the moment is to sacrifice the perceived advantages of superiority. And for the loyal advocates of the rank-and-file structure who've been conditioned to reflexively adhere to its customs, this vulnerability is often too much to bear.

Dealing with an Addiction. In my first book, *HR Management in the Forensic Science Laboratory – A 21st Century Approach to Effective Crime Lab Leadership*, I wrote about the tragic story of Joseph Graves, an employee of the Pensacola forensic science laboratory operated by the Florida Department of Law Enforcement. Graves was discovered to have been stealing and using drugs held as evidence in the laboratory's custody. To account for the change in weight of the evidence, he allegedly replaced the illicit drugs he was using with over-the-counter pills. As I wrote in my book, the explosive story made national news:

"Reporter Susan Jacobson, writing for the Orlando Sentinel on February 4, 2014, established the context and proportion of the story when she reported 'about 2600 cases dating to 2006 are being reviewed, including at least 16 in Osceola County and at least five in Lake County, the FDLE said.'"

Clearly, the situation was dire for the Florida Department of Law Enforcement, now forced to exhaust huge portions of its already strained budgets to respond. But I expressed discontent with public statements made by the FDLE Commissioner, which wreaked of self-righteous indignation. Here's what I wrote:

"FDLE may have missed a valuable opportunity to gain sympathy from the public when it chose to attack its own employee and characterize the misconduct as being bad behavior committed by a bad person. In a statement released by the FDLE, Commissioner Gerald Baily said, 'the actions of Joseph Graves are disgraceful.' Of course, they were. But in

taking this authoritarian approach, the FDLE implicated itself as well, leaving open considerable space in the public domain to speculate about why such a prominent law enforcement agency would ever hire such a bad person in the first place. A different approach would have been for the FDLE to present itself, truthfully so, as another American employer coping with the growing epidemic of prescription-drug addiction in the United States, which was reportedly a key factor contributing to the scandal."

In expressing my thoughts, the degree of misconduct in which Joseph Graves engaged was not lost on me. What he did was terminal in its severity, meaning there were few options, if any, but to end his employment and investigate the possibility that a crime was committed. It's a cliff from which you can't *unjump.* And although reasonable people can be both angry with Graves and hopeful that he can put his life back together, severe consequences follow severe incidents in due course. The FDLE was justified in taking it so seriously.

But an interesting thing happens when severe misconduct occurs under the watch of those with a superiority complex. They succumb to the temptation of using the situation to showcase their superiority. In doing so, they make it about them – projecting outrage and a resolve to hold guilty individuals accountable. *I refuse to stand by and allow something this horrible to happen on my watch*, is the underlying message. And it has a remarkable way of making the responding superiors look like victims of sorts, such that doing the right thing and taking swift action is somehow a monumental act of courage for which the rest of us should feel grateful.

Intentional Anger. This kind of opportunistic reaction to catastrophe was exactly what we witnessed when the 11,000 rape kits were discovered in Detroit, which, by the way, occurred one year after its crime laboratory was shuttered. In my judgement, the two incidents stemmed from the same systemic failure to take forensic evidence seriously and ensure that it be treated with the respect it's due. The individuals who feigned the most outrage were the most derelict in their duties, caring little about how forensic evidence was being handled in Detroit until the catastrophe gave them a chance to grandstand.

Years after the Detroit laboratory closed and the rape kit stockpile was being resolved, I had an opportunity to chat with a forensic biologist who worked in the old Detroit laboratory where thousands of items of crime scene evidence were analyzed each year. "We actually had a pretty good lab," she explained. "But we just couldn't get the funding and support we needed. Our own commanders didn't seem to care much about what we were doing, and the prosecutors were notorious for bullying our scientists. We didn't need to shut down the lab, we just needed some help."

Everything she explained to me aligned with what I was personally observing as Director of the Michigan laboratories. Forensic science was an inferior enterprise in Michigan, taking a distant back seat to the traditional policing and prosecution priorities that seemed to dominate how criminal justice was administered. In one instance, an elected prosecutor with over 30 years of experience directly threatened me when our DNA experts complained that he was demanding unnecessary, redundant forensic testing in a case that his office was prosecuting. As a result, our DNA team advised his office that we wouldn't do further testing because it was impeding our ability to assist in other serious cases that needed attention.

I supported the decision made by our team. But, as I expected, the prosecutor called me at my office. What I did not expect was for him to threaten me, suggesting ever-so-subtly that he would interfere with my annual budget negotiations at the State Capitol if we didn't honor his wishes. I was mortified by his clear and egregious abuse of power, but I knew that my options were limited. If he couldn't get me to bend, his next call would surely be to the Governor's office where a 20-something-year-old bureaucrat would call and order me to do what the prosecutor wanted. So, I negotiated a limited plan of additional testing – expensive and time-consuming testing, by the way – which produced no results of any forensic or investigative value. The superior had successfully bullied who he regarded as his inferior and the cost was high.

A Matter of Human Nature

If you forced me to share just one lesson that I've learned over the course of my career – just one lesson that stands out among all the rest – it is that effective people despise being treated like inferiors. They want their expertise and skills to be recognized, and they want to have a seat at a table where they can make contributions that have value to the team. They want to have trust in the culture, such that it's safe to step forward and politely challenge conventional thinking when it might be necessary. To create this kind of culture, however, requires that leaders have a high tolerance for risk – that being the risk that comes with giving other people power. In giving other people power, leaders become more powerful themselves because they surround themselves with willing contributors, contributors who gain skills and experience that only come from working in an environment where they are permitted to accrue them and apply them.

Chapter 7

Superiority Signaling

One of the most irritating moments I ever experienced happened when I was filling a position responsible for the administration of our division's quality assurance system, recently vacated by a gentleman who was promoted into another position within the organization. To my delight, I now had the opportunity to open this position to applicants and choose a candidate, most likely from among the current members of our team, who could help our laboratories make some of the improvements they were hungry for. We were also in the process of transitioning into a new and more rigorous accreditation program that would require a talented and hardworking leader who cared about quality and could inspire the commitment we would need to earn accreditation under the new international system.

One of the candidates who applied was a man I liked and respected – I'll call him Gary. Gary always struck me as being kind and I enjoyed his company. He was a sworn trooper, the highest-ranking applicant, and had the most seniority. Common sense would have predicted that the position belonged to Gary if he wanted it. But in his interview, Gary was clumsy in the answering of his questions and seemed to lack any strategic vision for how our laboratories would restructure their quality assurance systems in preparation for the new accreditation. In fact, I don't think he fully understood what the new accreditation standards were. Sure, he was friendly and energetic, but he left me little confidence that he could give us the leadership and insight we would need from our quality assurance director. I didn't trust that he could earn and retain the respect of our laboratory directors who'd be counting on him to make sure that our evolving work processes would continue to be reliable. The last thing any forensic administrator wants to hear is that a scientist made a mistake in a criminal case where a defendant's freedom is on the line. Gary just wasn't the guy for the job, even though I had the clear sense he felt entitled to it.

Julie, however, was a different kind of candidate, and when I interviewed her, she overpowered me with confidence, clarity, knowledge, and vision. She explained exactly how we would transition our accreditation and was able to anticipate some of the challenges we might encounter along the way. She had the perfect blend of authoritativeness and approachability, something that's always been important to me when considering candidates for leadership positions. Unlike Gary, Julie seemed to recognize the responsibilities to which she would be *entrusted*, and despite her youth – Julie was in her early 30s, I'd say – she was remarkably mature and thoughtful in her answers, sharing perspectives that I would expect from someone with much more experience.

When it was all over, Julie was named the new Assistant Division Director in charge of quality assurance, and I couldn't wait to help her get started. But first, I had to break the news to Gary, uncertain of how he might respond and hopeful he would understand that the demands of the position were over his head.

As soon as I could, I called Gary and asked him to meet me in my office. When he arrived, he was jovial and confident, taking a seat in one of the two chairs across from my desk. As I told him about my decision, his eyebrows raised and his jaw clenched in a show of confused irritation. "Is that so?" he inquired with a calmness that failed to mask the intense disappointment I know he felt.

"Gary," I continued. "I appreciate you and what you've done for our organization. You bring a lot to the table, and I'll continue to enjoy working with you. But we've got some challenges ahead that are going to require the kind of knowledge and skills that only Julie seemed to demonstrate in the interviews. She's going to do a great job for us and she'll need your support."

Gary was unmoved. He proceeded to remind me of his rank and the years of service he'd given to our organization. He voiced his disagreement with my decision and made his case for why he should have been selected. Wanting to defuse the tension, I allowed him to vent until he said something that caught me by surprise.

"John," he said. "I am a man of God."

Dumbfounded, all I could do was look at him and wait for some kind of clarification that would make what I just heard even marginally appropriate. It didn't happen. Instead, Gary explained how he was an ordained minister and could provide the kind of moral leadership that our team needed. Julie, he argued, was too young and inexperienced for this kind of position and that my poor decision would have serious consequences.

What Gary didn't realize was that as I sat and listened to his sermon, I privately celebrated my relief that I did not select him for the position. By his own doing, he further validated my decision to promote Julie who, by the way, turned out to be every bit the administrator that I knew she would be, and more. Gary, on the other hand, was mentally and emotionally entangled in his own entitlement, which accounted for his poor performance during his interview. He just wasn't prepared, and the reason he wasn't prepared was because he made the mistake of anticipating that my selection would be based on factors unrelated to competence, that I was somehow obliged to fill the position with the candidate having the highest rank and the most seniority – the next in line, you might say – even if the candidate was only marginally qualified. After all, there's no motivation to prepare for an interview when you believe in your heart-of-hearts that you're entitled to the position. Gary was an *entitled* job candidate. Julie was *entrusted*.

In that moment, when I informed Gary about my selection of Julie for the quality assurance position, he felt cheated. He saw himself as the superior and Julie as the inferior, which could only mean he was the rightful heir to the quality assurance throne. So, when I informed him that Julie was selected for the position, his entitled ears heard something different, that I had anointed Julie as the superior and Gary as the inferior. This, of course, offended him because it was contrary to what he thought was true, which could only mean there was something wrong with *me*. Clearly, I must not have fully understood what I was doing. In Gary's mind, I was confused about who was superior and who was inferior. So, in his own way, he took it upon himself to politely correct me.

I am a man of God was Gary's way of signaling his superiority not just over Julie, but over me as well. It was an immature, entitled way to protest a decision he interpreted as an attack on his sense of self-worth. It didn't matter that he was ill-suited for the position. He felt like an inferior and it hurt. So, positioning himself as *a man of God* returned order to his shaken universe and afforded him the opportunity to reclaim the superiority he so desperately needed.

Common Types of Signaling

Superiority signaling is a behavior in which a person seeks to reassert his standing over those he regards as inferior. I say *re*assert because the signaling is motivated by a feeling of having lost it or being close to losing it. Superiority signalers are people who feel insecure with how they're perceived, how they compare to others, or how much control they have. As a result, they display forms of conduct that serve to remind us of how great they are and how deserving they are of our praise and adoration. To observers, their conduct may seem awkward or contrived, but to the signaler it feels entirely appropriate, even medicinal. The signaler feels inferior in the moment and the discomfort is too much to bear. Signaling, therefore, serves to soothe the signaler who, for whatever reason, feels bad about himself.

Superiority signaling comes in many different forms but always results in a common outcome for the signaler, the loss of trust. Although the signaler feels an unmistakable pleasure, akin to the scratching of an itch, observers of the signaling eventually recognize it for what it is – self-promoting behavior intended to compensate for an insecurity. But it's not the insecurity that causes the loss of trust. It's the deception. The reason superiority signalers conduct themselves as they do is because they are trying to send a message, that message being that they are superior or worthy of praise and adoration. But they're also smart enough to know that they'd be branded as narcissists if they simply blurted out to people, *Hey! I am superior and worthy of everyone's praise and adoration!* That would be ridiculous and sure to offend observers.

Signalers have a message they desperately want to communicate but are unwilling to say it aloud. So, they encrypt the message within a pattern of behaviors displayed before unsuspecting observers, behaviors that express the desired message without having to say it. In essence, they're lying, and lying disqualifies them from being trusted.

In my coaching practice, I encounter six types of signaling behaviors that are worth explaining in more detail. There are others, but the ones I will explain here are quite common in professional settings. By recognizing them in yourself and others, you can become more effective in the personal and professional domains of your life. You might also become more effective in dealing with superiority signalers when you cross paths with them.

Physical Signaling. President Lyndon Johnson was famous in Washington for being quite a tall and imposing figure. He was known to lean into people when talking to them, sometimes getting into their personal space as a show of strength. This habit made him rather intimidating to those with whom he interacted.

We might describe President Johnson's behavior as *physical signaling*. And, although it may seem like a rather childish and primitive way to signal one's superiority, it is remarkably effective. In any environment where people interact with each other in person, one's physicality is always noticed. Especially when we meet people for the first time and have no basis upon which to make any reliable judgements, we take notice of their physical attributes, including their size and shape. People who are tall or muscular strike us as being more vibrant and energetic. Tall people seem to command a degree of respect simply because they are tall. Every U.S. president since and including Ronald Reagan has been over six feet tall. President Johnson was the second-tallest president at 6 feet 3 ½ inches, and he used it to his advantage.

According to Economic Times, while 14.5% of men in the United States are six feet or taller, among CEOs of Fortune 500 companies, that number goes up to 58%. That someone is tall, of course, does not mean he is signaling. He can't control how tall he is. But President Johnson's behavior was, in fact, signaling because he used his physical stature as a way to make other people feel inferior, thereby positioning himself as the superior.

Weightlifters who wear skin-tight shirts and walk with their arms flared out wide from their bodies are often signaling their strength and superior physiques – and perhaps they have every right to, considering how hard they work to achieve them. But for many, it is a way to use their physique to intimidate or impress. Some women may engage in similar behaviors by flaunting a well-tanned and chiseled beach body as a way to show their superiority over other women, or to arouse the sexual energies of potential partners. In fact, this kind of physical signaling is not limited to humans. We see physical signaling throughout the animal kingdom as a necessary way for suitable mates to find each other and reproduce.

Moral Signaling. My encounter with Gary, as I explained earlier, was a clear example of *moral signaling*, which is a pattern of behaviors through which people seek to position themselves as being more righteous and, therefore, more qualified to judge others. Sometimes called *virtue signaling*, it is a very powerful and offensive form of signaling because it cannot be contested. When Gary told me he was *a man of God*, there was no evidence I could present and no argument I could make to prove that he was wrong or misguided in how he viewed himself. At that point, the conversation was over, and the sermon began. By positioning himself as the moral superior, he sought to strip me of all my power and influence in the moment, restoring the sense of superiority he lost when learning that he wasn't selected for the job he wanted.

Moral signalers see the world as a hierarchy of people having varying degrees of significance based on their standing to either judge or be judged. As judges, they feel a sense of power and control. They feel righteous. They feel like better human beings. They're not as interested in organizational rank or social stature, but rather in assuming an elite state of transcendence that distinguishes them from the rest of us.

An interesting thing about moral signaling is that it can actually make observers feel bad about themselves even when it's not justified. Moral signalers are remarkably effective at portraying themselves as decent, honorable, and wholesome individuals who seem qualified to judge others. But what they fail to acknowledge is that their signaling is *im*moral and *un*justified, and that they are not, in fact, qualified to judge anyone. As people, moral signalers can be very likable and engaging, but given enough time, they will lose friends because those friends don't appreciate being judged and made to feel like there's something wrong with them. As leaders, moral signalers will struggle to retain the trust and confidence of their teams because their team members will come to notice that signalers never seem to judge themselves, only others. This perpetuates suspicions that signalers lack self-awareness and are therefore poorly equipped to navigate more complex situations and challenges when they arise, something any reasonable person would expect of a competent leader.

Intellectual Signaling. *Intellectual signaling* is the effort to showcase one's intelligence. Intellectual signalers have an emotional need to be among the smartest people in the room – if not, *the* smartest. They like to use big words when they speak, discuss complex issues in complex ways, utter abbreviations to listeners without explaining what they stand for, and reject what they perceive as the naiveté of their intellectual inferiors by refusing to give them the time of day.

I want to disclose something here before I continue. I was the victim of intellectual signaling early in my life and I believe that it still affects me today. I was a college athlete, a discus thrower, and I wanted to wear my varsity jacket as often as I could. I was proud of it. And, I was a bit of a meathead, muscular, and physically imposing at the time. In fact, I may have been guilty of some physical signaling in my youth mainly because I was bullied in elementary school. I wanted people to think of me as physically superior so they'd leave me alone. But in college, I noticed that many of my professors spoke down to me when I visited them for help or to get some questions answered. It was as if they didn't want me there and seemed annoyed by my presence. Some wouldn't look at me when speaking to me. Others spoke to me over the tops of their reading glasses, as if to say *What I'm reading here is far more important than me talking to you.* Now that I wear reading glasses, I always remove them before speaking with people.

Whether I was being hypersensitive or not, I chose to stop wearing my varsity jacket to class, and I did whatever I could to signal my intelligence to people in positions of authority. As I got older and started my career, my physical signaling went away, but my intellectual signaling continued. For example, when I realized my young son was afflicted with a disability, I found myself having to interact with a variety of doctors and other healthcare professionals. I was very intentional about signaling my intelligence because I wanted them to be honest with me and my family. My forensic career really helped me in this regard because I spent a lot of time reading autopsy reports and becoming familiar with medical jargon, expanding my vocabulary further and allowing me to sound like I really knew a lot about medicine – which, of course, I didn't, at least not to the degree that practicing physicians do. Even today, if I'm not careful, I can easily revert back to using big vocabulary when I'm trying to impress people. Because I want to avoid the temptations of signaling, I try to use common language as much as possible, not only in my personal interactions, but in my writing as well.

Dogmatic Signaling. I can't help but wonder if there's ever been a time when the social and economic engines of life have been more impaired by entrenched belief systems than they are now. Especially worth noting are the deep political and religious divides that hold some people together while driving others apart. What makes the phenomenon so troubling, though, is how confident people can be in their beliefs when that confidence has no basis. This is not to suggest that confident people are always wrong or unreasonable; indeed, they are not. It does mean, however, that some will position themselves as unrelenting advocates for a set of principles even when they have limited or no personal awareness of why those principles should be construed as true, and they will quickly shun or judge those they perceive to not share the same beliefs.

Dogma is a word used to describe a principle or set of principles that are viewed as being incontrovertibly true, often championed by an authority of some sort that keeps believers organized and united. Of course, there is nothing wrong with this, assuming believers don't adversely and unfairly impact the quality of life for nonbelievers. But, in fact, this is often what happens. For the overzealous believer, it's not good enough to just believe; he must also establish the superiority of his beliefs over those of others. He will also go so far as to establish his own superiority and the superiority of his fellow believers over nonbelievers who are then summarily discounted as mere inferiors.

This is *dogmatic signaling*, the need to establish one's belief system as being superior so that its believers can, as a matter of consequence, be viewed as superior themselves. Note that the goal here is the superiority of the believers. The beliefs themselves are but a conduit through which the desired superiority can be achieved. Dogmatic signalers can be quite aggressive and offensive in how they interact with others. They take seriously their social connections to other believers and draw great strength and feelings of personal relevance from these associations. What's more, their sense of purpose, self-worth, and personal identity are firmly based on these foundations. Anyone who refuses to recognize the validity of an underlying belief is mistaken for rejecting the personal legitimacy of the believers. This means that to compromise or engage in discussions in which closely held principles or beliefs are scrutinized for their validity is to entirely dishonor oneself and his community of believers. Some would rather die than give in to such cowardice.

Dogmatic signaling exists in all walks of life and can have both personal and professional origins. It can also be very offensive. The reason for this is because dogmatic signalers cloak themselves and their rhetoric within a thick blanket of certainty and confidence while dismissing the potential validity of competing perspectives. Observers to this behavior are smart enough to recognize that refusing to engage in conversation limits one's access to information and insight. This means that the certainty and confidence that signalers project are likely not justified. But because so many dogmatic signalers refuse to give serious consideration to opposing viewpoints, nonbelievers will often agree to disagree and move on, leaving the signalers feeling that they've won and that it's time to find some other confused mind to educate.

Organizational Signaling. Hale Cermak was the chief of a small police department in the Midwest. As part of his duties, he served on an executive leadership team with other public officials in his jurisdiction who met regularly to discuss a variety of topics of strategic significance. When I began working with Hale, he complained that other members of the leadership team seemed hesitant to warm up to him. When he gave his reports, they didn't ask many questions. During general conversations, they didn't go out of their way to seek his input on key issues, even when they pertained to public safety. He was confused and I could tell that it was bothering him.

Hale was a friendly guy. Our coaching sessions were usually energetic, and he enjoyed talking about leadership, having several well-known books about leadership and management resting on the credenza behind his desk. As a military veteran, he was a bit rigid and formal in how he carried himself, but I found it easy to make him laugh or smile. There was nothing about him I found to be off-putting that could explain why he was encountering friction with his colleagues on the executive leadership team. Well, except for one thing.

Whenever Hale and I met for our monthly coaching sessions, he wore his full police commander's uniform, comprised of a crisply ironed white shirt, a badge on his chest, and a radio on his belt that was tethered to a handpiece secured to his left shoulder. Also secured to his belt on the other side of his waist was a firearm. Keep in mind that Hale worked in an office setting. Also keep in mind that the other members of the executive leadership team were not police officers.

So, one day I asked Hale if there was a specific reason he found it necessary to dress in his uniform each day. He responded by saying that it was really just a matter of habit, and that he liked to be in uniform when his officers came to visit him. Hale wanted them to feel that he was still one of them.

I also asked him if there was a safety threat that required him to carry his service firearm while he was in the office. He admitted there wasn't, and that the firearm was simply part of the uniform and a fixture to which he'd become accustomed. Something unexpected could happen at any time, of course, but the chance of a situation erupting in which he needed to draw his gun from its holster was remote at best.

"I'll bet you stand out like a sore thumb at your executive leadership meetings, Hale," I remarked with a smile on my face, but curious how he might react to my observation.

"Yeah, I suppose I do," he replied. "But I feel better in uniform and I like knowing that I can respond to a situation if I need to."

I nodded to convey my understanding, but I wanted to force Hale to make a choice between two mutually exclusive options.

"Hale," I began, "does the benefit of you looking like a cop and being able to respond to a dangerous situation justify the barrier that your uniform creates for your colleagues on the executive leadership team?"

A mix of confusion and curiosity washed across Hale's face. "What do you mean by barrier," he asked.

"Hale, everything about your uniform is a barrier because it's specifically intended to set you apart from everyone else. On the street, this barrier has value because it protects you from harm and makes you more visible to people who may need your help. But it also signals your rank and superiority, which may be unsettling to the other leaders who are supposed to be acting as your equal when you meet in the boardroom. I wonder, do you carry your firearm with you into the leadership meetings?"

With a knowing smile he admitted that he did. "Yeah, I guess I never really thought about how my appearance might be affecting the other folks in the room."

From that moment on, Hale took it upon himself to completely change his appearance, not only for the executive leadership meetings but also when working in the office. He began wearing soft, pastel colored dress shirts with stylish ties that complimented his shirt selections. His leather waist belt matched his shoes, the kind of dress shoes you might expect the CEO of a large bank to be wearing. Gone was the utility belt and service shoes Hale wore each day. When arriving to work in the morning, he locked his gun in a cabinet above his desk. His badge, previously pinned to his chest, was now clipped to his belt. Overnight, Hale went from looking like an intimidating police chief to looking like a business executive. He looked approachable, kind, and unassuming – the kind of guy that likes to collaborate with people in a professional setting rather than a cop who's waiting to take someone down.

Hale admitted that the change took some getting used to, but the impact was unmistakable. At his executive leadership meetings, his colleagues smiled and greeted him with more warmth. They seemed to pay more attention to his reports and asked him questions after he spoke. They joked with him and laughed with him. And, perhaps more importantly, Hale felt better about himself. He felt like he belonged, like he was part of something bigger than himself, and this brought him comfort. The deeper connections he was establishing with his colleagues infused him with energy and feelings of contentment that were empowering. Hale was a new man.

What Hale didn't realize prior to the change of his wardrobe was that he had been signaling. In police culture, signaling is as normal as a traffic light at a busy intersection. In public, the uniform, the gun, the badge, and the stripes help to signal that a person is, in fact, a police officer. In the office, however, the uniform does nothing but to signal where in the organization the officer is ranked. The highest-ranking officer, usually the chief or sheriff, often wears a white shirt when in uniform, making it clear who is in charge. This is *organizational signaling*, intended to facilitate the quick recognition of individual power and influence in a hierarchy.

Hale didn't do anything careless or inappropriate by wearing his uniform as often as he did. He was a consummate professional and cared deeply about his work and how he represented his agency. But his uniform caused him to encounter a problem that, in my opinion, confronts most police officers today. They habitually signal their superiority in quarters where it has the opposite of the desired effect. Instead of cultivating trust and confidence, it foments tension and suspicion. Superiority signaling is often interpreted as aggression, defensiveness, or a show of strength, and it leads reasonable people to believe that the signaler intends to act out his superiority. For Hale, his uniform was an organizational signal that alienated him from his fellow executive leaders. By turning off that signal and presenting himself as an equal in the moment, Hale dramatically improved how he was perceived and, as a matter of consequence, how he perceived himself. When he stopped his organizational signaling, his peers responded by welcoming him as one of their own.

Social Signaling. The story of Hale provides us with a useful example of how superiority signaling of the organizational type can offend and marginalize people to the point that it impairs relationships in a professional setting or on a team. *Social signaling*, however, is behavior intended as a demonstration of where one stands within a particular social circle. The motive behind social signaling is the desire or need to be perceived as successful, attractive, and influential. A social signaler wants respect and admiration, and she seeks it out by continuously comparing herself to others in her neighborhood, community, or network. She strives to be *like* the people she respects and admires while distinguishing herself from those she doesn't. And to further reinforce the image she wants to project, she is careful and discriminating about those with whom she is seen. She recognizes that her own social stature depends heavily on mingling with the social superiors while shunning the inferiors.

Social signaling, however, can get much worse than this. It is my view that *gender signaling* has become a modern plague. We might describe it as the signaling of one's masculinity or femininity as being superior to the other. In fact, many women feel especially vulnerable to the signaling of superiority by men, which can do significant harm to organizational cultures and lead to sexual harassment or other forms of abuse perpetrated on women by men. The reason I do not include it as its own form of signaling, however, is because gender signaling seems to be an especially insidious form of social signaling that can originate from a sense of physical superiority. Men guilty of this kind of behavior are not signaling to let everyone know that they have a penis and want to have sex. They signal because they fancy themselves as being both physically and socially superior because they are men, and their behaviors reflect it. Women, however, can be guilty of this kind of signaling as well. Depending on the situation or circumstances, women can signal their superiority in ways that marginalize men or make them feel like second-class citizens – and it can hurt just as much as when men inflict it upon women.

Signaling and Leadership

When it comes to superiority signaling, whatever the type, the best policy is to not do it, and I mean *never*. Superiority signaling is nothing more than a childish, immature attempt to create a hierarchy where one doesn't exist, often perpetuated by people who judge their own self-worth by how they compare to others. They feel lost without a formal ranking system that clearly distinguishes the superiors from the inferiors – like soldiers without a war to fight. Tempted by the empty promises of the old superior, they imagine ways to compare themselves to others and establish whatever form of dominance makes them feel good about themselves.

Signalers may be decent people, of course, but they sense that something is missing within themselves and don't know how to find it. They feel irrelevant to some degree and discover they can medicate this pain by acting out behaviors that make them feel artificially relevant, at least in the short term. But, once again, because these behaviors are deceptive and come at the expense of others, the signaler eventually does grave damage to herself, whether she realizes it or not.

Superiority signaling is like a drug for wayward souls. When the pleasure it brings to the signaler becomes so great that it masks the damage it's causing her, she will begin a downward spiral that stains her reputation and impairs her ability to influence others. If she's lucky, her behaviors might bring pleasure and comfort to a small cadre of allies who benefit from her proclivities and therefore hold her in high regard. But within a more diverse and well-represented population, she will likely be met with disdain.

Superiority signalers are the special-ops forces of the old superior, and they poison the powerful alliances that might otherwise form among selfless individuals who find strength in collaboration and mutual commitment. The notion that our personal power and influence amplify in proportion to our willingness to be equals in the moment is offensive to the old superior, whose legitimacy and relevance require the existence of hierarchies. The old superior revels in the delight of watching people compete for their survival, whether literal or figurative, just as animals do in the natural world. To the old superior, there is beauty and elegance to a system in which people must compete against one another for the right to dominate and, most certainly, for the right to survive. This is the way of the natural world and, therefore, must also be the way of humanity. Right?

Wrong. As I explained at the beginning of this book, hierarchies are natural, teams are not. Dominance is natural; leadership is not. But both experience and research show that people thrive and accelerate the improvement of their conditions when they collaborate as teams in the presence of entrusted leaders. Businesses, for example, increase their market share and profitability when they prioritize teamwork and leadership. But they struggle when the creativity and communication needed to succeed are stifled by bureaucracies that reward personal ambitions over interpersonal collaboration.

A Scientific Perspective on Signaling

Hierarchies and hierarchical behaviors such as superiority signaling exist all throughout nature, including among humans who use them to keep each other organized and compliant with established rules. Hierarchy provides a framework in which superiors can compete for prominence, allowing their personal talents and contributions to have the greatest benefit. In fact, a 2008 study by the National Institutes of Health found that upward changes to a person's hierarchical stature activate brain circuits in ways that are similar to people who've just won money. Other studies find that stature correlates directly with physical, mental, and emotional health. Humans, you might say, are wired for hierarchy in ways that we see in other species. Even trees in a forest compete for sunlight and water. The healthiest trees outgrow the others, resulting in the eventual deaths of the weaker ones. This ensures a forest full of healthy trees. Thanks to hierarchies, the best emerge from the masses, making it more likely that the masses will survive. Everybody wins.

Well, not exactly. A forest full of trees is not the same as a team of people; and a team of people aspire to more than just survival. Think of it this way. The overall well-being of a forest is not dependent on the inferior trees collaborating with one another. In fact, the forest wants the inferior trees to die-off and make room for the superior trees. All the forest cares about is giving all trees the opportunity to compete for whatever soil, water, and sunlight might be available. The winners will grow to occupy the space, the losers will die, and the forest will survive regardless of who wins or loses. All that matters in the hierarchy is that someone – *anyone* – wins. By establishing the deserved winners, the forest survives.

Survival, however, is not the goal of most teams. Teams exist to accomplish things far more impressive than simply getting by. They want to thrive. They want to *achieve*. A byproduct of achievement, of course, is a higher probability of survival, but survival is not the unifying objective. Teams are more than the sums of their parts, meaning that they perform with a degree of effectiveness that could not be achieved by the same individuals acting on their own.

The Distinctions of Teamwork. The amplifying factors that give a team its power are collaboration and communication. When a group of people are united by a shared vision, mutual trust and respect, and generous doses of encouragement, there is an almost magical unleashing of creative and productive energies. These energies direct the group's members to find joy in committing themselves to the group's mission, tempering the distracting impulses of self-interest. With personal ambitions held in check, working conditions are further optimized, more collaboration is enabled, and even greater success is made possible. What began as a group has now become a team.

Successful teams, of course, often have hierarchies. Members may have rank and know their place in the power scheme. Decision-making authority may be distributed according to certain rules or policies. But we find within these high-functioning hierarchies that the structures and customs have an energizing influence on their members. The hierarchies do what they're supposed to do, they keep people organized. But it is the commitment to teamwork that enables *everyone* to thrive, not just the superiors.

But as we know and often experience, many hierarchies fail to function as a team. When they do, we invariably find signaling and other dominance behaviors by a few superiors that cause the resulting inferiors to feel like they are being mistreated or forced into subordination. This inflames resentments toward the hierarchy and the superiors in charge of it. The result is a remarkable loss of energy and motivation among the inferiors and, in the worst instances, protest behaviors or even sabotage.

Whatever the case may be, at a minimum, there is the suppression of desire among inferiors to collaborate and contribute on behalf of the hierarchy. This follows a basic rule of human motivation, that it is nearly impossible to inspire superior performance among people made to feel inferior.

The Games People Play. The adverse impact of hierarchical behaviors on individual performance was measured and explained in 2015 by researchers Katherine Cronin, Daniel Acheson, Penélope Hernández, and Angel Sánchez, who studied the behavior of human subjects to measure how teamwork and collaboration are adversely affected by primitive shows of dominance. Their groundbreaking work appeared in a scientific report published by *Nature* in December 2015 titled *Hierarchy is Detrimental for Human Cooperation.* They applied a creative twist to behavioral studies previously conducted on nonhuman primates. Cronin, whose work at the University of Chicago focuses on primates, knew that chimpanzees, for example, work together as a team to hunt and kill monkeys. But once the kill is complete, it is the higher-ranking chimps in the hierarchy who determine how the meat is distributed. As higher-ranking chimps engage in more abusive or heavy-handed behaviors, there is a concomitant reduction in the amount of effort that lower-ranking chimps are willing to invest in future kills. As a result, the collective effectiveness of the group suffers.

Curious to know if similar results might be observed in the study of humans, Cronin and her colleagues equipped several human subjects with computers on which the subjects were administered a series of skill tests lasting 3 minutes each. These included basic math problems, a game of Tetris, and a general culture quiz. Participants competed to achieve a higher rank than their fellow participants, which would give them potential advantages later in the study.

In the second phase, all participants were grouped into pairs, with one partner in each pair having a higher rank than the other. After being awarded an allowance of experimental currency, the partners were both instructed to play a bidding game in which they would play off each other to make deposits into a central pot. The terms of the game were such that the partners would benefit individually and mutually by collaborating to maximize the amount of currency deposited into the pot. If the pot reached a threshold of 20 currency units, both partners would share a mutual payout of an additional 20 currency units and would be allowed to proceed to the next phase of the study. In other words, collaboration resulted in personal *and* collective profits.

It was in the next phase of the study, however, that researchers began to see the adverse impact of hierarchy. In the previous round, both partners were informed of where each other ranked in the skill tests, but the rankings had no significance to how the bids were made or how the payoffs were awarded. But in the third round, the players were required to come to an agreement about how the bidding would be performed, with the higher-ranking player being given more control and influence in negotiating the terms, which the lower-ranking player could accept or reject. Higher rank was rewarded with more control in the negotiation. Lower rank was punished with less control. Once an agreement was made, the game was played the same as before.

When hierarchy was permitted to influence the playing of the game, the individual payouts to the higher-ranking players were greater than those awarded to the lower-ranking players. More important, however, they also found that the awarding of mutually shared payouts based on collaboration declined remarkably. But why? Why exactly did collaboration decline in the presence of hierarchy when all other variables were controlled? According to the study's published report, "the main reason for the decrease in successful cooperation events can be traced to diminishing contributions by lower-ranked individuals."

This finding can also help deepen our understanding of how hierarchy influences human performance in professional environments, especially those in which the stakes are high. When circumstances require a group of people to perform at their best or react effectively to an emergency, hierarchy on its own will not sabotage the effort. What *will* sabotage the effort are signaling or other dominance behaviors among higher-ranking officials that offend or harm lower-ranking contributors, deflating the intensity and quality of their contributions. Over time, this loss of individual investment in the collective good impairs the overall effectiveness of the hierarchy and, as a matter of consequence, its ability to function as a team.

We should expect that dominators will emerge from within hierarchies, but those dominators must resist their natural tendencies to signal their superiority and instead direct their energies toward the encouragement, enabling, and empowerment of others. It now becomes clear why superiority signaling of any kind is so costly and damaging. It subjects observers to the indignity of being made to feel inferior, which dulls the motivation and energy they need to volunteer their best efforts for the good of the group.

Chapter 8

Abuse and Violence

If we step back and observe superiority signaling from a distance, we can begin to see it for what it really is, a form of control. Signaling is a behavior adopted by an individual who intends to control how others feel and think. To some degree, he distrusts his own environment and the people in it, and he is no longer willing to leave his own sense of confidence and emotional security to chance. So, he seizes control of it through passive-aggressive behaviors aimed at exerting steady influence on those who are significant to him, expecting that the underlying insecurities will go unnoticed. But a critical inflection point exists at which superiority signaling ceases to be a mere annoyance and devolves into something more serious. It is at this point where innocent, unsuspecting people can no longer ignore the behavior because they now suffer from it.

Recall in the introduction my overview of the ongoing sexual assault crisis and the meeting we held in Washington, DC to discuss it. Contributing to the problem was the fact that police and military personnel are trained to be superiority signalers of the organizational type. Their work requires their rank to be easily recognized so that, when necessary, it's abundantly clear who gives the orders and who follows them. This kind of signaling has legitimacy and is not necessarily intended to demoralize anyone. But the institutionalized *habit* of signaling, useful or valid as it may be, creates temptations to engage in illegitimate forms of signaling that bring harm to those who don't deserve it.

As you can probably tell, I care deeply about the competent investigation of sexual violence, sexual abuse, and our public responses to it. Except for child abuse or child trafficking, this form of violence is perhaps the most egregious form of human exploitation – instances of pure evil in which predators overwhelm the physical, mental, and emotional senses of their prey. I've worked with survivors and survivor advocates and have partnered with the federal government of the United States in its attempts to understand why these crimes happen and how they can be prevented.

It is my opinion that the sexual assault crisis was enabled by police and military personnel who made victims feel like they were second-class citizens. In macho, male-dominated police and military cultures, softening one's heart to tend to the physical and emotional needs of a woman reporting to have been raped is not exactly a cultural priority, or at least it wasn't. For a police chief or base commander to meet the unique demands that reports of sexual crimes and abuse present, they would have to be willing to work collaboratively and thoughtfully with survivors as equals in the moment. Unfortunately, in so many cases this didn't happen.

Sociopaths and Predators

I believe that sexual predators are sociopaths and that there are virtually no exceptions to this rule. Sociopaths are not restrained by any sense of empathy or responsibility that might otherwise ameliorate their impulses. And because they are largely incapable of considering the interests of others, they will not be deterred in their seeking of pleasure, using whatever methods they find acceptable.

In 2006, Paul Babiak and Robert Hare published what I believe is a book of great professional importance. *Snakes in Suits – When Psychopaths Go to Work*, explores the prevalence and effects of sociopathy in the modern workforce. They estimate that between 2 to 4% of the human population are sociopaths or exhibit strong sociopathic tendencies. The implications of this should be obvious, with every two to four people you meet out of a hundred, on average, having a significantly impaired capacity to empathize. This, of course, does not necessarily mean they are violent, as Babiak and Hare explain, but it does suggest that our personal and professional lives are always exposed to the variety of threats that these pseudo-humans, if you'll permit the characterization, present to the rest of us.

The odds of crossing paths with a sociopath, however, rise considerably as researchers examine the prevalence of sociopathy in specific industries and professions. In 2011, British psychologist and expert on psychopaths (a name used interchangeably with sociopath, especially when violence is involved), Dr. Kevin Dutton, published the *Great British Psychopath Survey* in which he measured and reported the prevalence of psychopathy in various lines of work. According to Dutton, the following job titles have the highest rates of psychopathy:

1. Chief Executive Officers
2. Lawyers
3. Television and Radio Personalities
4. Salespeople
5. Surgeons
6. Journalists
7. Police officers
8. Clergy

9.   Chefs

10.   Civil servants

The Sociopath's Lifeline. As you examine the above list, ask yourself what these titles or positions have in common. Why would they tend to attract sociopaths?

What they have in common is the condition all sociopaths need to stay reasonably functional in their lives and careers – the opportunity to dominate others. Only through dominance can they keep their disorder a secret. As sociopaths, they lack both empathy and the ability to sense what others around them may be thinking or feeling. They struggle with reading facial expressions, tones of voice, body language, and other subtle social queues. They fail to say the appropriate things at the appropriate times, and often say the most inappropriate things at the most inappropriate times. The result is significant social awkwardness and a tendency toward withdrawal in intimate settings. And because social awkwardness is a strong limiter of career progression, sociopaths will seek out positions that neutralize the disadvantages caused by their sociopathy. In other words, they seek out positions that allow them to talk *to* people rather than *with* people.

Remember that to dominate is to assume a position of superiority over someone else. In each of the job titles identified by Dutton, incumbents don't need advanced interpersonal skills to get the work done. They simply need to be smart. The positions themselves provide the necessary rank, stature, and authority that a sociopath would need to fake their way through them, at least for as long as possible.

When I present Dutton's list at my executive leadership workshops, participants are often surprised, as I was, to see *clergy* on the list. But with some additional reflection it becomes clear why it is. In a ministerial role, sociopaths can assume dominance or superiority over their congregants and, in some ways, are expected to do so. Church pastors are viewed as moral superiors and are expected to deliver messages that congregants find inspiring and insightful. Empathy, however, is not a personal trait that's necessary to pull this off. A high-functioning sociopath may, in fact, be a moral superior and quite effective at delivering inspiring and insightful messages, while never actually feeling any emotional connection to her congregants or empathizing with them in any way. True, many congregants may find the sociopathic pastor to be strange or awkward and therefore may avoid personal interactions with her, but they may continue to attend their church out of a sense of duty or tradition. So, it is from this position of superiority and the cover it provides that a member of the clergy can be sociopathic, keep her disorder a secret, while mustering a marginally competent performance that allows her to remain gainfully employed for as long as possible.

Somebodies and Nobodies

This, of course, is not a book about sociopathy – I wouldn't dare encroach on the impressive contributions that Babiak, Hare, and Dutton have put forth to expand our understanding of the darkest corners of the human the psyche. But within these corners exist types of behaviors that, while not necessarily sociopathic in their entirety, include elements of sociopathy – also called *antisocial personality disorder* – that seem to arise in certain situations. Superiority signaling is among them, for it represents a kind of behavior in which the perpetrator's impulse to self-gratify overwhelms his impulse to empathize, resulting in behaviors that offend or harm those around him. As such, I regard superiority signaling as a kind of *situational sociopathy* in which the well-being and interests of others are ignored or judged to be inferior to those of the signaler. By recognizing the sociopathy that exists within illegitimate or counterproductive displays of superiority, we can then appreciate why superiority signalers cause so much damage to themselves and others.

Questions and Answers. In December 2017, I had just finished writing the manuscript for my first book, *HR Management in the Forensic Science Laboratory*. As many authors experience during a writing project, the expression of ideas can inspire the asking of new questions that still long to be answered even after the project is completed.

In *HR Management*, I wrote extensively about the problems of harassment and hostility in the workplace, as well as solutions for correcting and preventing them – something you might expect to see in an HR book. But there were strong emotions behind my dissertation. Throughout my own professional career, I directly observed some of the worst instances of workplace misbehavior that I could ever imagine. This included overt acts of racism, sexism, and ageism. I worked for supervisors who were abusive, hostile, and seemed to enjoy inflicting emotional pain on their people. In one instance, a top-ranking official retaliated against me for politely and professionally bringing to his attention a departmental policy that I sincerely believed, and now know, exposed our office to serious legal sanctions. In another instance, I reported a high-level director to our HR department for what was the clear mistreatment of female employees under his span of control. He was eventually forced out but received a handsome retirement pension and a generous severance package as an incentive to go away.

I couldn't help but notice a common thread in these painful experiences. They happened in organizations where there was a strict adherence to rank and an almost apostolic genuflecting to professional stature, leaving them vulnerable to ignoring or even encouraging abusive behaviors. The following passage in *HR Management* captured my raw sentiments on the subject while opening an entirely new channel of inquiry that gave rise to the book you are reading now. Here's what I wrote:

"A common problem in today's workforce is the inappropriate treatment or judgment of employees based upon their rank or seniority within their organizations. This sets up a very dangerous set of circumstances where the degree of goodwill, encouragement, or support shown to employees is somehow dependent upon their rank within an organizational structure or is perhaps based on their lengths of service within their organizations. This, of course, is not to say that rank or seniority should not be respected. But when there is excessive emphasis on rank or seniority, it becomes difficult to encourage meritorious achievements in performance since the organizational culture tends to regard performance as being of limited importance anyway."

A Friend and Mentor. After submitting the final manuscript to my publisher, I continued to reflect on the relationship between an organization's reverence for rank and its susceptibility to abusive behavior, however unintentional it might be. Like it was yesterday, I remember typing the words *rank* and *abuse* in my Google search bar. When I clicked the return key on my laptop, there it was – *Somebodies and Nobodies: Overcoming the Abuse of Rank* by Robert W. Fuller. Reading the book flooded me with feelings of relief and validation.

Within days of finishing *Somebodies and Nobodies,* I sent a heartfelt message to Dr. Fuller to express my thanks for his work and to request the opportunity to speak with him. He responded immediately and graciously, allowing me to explain who I was and why I contacted him.

Despite having a Ph.D. in Physics from Princeton University and being the former President of Oberlin College in Ohio, he insisted that I call him *Bob*. We spoke for about an hour on a video conference call during which he went into more detail about his book and shared his own experiences with the many abuses of rank that he witnessed during his extensive career in the stature-obsessed culture of academia.

As I sat glued to my computer monitor like a child watching his favorite cartoon, Bob expressed his own appreciation for the work I was doing and encouraged me to continue. Now in his 80s, but still committed to hundreds of speaking engagements each year, I hoped that perhaps Bob saw me as a future champion of the work he'd been doing for so many years. Bob is nothing short of a warrior. And his sworn enemy is the evil presence – the devil, if you will – who encroaches upon human dignity with such ruthlessness and nonchalance. In *Somebodies and Nobodies*, Bob became the first to call out the devil by name: Rankism.

Rankism, as Fuller explains, is the mother of all forms of abuse, harassment, and hostility. Racism, for example, is rankism based on race, where the members of one race regard themselves as *outranking* the members of another race. Sexism, in a similar vein, is rankism based on sex, where men believe they outrank women or women believe they outrank men.

The problem with this *outranking* of each other is that it perpetuates disrespectful behaviors that can eventually lead to abuse, even violence. You may recall that I began this chapter talking about my belief that sexual predators are sociopaths. They are. But the reason they act out their aggressions in this way is that they genuinely believe they *outrank* their victims and are entitled to the gratification they seek, something to be expected from a person incapable of empathy. They are the opposite of equals in the moment, and their behaviors are far worse than signaling. They are predators.

University Sex Scandals. During my conversation with Bob Fuller, we discussed how rankism was making international headlines by wreaking havoc just a few miles from where my office was located at the time. My beloved alma mater, Michigan State University, was embroiled in what *The Guardian* described as "the biggest sexual abuse scandal in sports history." Dr. Larry Nasser, a physician and associate professor in the College of Osteopathic Medicine, was fired in 2016 after repeated accusations that he sexually molested young female gymnasts and other patients under his medical care, including future Olympic gold medalists. Although the exact number of victims is not known, over 150 made personal impact statements during Nassar's criminal trial. He was eventually convicted and sentenced to 175 years in prison. The investigation is still underway and additional survivors continue to come forward as of this writing.

As you might expect, questions swirled about the enormity of the crimes that were committed. *How could Dr. Nassar have gotten away with abusing so many young women for so long? How did he get away with such misconduct right in his own office on the campus of such an esteemed university?* In some instances, the victim's parents were in the room while the abuse was taking place. *How did that happen?*

As we've come to learn, the problem is not unique to Michigan State. Other bombshell scandals at the University of Michigan, San Jose State, Ohio State, Penn State, California State, and other universities have also hit the headlines with their sordid and twisted details. In my view, these scandals are not that surprising. Institutions of higher learning these days are profoundly reverential toward professional rank and stature. Having lectured and taught at the collegiate level and having worked and collaborated with many academics during my forensic science career, I've come to realize that many college professors and administrators fancy themselves as intellectual elites and make a habit of signaling their superiority in a variety of strange and offensive ways. They hold in such high regard their own cognitive prowess that they can't fathom something really bad happening on their watch, especially at the hands of one of their own. Dr. Nassar, after all, was arguably the most respected physician in the world of international gymnastics, and his stature was a source of pride for his university and its alumni. To bring into question the integrity of *one* superior is to bring into question the integrity of *any* superior, which is why those with a superiority complex are so ill-equipped to hold other superiors accountable for their misconduct. And I can only suspect that it's emotionally easier to question the validity of the complaints than the integrity of an entire institution.

For this reason and others, the stories of one or two survivors are often insufficient to move a culpable institution to immediate action or to penetrate the protective barrier of a perpetrator's stature. Even more infuriating is a perpetrator's condescending regard for his victims. He has stature. He has authority. *He* is the superior. The survivors, in his mind, are inferior – that is until a *few* survivors become *many* survivors, and *many* survivors become an *army* of survivors. Eventually, the collective power of so many survivors speaking one unified message will help them to eventually assume their rightful place as the superior voice. When that happens, and when the perpetrator's stature can no longer withstand the pressure of the claims being made against him, *he* becomes the inferior, at which point his career and crime spree are over.

A Reason for Vigilance

Rank need not be a precursor to abuse or violence. And there are many legitimate ways to signal superiority such as when a police officer wears a badge, a professor writes the letters *Ph.D.* after her name, or a volleyball coach blows his whistle to command the attention of his players. In each of these examples, the signaling serves a purpose and is done neither for self-gratification nor any pathological need to dominate others. In these instances, the signaling has strategic value, something that illegitimate signaling does not.

When illegitimate dominance and signaling of superiority are tolerated or rewarded for too long, they become institutionalized. It is then that people come to believe that achieving the many perks that rank, stature, or authority bestow upon them depends on their willingness and ability to be effective dominators or signalers themselves. At best, what results are emotionally stunted hierarchies, entire cultures overrun by self-gratifying superiority signalers whose behaviors destroy the conditions needed for teamwork. At worst, and given enough time, we will eventually witness abusive, hostile, and sometimes criminal behaviors perpetrated by dominating signalers whose habits have grown so offensive or so dangerous that they violate the basic human dignities of those judged to be inferior. It is then that lawyers, police, or HR experts might be summoned to stop the damage and prevent it from ever happening again.

Chapter 9

Policing, Public Safety, and National Security

For all the criticisms the United States receives from inside and outside of its borders, it has a lot going for it. The influence it's able to exert on the international stage has its origins in a government whose power and scope are limited by design. Americans are reticent to trust political superiors with their well-being, as many made abundantly clear in the race to deal with the COVID-19 pandemic. With a comparatively weaker government, the people of the United States entrust *themselves* with the responsibility for their own individual and collective well-being. The result is a citizenry more motivated to secure the skills they need to take care of themselves and meet their own responsibilities. When America's leaders are then selected from among that citizenry, we expect their power to be leveraged with more fairness and effectiveness. Thanks to the mechanisms of American government, individuals are prevented from gaining too much authority, which means that American leaders are viewed as truly representing the people they are leading and, as a result, have more credibility on the world stage – at least in theory.

The opportunity to travel and work internationally can be quite eye-opening, especially when it gives you the opportunity to witness, with your own eyes and ears, the toxic impact that cultures steeped with superiority signaling can have on their public and private institutions.

Entire governments are hobbled by their destructive worshipping and accommodating of superiors, leaving them ill-equipped to protect the rights of their citizens and participate in the delicate matters of global affairs. This presents a clear danger to the entire world. Systems and styles of government based on the signaling of dominance by public officials have the effect of weakening the capacity of such regimes to react competently to national and international security threats when they emerge.

The Casablanca Bombings

In November 2016, immediately after the U.S. presidential elections, I flew to Casablanca, Morocco on behalf of the U.S. government to teach an organizational leadership workshop for local police officials. The intent of the trip was to support efforts by the Moroccan government to modernize its criminal justice system. Morocco has been a nation struggling with a chronic identity crisis, recognizing international pressures to promote freedom and human rights, but also keeping a firm grip on the traditions of its authoritarian past. Morocco underwent significant constitutional reforms in 2011 but preserved its existing monarchy. Despite these reforms, Morocco still remained largely ineffective in convincing the international community that it was serious about freedom and human rights.

Despite Morocco's poor record on human rights, there are very good reasons for the United States and its allies in Europe and Asia to care about Morocco and its government. Geographically, it sits at the far northwest corner of Africa and helps to guard the narrow mouth leading to the Mediterranean Sea. For this reason, Morocco has the potential to exert significant influence on trade, commerce, and security in the region. It is also well-positioned to have a stabilizing influence on its neighbors to the east (Libya, Egypt, Jordan, Syria, and Turkey) where the radicalization of international terrorists remains a grave concern. In these regions where radicalization is a threat, the United States and its allies hope to build strong criminal justice capabilities so that the most dangerous predators can be identified and brought to justice long before they radicalize.

Perhaps due to its modest attempts at reform, Morocco is now considered a hybrid-regime with considerable administrative remnants of its authoritarian past still evident in its hierarchies. Morocco is a kingdom and, as a kingdom, relies on hierarchy and superiority signaling for the exertion of political and governmental will. Unfortunately, the inherent weaknesses of this arrangement, combined with an unspeakable act of evil, led to international embarrassment for the small nation, raising questions about the effectiveness of its government.

On the night of May 16, 2003, twelve suicide bombers killed 33 innocent people in a coordinated attack at five different locations across Casablanca. The perpetrators were affiliates of Al Qaeda, the same organization responsible for the 9/11 attacks on the United States just a year and half earlier. But in the wake of the Casablanca bombings, international sympathy turned to scorn when it was discovered that Al Qaeda cells had been operating in Morocco all along. Not only was the monarchy of Morocco allowing for the safe harboring of terrorists, it made the grave mistake of assuming that its Islamic roots would protect it from the savagery of Islamic terrorism. When teams of international investigators arrived in Casablanca to provide their assistance, they discovered that the crime scenes had been poorly secured and improperly processed, making it nearly impossible to fully leverage any forensic evidence needed to identify and capture those responsible.

The Casablanca bombings were devastating both to the credibility of the Moroccan monarchy and the confidence the international community could afford to have in the monarchy's willingness to confront terrorism.

The United States, however, recognized an opportunity to leverage the power of collaboration to improve the situation. It could share its investigative expertise with authorities in Morocco as a way to enhance the integrity of Morocco's criminal justice system, making it difficult for terrorists to operate there with impunity. Over a decade later, these collaborative efforts continue, with criminal justice representatives of the United States spending considerable time in Casablanca helping authorities improve their investigative competencies. As part of this ongoing effort, I was again tapped by the U.S. Departments of Justice and State to facilitate an educational workshop where police officials could discuss and learn some contemporary leadership principles that would help improve the communication and collaboration needed to make lasting improvements to the criminal justice system of Morocco.

What struck me about my experience in Morocco was the degree to which the hierarchical superiority culture of its monarchy was reflected in the cultures of its law enforcement agencies. Superiority complexes, apparently, can be inherited. Just as Morocco was a kingdom led by a king, some of its criminal justice officials seemed to think of themselves as kings in their own departments, making it difficult for them to understand why my lessons on leadership were relevant to them. *Kings don't need leadership skills; they're kings!*

Some of what I observed in Morocco is not unlike what we see in the United States and in other countries. But the absence of accountability in Morocco was striking. According to an August 2008 report by the Carnegie Endowment for International Peace, the King in Morocco "still both rules and governs and is accountable to no one. His representatives in the state's central administration, government ministries, justice system, and security apparatus maintain tremendous powers and are accountable only to him." Such a culture will tend to inspire others in positions of power throughout the government, ones who might fairly be described as *copycat leaders,* to maximize their own autonomy by relieving themselves of the burdens of accountability just as they perceive their king to do.

The ineffectiveness of authorities in responding to the 2003 bombings in Casablanca was the result of hierarchies that didn't know how to function as teams, chronically weakened by dominators who didn't know how to lead and professionals who didn't know how to contribute. The criminal justice officials we'd expect to have been driven by the urgency reflex were perhaps numb to the situation's demands. For decades, they endured the authoritarian pressures of a government whose energies were focused more on the exercise of power than on the demonstration of competence. The King and his kingdom were superior. The agencies directly responsible for serving the people were inferior. Enter, then, an unspeakable act of terrorism and the consequences speak for themselves.

Policing in the United States

It isn't necessary to travel overseas to observe dysfunctional superiority in action. We see plenty of it right here in the United States, and among those American institutions most impaired by unhealthy attitudes about superiority are those we hold responsible for enforcing our laws and keeping our communities safe. The policing profession has struggled in recent years to maintain the trust of the public. And in my frequent conversations with police officials about this problem, it's clear that the more intelligent and thoughtful among them understand exactly why these struggles are happening. Police, they argue, have become too paramilitary, too paternalistic, too hierarchical, and too dominant over the people they're supposed to serve. But the efforts of these would-be disruptors of the status quo are met with the vigorous defiance of traditionalists who like it just how it is and who retain control over many of the training academies that feed new police officers into our communities.

Objectification

Dominance behaviors having no legitimate purpose cause remarkable damage by dehumanizing people, whether they occur within an organization or out in a community. Dominators often struggle to see people as *people*. They instead see people as objects, categories, or rungs in a ladder. When patrolling streets, police officers having different priorities than those of the surrounding community will be vulnerable to the same blindness, dismissing fellow human beings as nothing more than tactical impediments. Especially in underserved or disadvantaged neighborhoods where the top priority of citizens is their own survival, the authority of police will have no legitimacy if law enforcement officers seem distracted by their own desire for superiority. This, of course, also puts police at risk because it is the police who will then become objectified by the people they are supposed to protect. A bunch of objects slamming into each other do not make for peaceful coexistence.

This penchant for police dominators to objectify citizens will tend to manifest itself in communities after it's already been practiced and conditioned internally within police organizations. And this is exactly what happens. Police hierarchies reinforce the notion of officers as rungs in the organizational ladder, objects taking up space in the structure. It makes complete sense that the institutionalization of this objectification will eventually come to compromise how officers conduct themselves in their communities. Objectification on the inside leads to the same on the outside.

The priorities of change-minded police commanders, therefore, is clear. They must recognize any illegitimate hierarchical behaviors within their own agencies, behaviors that tempt the mistreatment of team members based on their rank. They must then decondition their cultures of any toxic attitudes about what it means to have rank, stature, and authority in the organization as well as in the community.

If you find yourself attempting to lead a similar change effort, begin by being aware of how your people treat each other. Pay attention, for example, to how your professional superstars treat the custodians who mop your floors and clean your washrooms. Notice how new employees are treated by those who've been around a long time. How are the younger treated by the older, the men by the women, and the women by the men? Observe how your recently promoted leaders apply their new rank, stature, and authority. Do they behave as if they've been entrusted with a great responsibility or do they act as if they are owed something? The more attention you pay to these dynamics, the more accurately you can assess the health and condition of your team and its capacity to treat customers, clients, and stakeholders with care and respect.

Deconditioning

Just as the old superior gains its strength through a sustained process of conditioning people to accept its value and legitimacy, it can be weakened and eliminated through *deconditioning*. To accomplish this, leaders have more options available to them than they realize. Remember, the old superior can only survive in hierarchies. It needs people to be stratified into graduated layers of power and influence, whereby superiors can be clearly distinguished from inferiors and where superiors enjoy privileges to which inferiors are denied access. This means that the old superior feeds off the innate ambitions that people have to gain superiority and the privileges that come with it. By softening the role of hierarchy in governing how people communicate and interact with each other, the old superior is cut off from the air it needs to breath, and eventually it dies.

This is precisely how some forward-thinking police leaders in the United States are trying to change untrustworthy attitudes and cultures as quickly as possible. It's not easy, and the challenges they face are not unlike those confronted by organizational leaders in other professions or industries who've also been entrusted with teams having great potential but a history of dysfunction. All of us have much to learn from what's happening in policing today because it represents some of the highest stakes and pressures in which a change initiative could ever be attempted. The quality and duration of people's lives are on the line, and there is no doubt that change is needed.

A Champion of Change. David Couper is a retired chief of police for Madison, Wisconsin, known for revolutionizing his department and its strategies for maintaining a more trustworthy presence in the community. He is the author of *Arrested Development – A Veteran Police Chief Sounds Off About Racism, Protest, Corruption, and the Seven Steps Necessary to Improve Our Nation's Police*. An outspoken advocate for more professionalism and education in policing, Couper argues that police officers must work in partnership with community members – as equals in the moment, we might say. In a 2014 PBS interview following the shooting of an unarmed black man in Ferguson, Missouri, Couper explained that there are better ways for police to deal with dangerous situations:

"Ninety percent of a police job is relational. It's how you maintain your contact with somebody that might be disturbed, or who might be angry. That first contact is extremely important. And I've criticized the protocol today that everybody who seems to have a knife or who's not obeying police commands ends up being shot and killed... And I have really tried to push, and will continue to push, police leaders and police trainers to think about alternatives to that."

Police who adopt a superior presence in a community create a destabilizing effect over the long term, a consequence of causing the community's members to feel inferior. When made to feel inferior, they will come to resent and resist police, seeing them as a controlling or occupying force rather than partners engaged in a common cause. Any act of aggression, then, taken by police against one or more members of that community is more likely to be perceived as predatory than peacekeeping, and will worsen the tensions that already exist.

The Standard Approach. In seeking to turn around a police culture, there are formidable obstacles that must be overcome, the worst of which are the existing mindsets about the role police should play in a community and how police should conduct themselves when interacting with some of the more troubled or outspoken members of that community.

Attempts at police reform, unfortunately, have become about as predictable as they are daunting, with some all-too common outcomes that leave many champions of change scratching their heads or licking their wounds. With the best of intentions, a new police commander with new ideas will assume her position, meet with her team, identify challenges, look ahead to potential opportunities, and communicate a vision of how wonderful things could be if new ways of working and thinking could be adopted at scale. Once that vision is communicated, she'll call upon her team to commit to what she's trying to accomplish. Her vision may be based on good data, reliable intuition, and the input of her team's members. It might even be nothing short of obvious that the direction she wants to lead her team is the direction it needs to go and may be exactly what the members of the community want. But something strange happens. The rank-and-file dig in their feet. The police union stands up against her. She can't get them to budge. They fight and complain. They file grievances. *She doesn't know what she's doing! How dare she destroy what we've built here!* Using passive-aggressive tactics, the resistance seems to revel in making life difficult not only for its new leader but for the members of the team who want to commit to the leader's vision. The culture seems contaminated by the toxic attitudes of a few or more obstructionists hell-bent on causing problems for everyone else. *Change, be damned.*

Change Management. The inability or unwillingness of team members to commit to a new approach or new vision is often described as *resistance to change*. In fact, an entire consulting and training industry is dedicated to what is called *change management*, a set of methods and principles focused on creating the conditions in which teams can actuate progress without being impeded by resistance. There's even change management certifications that can be obtained, arming administrators or practitioners with skills and knowledge that can help team members flow through the normal cycles of change that happen in any organization.

Without question, change can be difficult for teams and their leaders, the resistance to which is made more alarming when changes are needed to protect people's lives. It is when the stakes are at their highest, as they certainly are in policing, that leaders cannot afford to accept any inadequacies in the status quo. Progress is needed and a trusting public is depending on effective police leaders and teams for their well-being. Fortunately, there are strategies and attitudes that can help overcome the resistance that's often encountered when leaders in positions of public trust find themselves struggling to turn around an underperforming culture, especially when that culture has a history of being poisoned by the old superior. We'll get to that soon.

A Different Kind of Sheriff

Several years ago, I was hired to consult with the forensic science laboratory at the Richland County Sheriff's Office in Columbia, South Carolina. The purpose of my engagement was to provide some assistance to the laboratory in its ongoing efforts to keep its quality assurance systems in compliance with accreditation standards that were quickly evolving at the time. With the advent of forensic DNA analysis in the 1980s and its widespread adoption in the early-to-mid 1990s, forensic science laboratories around the world were beefing up their quality assurance practices to accommodate this new and exciting forensic method. Then, in 1995, the infamous murder trial of football star O.J. Simpson exposed the public to courtroom theatrics that made forensic DNA evidence appear especially vulnerable to contamination. And, in some respects, it was. But through enhanced laboratory practices and the improved collection and preservation of DNA evidence at crime scenes, these risks were successfully mitigated.

Preparing for my trip to Columbia, I found myself struggling with feelings of cynicism that were uncommon for me. Having spent so many years working with a sheriff who I perceived as a loyal disciple of the old superior, I had come to develop negative attitudes about sheriffs in general. And make no mistake, there were some legitimate reasons for feeling as I did.

Sheriffs in the United States are usually elected law enforcement officials with constitutional powers and responsibilities that make them nearly untouchable in their respective states, assuming federal laws aren't violated. Unlike police chiefs who are appointed, sheriffs are elected and, therefore, accountable directly to voters in their jurisdictions, voters who tend to be hawkish about law enforcement and criminal justice. As a result, many sheriffs who portray themselves as stubborn, grumpy, uncompromising guardians of their communities often do quite well on election day. Almost always white males, they are like kings in charge of their kingdoms, which tends to disincentivize collaboration with other agencies and authorities in the criminal justice system. Indeed, over the course of my career, I found many sheriffs and their underlings to be challenging personalities to work with.

When I arrived at the Richland County Sheriff's Office, I was greeted by a team of professionals who were upbeat, enthusiastic, and appreciative to have me join them. We got right to work, and I found the experience to be enjoyable and rewarding. The environment felt buoyant and energized.

One morning, the laboratory staff invited me to join them for an annual Christmas lunch hosted by the sheriff himself. Of course, I agreed. When it came time to break for lunch, we made our way to a large room where members of the office were beginning to gather. Food on trays and trays in hand, we found a table and sat down to eat. Within moments, our conversation was interrupted by a buzz coming from the other side of the room. Looking up, I saw a man dressed in a Santa Claus outfit and a red bag slung over his shoulder. He made his way through the room, stopping at each table, one by one, to say hello to the employees and to extend some good-old-fashioned holiday cheer. The joy and goodwill I felt was unmistakable.

"That's our sheriff," chimed a woman sitting across from me, glancing my way to make sure I heard. Others nodded in agreement.

Before long, he made his way to our table, where he greeted everyone with a warm smile and a hearty welcome. The laboratory director got his attention and introduced me. He smiled, shook my hand, and thanked me for being there. There was something about him. *This is a different kind of sheriff,* I thought.

Indeed, he was a different kind of sheriff. After winning the 1996 election to cap his successful bid for office, Leon Lott orchestrated a major shift in the policing priorities of his agency. Among those priorities was an organizational focus on community-oriented policing – often called *community policing* – a philosophy that emphasizes the building and nurturing of relationships within the various neighborhoods and districts being served by the police, especially where socioeconomic challenges tend to raise both community anxiety and suspicions about police authority. As part of his public safety vision, Lott implemented a variety of innovative programs aimed at transforming how the authority of his office was leveraged and perceived.

South Carolina's governor, Henry McMaster, announced that Sheriff Lott would be the recipient of the 2021 South Carolina Sheriff of the Year Award. "South Carolina is a safer place today because of Sheriff Lott's strong leadership and collaborative efforts."

The announcement continued, explaining more about some of the specific initiatives Lott prioritized during his time as sheriff:

"Upon taking office in 1997, Sheriff Lott launched a series of innovative programs designed to uplift, support, and protect all communities in his jurisdiction. Community-Oriented Policing was introduced as a holistic approach to address degenerative community conditions and reduce fear of victimization. Project H.O.P.E. was initiated to support seniors lacking needed assistance from family and friends through volunteers who call and visit hundreds of disabled citizens each month. The Community Action Team was formed to further 'build bridges between citizens and law enforcement so that both groups had a sense of ownership' in their communities."

The announcement, released just a few months before the initial drafting of this chapter, went on to explain how Lott also serves as the Brigadier General in command of the South Carolina State Guard, described as a "national model for emergency preparedness and disaster response."

What strikes me about Sheriff Leon Lott is that he models what I believe is a prototypical approach to leadership in public safety, one that I hope will be embraced more readily by future sheriffs and future chiefs of police. This is not to say that community policing is new; it is not. Its origins can be traced back to the early 1900s, but it gained momentum after the riots of the 1960s overtook many of America's major cities. Thought leaders in the field of criminal justice correctly recognized the opportunity before them. Police commanders could help stabilize and secure challenged communities by prioritizing collaboration and partnerships over enforcement. Through experience and research, it became clear that the adversarial, paramilitary signaling of superiority was fomenting community anger and delegitimizing police authority in the eyes of the public. Something had to change. The status quo was not sustainable.

Community Policing

While some police agencies have adopted the fundamental principles of community policing with great success, producing remarkable reductions in crime, social disorder, and other forms of physical decay, others couldn't seem to make it work, or perhaps only observed marginal improvements that failed to justify, in their minds, its continued prioritization and funding.

A 2018 study on the implementation and monitoring of community policing in Malaysia revealed some eye-opening facts about why it fails. Writing in the *International Journal of Social Sciences and Humanities Invention,* researchers Mohammad Mujaheed Hassan and Aldrin Abdullah found that in those police agencies where community policing failed to produce the desired results, internal cultural barriers tended to suppress the energy and creativity needed to move beyond traditional approaches to policing. Hassan and Abdullah noted that opposition from officers and mid-level management had the effect of sabotaging organizational efforts to move toward a policing style that emphasized community relationships and interactions. Referencing past research on the cultural challenges faced by community-policing advocates, they noted the following:

"The initiatives associated with community policing cannot survive in a police agency managed in traditional ways. If changes are not made, the agency sets itself up for failure ... Officers will not be creative ... if a high value continues to be placed on conformity. They will not be thoughtful if they are required to adhere to regulations that are thoughtless. Moreover, they will not aspire to act like mature, responsible adults if their superiors treat them like children."

Ah, yes. Superiors treating their people like children. What Hassan and Abdullah identified as being the primary barrier to community policing is – you probably guessed it – the old superior, the culturally reinforced sorting of conformers into an exploitable hierarchy, then rewarding its loyalists with internal rank and authority. Because community policing requires sensitivity to community feelings and sentiments and the ability to solve challenging problems in creative ways, the old superior has little to offer in support of such a nuanced and refined way of interacting with community stakeholders. Guardians of the old superior want to *enforce*, not serve. So, when entrusted with the demands of a community policing strategy, they will drag their feet in silent protest then blame the inevitable failures on the strategy itself.

A Disruptive Idea. The leading academic advocate for community policing was Robert Trojanowicz, a criminal justice educator who pioneered what became known as the *Flint Foot Patrol Study* in 1979. According to an online retrospective on the study:

"... the Flint Police Department instigated foot patrols intended to get officers more integrated in the city's neighborhoods, improve citizen-police relations and reduce crime. It was a success on many levels. Flint citizens had a more positive perception of police, a reduced fear of crime and a better sense of community."

Upon his untimely death from a heart attack in 1994 at the age of 52, *The New York Times* and other news outlets credited Trojanowicz for the profound impact he had on the rethinking of police strategies for reducing crime. In 1983, with the success of the Flint Foot Patrol study in clearly demonstrating the value of community policing, Trojanowicz founded the National Center for Community Policing.

Trojanowicz was passionate about the potential for all police agencies to produce remarkably positive effects for the communities they serve, and he had the data and case studies to prove it. Violent crimes, property crimes, physical blight, societal decay, youth delinquency, neighbor isolation, sexual and domestic abuse – all mitigated to a statistically significant degree by the implementation and sustained administration of community policing strategies. But I also know that Trojanowicz and other champions of community policing were keenly aware of how divergent its foundational principles were from existing law enforcement cultures, attitudes, and traditions – an entirely different kind of problem requiring a different kind of solution.

Public Safety Through Public Trust. The challenge that community policing presents to traditional police culture is that it requires police to act as neighbors, not occupiers. As we discussed earlier, an occupying force assumes a superior position within a community, asserting its will by leveraging its authority. As such, it's an approach far less dependent on thoughtfulness and relatability. Members of the community are given no choice but to subordinate themselves to the inferior role, an indignity that foments resentments and distrust, further destabilizing the channels of communication between police and citizens that are needed to prevent crime.

There's a message and lessons in this for all of us. Law enforcement is an ideal context in which to explore how superiority signaling and dominance behaviors adversely impact the human condition. We can observe and measure the outcomes, and those outcomes represent lives that are saved or lost. As police adhere to oppressive, militaristic behaviors in the communities they serve – in other words, when their routine methods are motivated by the intent to dominate – we can expect a worsening of the public safety conditions in those communities. But when committing to more humane and collaborative methods, methods that position police as trusted friends and neighbors, crime abates and lives are saved.

Watching Sheriff Lott prance around in a Santa Claus costume was to behold something more than just a boss playing nice with his people, which, of course, it was. He was setting an example, an example of what it looks like, sounds like, and feels like when a person of authority humbles himself before the people he is leading. By being an equal in the moment, Sheriff Lott was making meaningful connections, building trust, and raising morale, knowing it would help to make his people more effective in their jobs and more sensitive to the needs of the communities they serve. This does not mean that Sheriff Lott is perfect; and it doesn't mean that he isn't willing to pull rank or signal his superiority when he believes a situation calls for it. Certainly, he will, but not as a chronic, reflexive way of engaging others. To those like him, self-gratifying dominance serves only the egos of insecure leaders trying to inflate their sense of self-importance at the expense of others. This, of course, is not how you build and maintain a culture in which people feel motivated to volunteer their best efforts, make the right decisions, and do the right things, even when no one is watching.

Changing Hearts and Minds

When I think back on my experience in Richland County, as I enjoyed a festive and inspiring Christmas lunch with my forensic colleagues, I can't help but wonder how many people in that cafeteria were frustrated guardians of the old superior who looked upon Sheriff Leon Lott with disdain. How many sat and stewed over the indignity of having to watch such a pathetic excuse for a law enforcement officer desecrate his uniform and his entire office right before their very eyes. *A Santa Claus costume? Are you kidding me?* I can imagine their senses being flooded with anger as they watched their superior commander dishonor the structured hierarchy that's supposed to keep a healthy distance between him and those ordinary employees who haven't yet earned the right to get that close to him.

How dare he do this to us? We depend on that hierarchy for our own sense of self-worth. It's our roadmap. We've spent our entire careers preserving and protecting this hierarchy, and now he's turning his back on it and us!

Hopefully, there was no one in the room with such poison coursing through them. Then again, you'll never hear the old superior use those words aloud in mixed company. But you'll certainly see the underlying thoughts and feelings manifest themselves in behaviors that sabotage efforts to build a different kind of police organization with a different kind of police culture. And if you happen to be one of those leaders trying to energize your team by deconstructing the cultural barriers that keep people sorted and siloed in their individual spaces, then I have some important news for you: You cannot negotiate with the old superior. It won't listen and it won't play nice. The only thing you can do is pry open the grip it has on your people. Expose it to the truth. Like mold, it will die in presence of sunlight, and you should expect that some of your people will not survive the experience. They will have no recourse but to leave your organization by choice or by dismissal. That's okay; let them go because they cannot be saved. Fortunately, many *can* be saved and will.

PART 2

SOLUTIONS AND STRATEGIES

"In complexity, our job isn't perfection, it's building a culture that is always learning. And that requires letting go."

Aaron Dignan
Brave New Work
Portfolio/Penguin, 2019

Chapter 10

Focus on Fundamentals

Fundamentals are the basics of successful execution. Execution is what you do to achieve an outcome, to build something, or to make something happen. When you execute well, your outcomes are desirable. When you don't, they aren't. Leadership is no exception; it requires execution. In fact, one of the things that makes leadership so challenging is that you're always executing. You are always a leader. You are always trying to spark high levels of motivation and engagement among the people you lead. Even if you aren't leading, you're thinking about it. When you're not thinking about it, you very well may be dreaming about it.

Fundamentals of Leadership

If your purpose is *why*, then your fundamentals are *how*. How are you supposed to lead? How are you supposed to conduct yourself? What are you supposed to say to people, and how are you supposed to say it? We can talk all day long about leadership and its importance – and some people do, by the way – but eventually you must execute. You must be the leader that your team needs, not just the leader you want to be. To some extent, your execution will depend on the nature of your work, the problems you're trying to solve, and the opportunities you're trying to exploit. It will also depend on the people with whom you're working, their tendencies, and their expectations. But there's also some basics to the execution of leadership – especially in this modern, professional, high-tech, fast-paced era we find ourselves in right now – that apply to everyone, including you.

These *leadership fundamentals* are ways of speaking, behaving, and thinking that have the effect of bringing the best out of your people and yourself. They inform how you carry yourself, how you interact with others, when you seek input, and when it's time to make decisions. When you adhere to leadership fundamentals, you build healthy professional habits, maintain trusting relationships, and set the conditions for teamwork to grow.

Below is a list of ten leadership fundamentals that you can and should follow to maximize the positive impact you have on your team, your work environment, and your reputation as a leader:

1.   Treat every team member like a superior – Even though you may be the one in charge, each member of your team oversees his own decisions and behaviors. Have respect for this personal autonomy and the responsibility that comes with it. There should be little difference between how you treat your lowest-ranking people and how you treat the top executive officer of your organization. Treating people with respect and dignity gives them energy, energy they will use to make your team's vision a reality.

2.   Be present in your conversations – Every conversation you have is an opportunity for you to earn more trust. Don't waste this opportunity by acting distracted or wishing you were doing something else. Stop and engage. Too many leaders claim to have what they call an *open-door policy* only to treat visitors like intruders. Have an *open-heart policy*. Listen to your people and embrace the opportunity to hear them. Allow yourself to be impacted by what they share. If you truly have more important things to do, be gracious by explaining your situation and ask to schedule a time when you can give the person your full attention. When somebody stops by your office to see you, turn around, face the person, smile, and ask her how she's doing. If you're cramped for time, tell her you only have a minute but that you're glad to see her. Every time your people speak with you, they should feel like it was a good use of their time and yours. They should feel like you appreciate them.

3. Enjoy your people – To enjoy someone is to make him relevant to you in a special way. Your number-one goal is to be a trustworthy influencer of people, but this cannot happen if you are perceived as being irritated or bored by your interpersonal exchanges. When you enjoy your people, they will feel the genuine interest you have in them and will correctly presume that you want what's best for them. They will see you as a person they can trust and will volunteer their best efforts in support of *your* interests. To enjoy someone is to give him one of the greatest gifts that can be given to a fellow human being. In fact, it's more than a gift. It's an investment with a high rate of return.

4. Expect the unexpected – A phrase I've grown tired of hearing over the years is *I don't like surprises.* I can't tell you how many times I've heard it said by individuals at the highest levels of organizational leadership. Well, guess what: Leaders get paid to be surprised, but they send a trust-deflating message to their teams when they act like they aren't prepared to handle the unexpected. To act surprised in front of your people is to say that you were not prepared. When the unexpected happens, act like you expected it even if you didn't. It may not be easy; your insides may be quaking. But by acting prepared, you can take advantage of a surprise by demonstrating a cool, calm, confidence that your people will notice and appreciate. Even better, by putting yourself and your people at ease, you are more likely to respond to the surprise with greater effectiveness.

5. **Brighten your physical expressions** – As I encouraged one of my clients whose story I will share later in this chapter, raise your eyebrows, smile, and laugh as often as appropriate. Think of your face and body as billboards that communicate to everyone how you're feeling and what you're thinking. Without saying a word, you can use your face and body to convey warmth, curiosity, encouragement, confidence, and goodwill. But it requires you to be aware of what your face and body are doing and be intentional about how you do it. People are watching you and looking for reasons to *not* trust you. That's what people do; they protect themselves from harm. Act like the leader you would want to trust and follow if you were in their shoes. They are watching you, so take advantage of it.

6. **Compliment your people behind their backs** – This may be one of the most under-utilized methods in contemporary leadership for two reasons. First, it requires leaders to be conversational, engaging, and attentive to what's going on, despite the many demands that compete for their time. Second, leaders don't often appreciate what a profound impact it has on their audience. When you compliment someone behind his back, the listener basks in your generosity, trusting that you are likely to compliment *her* behind *her* back. It's yet another reason to have confidence in you. Whenever possible, compliment people – *any* people – behind their backs when the compliment is justified. It says as much about you as it does about them, and few things you could ever do will have such an immediate and positive effect on how you are perceived.

7.   Emphasize the positive aspects of executive action – Even if you are the greatest of leaders, your people can lose faith if they feel that *your* managers don't know what they're doing or don't have their hearts in the right place. If you question the decisions being made at the top, articulate a positive message that explains what your executive leaders are *trying* to do and why. Never criticize your upper managers in front of your people. It may feel to you like you are connecting with your people or being supportive, but you're not. What they want to hear is evidence that the pilot of the plane isn't flying toward a rocky cliff. If there are instances when it's impossible to ignore that wildly poor decisions are being made by your organization's top leaders, simply remind people that they are doing the best they can, that their jobs are difficult, and that you will look for any opportunity to help them prioritize the goals of your team.

8.   Maintain collaborative relationships with upper management – Adding to what I've noted in the previous paragraph, keep your relationships with your upper managers cordial and collaborative. If you happen to be the top executive leader, this might mean having cordial and collaborative relationships with your clients, customers, and key stakeholders. Avoid any temptation to do or say things that cause your upper managers to question your loyalty or commitment to their mission. If you want the people reporting to you to trust you, they must know that you are trusted by the people to whom *you* report. All of this, of course, assumes that nothing hostile, abusive, or illegal is taking place. But, in general terms, being viewed as someone at odds with your upper managers makes you look impotent and irrelevant and, therefore, unworthy of trust.

9.   Facilitate conversation, and lots of it – A talking team is a team that's going places. Few leadership competencies are more valuable than the ability to get people talking about things that matter. Within those conversations, you give yourself access to information and perspectives that enhance the quality of your decision-making. Ask good questions. Invite feedback about things you are doing and things you are thinking about. Be provocative, in a respectful way. Give people a reason to speak their minds and make sure they know that what they express will be appreciated and considered. Leaders who make a habit of sealing themselves off from their people will have a hard time with this. But those who can spark the kinds of conversations that allow opportunities and threats to be recognized with greater speed will energize their people and earn their people's trust. As a result, the team will feel more confident in itself and its leader.

10.   Signal your intentions, not your superiority – By now, it should be clear that the signaling of superiority is too often done for the comfort of a fragile ego, not for the good of a team. The only time you should ever signal your superiority is when the moment requires you to make a decision, express a thought, or take an action of some sort. Your signaling should be courteous and respectful. It might even be a polite way of letting your people know that the conversation needs to come to an end and that you'll take it from here. Don't worry, people who know you are very aware of whatever rank, stature, and authority you possess. There is no need to remind them. Be an equal in the moment and adhere to this list of fundamentals. When it's time for you to do what needs to be done, do it, but be gracious in making sure your people know how much you appreciate them and their input. After all, you can't do it without them. Feel free to signal your intentions but rarely your superiority because all it does is make you look insecure and undeserving of your people's trust and confidence.

Leadership Fundamentals Assessment

Now that we've set forth these ten fundamental principles for establishing a strong and collaborative approach to leadership, let's see how well you're doing. Below, I've written out each fundamental in the form of a statement. Read each statement, then give yourself as honest a score as you can, using the scale below. At the end, add your scores.

10 – Outstanding: I'm truly better than everyone else around me

9 – Exemplary: I'm a good example for others to follow

8 – Accomplished: I'm habitually effective

7 – Respectable: It's obvious I'm making a sincere effort

6 – Reliable: I know what to do but I make mistakes

5 – Competent: I may need some help or coaching from time to time

4 – Marginal: I definitely need some help

3 – Deficient: I'm creating problems for myself and others

2 – Weak: Disciplinary action is possible

1 – Poor: Disciplinary action is justified

0 – Incompetent: Termination may be justified

1. ___ I treat every team member like a superior, like they are important to me and my team. I don't hold back basic courtesies and respect according to how much rank, stature, or authority someone has. I give everyone my best because I believe everyone deserves my best.

2. ___ I am present in my conversations with people. When I'm engaging with someone, I make that person my top priority in that moment. If I

have something else competing for my time, I'm likely to ask if we can put something on the schedule for later.

3. ___ I enjoy the people with whom I work. They know I take a sincere interest in them and their well-being, and I make it my responsibility to check on people often to see how they are doing, and to learn what's new in their lives and careers.

4. ___ I expect the unexpected. When things surprise me, I remain cool and calm, sending the message that I am always prepared to handle the many surprises that pop up from time to time. I never show signs of panic or disturbance.

5. ___ My facial expressions and body language are almost always welcoming and engaging. People see me as being confident, approachable, and in a reasonably good mood. When people look at me, they see a person who clearly enjoys what he or she is doing.

6. ___ I compliment people behind their backs. I make a point to share with others the good things that their fellow team members are doing, and I make this effort on a regular basis.

7. ___ I emphasize only the positive aspects of executive decisions and actions. Even if I don't agree with something that my upper managers are doing, I look for the underlying positives and make a point to remind my people that our upper managers have good intentions.

8. ___ I have and maintain cordial, collaborative relationships with my upper managers (or key clients). As often as possible, I try to be

supportive and understanding of what they are trying to accomplish and what challenges they are facing. They trust me to have their backs.

9. ___ I get my people talking. I often facilitate constructive conversations to make sure we are getting the full benefit of their ideas, perspectives, and input. I ask a lot of questions and invite people to share what they are thinking – even when it's hard to hear.

10. ___ I let people know when I must act or make a decision, but I never engage in superiority signaling that makes people feel inferior, disrespected, or unappreciated. They know who I am and what my responsibilities are. I don't feel an urge to remind them.

Write your total score: _____%

Scores above 90% are rare and evidence of either very high levels of leadership performance or dishonest scoring by participants. Scores of 75% or higher are commendable and should be what people strive to achieve. Scores around 60-75% are normal for people who take their leadership responsibilities seriously but may have less experience. If you scored below 60%, or if you scored any of the ten statements with a 5 or lower, I would encourage you to work one-on-one with a supervisor, coach, or other mentor who can help you identify your best opportunities to improve. Whatever your score, never stop trying to improve.

Slumps – When the Train Goes Off the Rails

Do you have any special skills or talents that allow you to excel in activities or hobbies that you find meaningful or enjoyable? Just for fun, I'm talking here about things outside of work, things that bring you lots of joy when you do them well. Perhaps you play golf. Maybe you play the piano or the guitar. How about running? Have you ever endured hours of slamming your feet against the pavement just so you can feel the thrill of finishing a demanding race or setting a new personal best? Maybe you're a chess player or a gamer, thriving on the intricate testing of your intellectual and strategic abilities. It could be anything.

Whatever it is, if there's a skill or talent that you sincerely desire to perform well, then you also know what it's like to experience slumps, those frustrating periods when you can't seem to get it right. It's as if your brain suddenly forgot how to do what you've done countless times before. On the golf course, this means you are spending more time in the woods because you can't hit the ball straight. On the guitar, you can't seem to nail that solo you used to shred without even thinking about it. In your Tuesday evening chess club down at the community center, you don't seem to anticipate your opponent's moves as well as you have in the past. In the more physically demanding sporting events, slumps can even result in injury as your now-flawed technique exposes your bones and joints to additional strain.

They Happen to the Best of Us. During my discus throwing days, I was all-too familiar with slumps. Worse, they never made any sense. Why was it that I could go weeks and weeks throwing at or near my best, only to find myself barely able to throw it past my own shadow? Slumps just seem to appear out of nowhere, and when they do, they leave you feeling confused and demoralized, as if you went back in time to a day when you didn't have a clue what you were doing.

Slumps, of course, appear in all aspects of our lives and careers. Out of the blue, things suddenly get difficult. What used to be easy is now hard. People with whom you once got along are now a source of irritation, as you are to them. The quality of your work is suddenly being called into question. Your marriage is on the rocks. Your health deteriorates. Your teenage daughter seems like she hates you. You're desperate to get back to your comfort zone where life was easier.

The slumps we experience in life and career are the same as the ones we experience in sports, music, and all the rest. And they seem to have two primary causes: *loss of enjoyment* and *inattention to fundamentals*. Let's take each of these, one by one, and see if you can recognize them in your own life or career.

Loss of Enjoyment. For just about any task or activity, if you stop enjoying it, your performance suffers. Few things will impair your ability to execute a task or technique more rapidly than displacing the enthusiasm you once felt for it. If what you once found pleasurable is now a laborious source of frustration, you will eventually find yourself surprised by the sudden loss of your competence, even if you are trying harder than ever to be good at it. Your mind and body, after all, are not stupid. They're looking out for you. They have no interest in wasting your precious energies on activities from which you don't derive joy. So they go on strike, hoping that you'll give up and find something better to do with your time.

Among the most dramatic slumps ever witnessed was the sudden and shocking inability of New York Yankees second-baseman, Chuck Knoblauch, to make a routine 90-foot throw to first base. Fans watched in horror as Knoblauch repeatedly botched the simplest of throws, throws he made over and over again since he was five years old. But over and over again, Knoblauch fielded ground balls hit by opposing batters, aimed at first base, then missed the first-baseman, sometimes throwing balls into the stands.

Knoblauch came to the Yankees with impressive credentials. According to Charean Williams and Mac Engel writing for the

Washington Post in 2001, "Knoblauch is a four-time all-star, a four-time World Series winner, a 1997 Gold Glove winner and the 1991 American League Rookie of the Year. He hit .341 in 1996, had 62 steals in '97, and his 45 doubles in the strike-shortened '94 season had him on pace to threaten one of baseball's most unbreakable records."

From 1992 to 1997, while playing for the Minnesota Twins, Knoblauch averaged only 8 errors per year, making him an annual candidate for the Gold Glove. Then in 1998, Knoblauch was part of a trade that would take him to New York in exchange for four players and $3 million, which is when his problems began. He averaged a stunning 18 errors per year over three years, including a disastrous game against the Chicago White Sox in which he committed three errors, the most for a single game in his career.

In his interview with Williams and Engle, Knoblauch, having now been relocated to left field, was resolute. "It's still a game that I enjoy or else I wouldn't be here. That's why I can deal with it, because every day I put on the uniform, I am prepared to play physically and mentally."

Being resolute is admirable but is not the same as having fun. For Knoblauch, the move to New York, whose fans are notorious for the harsh demands they place on players, was clearly the inflection point at which his game started to unravel. In Minnesota, he was home, he was known, and he was appreciated – about as fun as it gets for a professional athlete, I suppose. But in New York, things were different. He had to *prove* himself, and expectations were high. He was now playing for one of the most storied teams in the history of professional athletics, a team that took a financial and competitive risk on Knoblauch and his abilities. Knoblauch was likely being honest when he expressed his continued enjoyment of the *game*. But it's doubtful he enjoyed the expectations being heaped on his shoulders, and even more doubtful that his coping with those expectations didn't come at the expense of his performance.

And when he began losing control of his playing abilities, the war he waged with himself only accelerated the decline. As he once knew them, his days of playing competitive baseball were over.

You, like Chuck Knoblauch, have a silent witness who lives inside of you, who observes what is happening and carefully monitors how it impacts your health, safety, and security. As famed author and alternative-medicine advocate Deepak Chopra describes it, "the silent witness is the higher self....it is the experience of self-awareness." This witness cares only about you and your well-being. She knows what you need, what you can handle, and what you can't. She doesn't care about making more money than your friends, living in a luxurious house, or making sure that your neighbors are impressed with you. She doesn't expect you to be perfect or to be the very best at what you do. If she comes to the conclusion that you're on a path that will lead you to physical injury, mental anguish, or emotional instability, she will find a way to warn you. At first, the warnings may be gentle, but if you are too stubborn, too distracted, or too ambitious to get the message, you may leave her no choice but to shut down your systems until you make the necessary changes. I suspect you can probably imagine all of the subtle and not-so-subtle ways that your own silent witness might fight for your attention. Perhaps she already has.

Leadership is difficult, just like baseball, especially when the stakes are high and the risks are daunting. For leaders, slumps come in the form of frustrated team members, saying the wrong things at the wrong times, impaired relationships, ignoring signs of team stress or dysfunction, not paying attention to external threats, or failing to leverage an attractive opportunity. When leaders go into slumps, as I certainly have, it makes you feel like a spectator who's powerless to control what's happening in the game. And because of the enormous responsibilities that leaders have, this feeling of having lost one's edge is both painful and disturbing.

I encourage you, therefore, to be grateful for the opportunity you have to be a leader and to enjoy it! Leadership slumps will invariably arise and will persist when you stop having fun. Even in the most serious businesses and occupations, or when difficult situations bring with them feelings of heaviness or worry, you can pause and remind yourself of all the things you enjoy about your work, your people, and your responsibilities. By having fun, you will perform at a higher level and will be perceived by your people as more competent. Why? Because they are smart enough to know that *incompetent* people don't enjoy being incompetent. They know that if you are having fun, you are probably good at what you do and, therefore, more deserving of their trust.

Inattention to Fundamentals. This leads us to what is the second cause of slumps, the failure to practice fundamentals. Look, when times are good, we relax. It's pleasurable not having to work hard to do things well. In fact, it's heaven! You would rather get while the getting is good, squeezing as much enjoyment out of the fruits of your effectiveness as possible. When you're hitting on all cylinders and life feels like a Sunday morning drive along the beach, your confidence and sense of well-being reach their maximum. And this is good, right? After all, we just agreed that having fun is vital to high performance. But here's the problem. Adversity sharpens the senses. Its absence can hypnotize you into a destructive state of complacency if you allow it. In this state of hypnosis, you will lose your sensitivity to subtle hints that the quality of your performance may be in jeopardy, or that changing circumstances may require you to be attentive to what you're doing. Eventually, the deterioration of your abilities becomes too much to ignore, bringing an end to the fun and the beginning of worry and frustration. It is here that the severity of slumps can quickly worsen because you've now lost both your enjoyment of what you're doing and your adherence to fundamentals. With both out the window, the worsening of your performance can accelerate. Any enjoyment that may be left will turn to utter disdain, further impairing your willingness and ability to execute fundamentals with any degree of competence. You are now in a tailspin, a full-blown slump.

Several years ago, I had the distinct privilege of working with a client who was the elected president of a large national membership association. I'll call him Richard. Richard had impressive credentials and was more than competent in his core areas of professional expertise, which happened to be in an occupation with high levels of technical and scientific complexity. Richard had a great career, which explains why his employer entrusted him with the responsibilities of management. It also explains why his peers entrusted him with the presidency of their association. Richard's professional effectiveness was paying off.

But while he was thriving as the president, his employer was losing confidence, accusing him of behaviors that seemed curiously inconsistent with what I experienced as his coach. He struck me as being a very thoughtful, engaged, and loyal employee who was trying his best to do a good job. But the more I listened to his story, the more I felt like something was off. Richard explained that his direct supervisor put him on a performance improvement plan (PIP) , hoping to correct problems that seemed to be spiraling out of control. By the time he came to see me, his confidence was gone, his mood was sour, and his future was uncertain. He was convinced that he would either be fired or would eventually resign of his own volition. As his relationships with his upper management became increasingly strained, his own employees seemed to withdraw in turn, as if to suspect that Richard wouldn't be there much longer. Said another way, Richard was in a deep slump with no apparent path to lead him out.

During some of my earlier sessions with Richard, he gave me the unmistakable sense that the people with whom he worked most often were having a hard time connecting with him. So, I asked him some questions about his physical posture and facial expressions at work. First, he seemed confused by my interest in how he appeared to people, but with further exploration and prodding, he came to realize that, over time, he had started to give signals that were being interpreted as irritation. The result was that people didn't want to interact with him.

So, I asked him to perform an exercise that I've asked many clients to do, usually with great success. I asked him to spend a full month being aware of his body language and facial expressions, and to keep notes for us to review during our sessions. I also asked him to spend time in front of the mirror at home, replicating physical signals he was displaying at work. When we convened for our next meeting, he was melancholy. On one hand, he was shocked to realize how angry and irritable his facial expressions made him look. He made a habit of furrowing his eyebrows, not because he was angry, but because that's what he did when he was concentrating or listening. On the other hand, he was relieved because he was now aware of it, telling me, "Now I understand why people have been distant with me. I look like I'm pissed off all the time."

"Good," I replied. "But let me ask you another question." Richard paused in cautious anticipation. "When was the last time you expressed curiosity about something going on in the life of one of your employees?"

"What do you mean?" Richard asked.

"I mean, when was the last time you asked an employee or coworker how his daughter's volleyball game went, how the date night went with her husband, or whether or not she has any interesting vacations planned for next summer? In other words, how often do you show people that you're interested in *them*."

Richard's reaction was a cocktail of embarrassment and guilt. "Not nearly often enough," he admitted. "I don't think I've been giving people many good reasons to like me or trust me."

"You can change all that," I assured him.

Upon further discussion, I also learned that some complicated personal tensions were putting Richard at odds with his direct supervisor, who Richard explained had once been a close personal friend. It gave me the feeling that Richard's supervisor was struggling with his own feelings of inadequacy and was taking it out on Richard. I didn't know for sure, so I kept my suspicions to myself. But I made it clear that some unpleasant exchanges with his supervisor probably conspired to bleed the fun out of Richard's work, causing him to build up resentments and abandon some of the fundamental behaviors that competent leaders are expected to demonstrate. Richard needed to regain the trust of his team.

The good news is that Richard's story has a happy ending. During our time together, we focused on a few fundamental behaviors that I knew would help Richard make fast work of turning around the perceptions that people had of him, including his upper management. I encouraged him to raise his eyebrows when he spoke to people, a trick I learned as an expert witness when testifying in court. When you raise your eyebrows, it welcomes people into your space and shows a confident willingness to engage. In high-stakes, high-pressure situations, sour facial expressions are a problem because people often furrow their eyebrows when they are concentrating or listening carefully. By raising the eyebrows, it softens the face and conveys the warmth needed for quality conversations to unfold.

I also asked Richard to smile and laugh as often as he could without appearing awkward or inappropriate. Not only did I want Richard's peers and upper managers to see him enjoying himself, I knew that by smiling and laughing more often, Richard would start to feel better all around, allowing future smiles and future laughter to occur more naturally. I was under no illusion this would be easy, considering Richard was on a PIP, not exactly an enjoyable thing to experience. But I figured that if he could see the PIP as an opportunity and enjoy the personal and professional growth that comes from it, there was no reason why he couldn't find many legitimate reasons to smile and laugh with his colleagues.

Finally, Richard and I both agreed that he must pause and take time, whenever possible, to ask people about their work and their lives, showing genuine curiosity about them. In fact, his objective was about more than just being curious, Richard needed to *enjoy* his people! In my experience as a manager and a coach, you cannot maximize your influence over people when they don't believe you enjoy them. As I mentioned earlier, enjoying people is one of the greatest gifts you can give them because it fills them with feelings of connection and relevance. In return, they will give you their loyalty and trust.

By the time Richard and I finished working with each other, he made dramatic improvements in both his performance and how he was perceived. His relationship with his supervisor didn't improve quite as much as he hoped, but their problems didn't bear as heavily on Richard's morale as they did before. In fact, as Richard's reputation warmed, he took the initiative to organize social gatherings and play a more useful role in creating opportunities for employees to interact with each other. Soon, Richard's slump was over. He returned to being a productive, valued member of the team, even more so than before.

Sometimes the best advice you can give yourself and others is to refocus on fundamentals and get back to enjoying what you do and the people with whom you do it. Even better, if you can make these priorities a constant in all aspects of your life, you will avoid some of the slumps that might otherwise come to burden you when you least expect them.

As a leader, this advice is especially appropriate because you are confronted with the many mental and emotional strains that come with having the well-being of a team placed in your hands. It is imperative that you enjoy yourself, your people, and the responsibilities with which you've been entrusted. And it's equally imperative that you know and practice the key fundamentals of effective, trustworthy leadership that I've shared in this chapter. They will give you the confidence of knowing that, even when the stakes are high, you are doing what you need to do to be at your best.

Chapter 11

Play the Odds

I'd like you to imagine the CEO of a large hospital arriving to work in the morning. Her name is Denise. She parks her car, rides the elevator up to the top floor where the administrative offices are located, and then heads to the breakroom where her assistant, as she always does, has a pot of hot coffee brewed and ready to pour. Denise doesn't expect the coffee to be ready when she arrives, but she appreciates it nonetheless. Stirring in her favorite creamer, she turns and glances over her shoulder at a thermometer-like device hanging across the hallway on the wall outside of her office. The red column of mercury is graduated on a scale of 0 to 100. This morning it reads 68.

Only 68? she thinks to herself in dismay. It hasn't been this low in over a year. When the gauge reads 80 or higher, she feels confident, but anything lower than 70, in her experience, requires immediate attention. *What the heck happened?* she wonders. *What did I do?*

Denise relies heavily on her personal leadership gauge, which keeps an up-to-date measure of how her decisions, behaviors, and communications are impacting the hospital and its employees. Setting her coffee on her desk, she sits down and ponders. *I wonder if the email I sent out to the division directors last night was too harsh.* In fact, it was. Denise was frustrated by the hospital's infection stats for the previous month and was looking to refocus her management team on the mitigation strategies they implemented after the first of the year. *Perhaps my email was too distant or impersonal. I probably should have gotten out and spoken individually with my directors to get their perspectives.*

So, she decides to clear her morning schedule and tour the administrative suite, stopping to say hello to her team members and asking for their input about how the infection rates can be kept at their target thresholds. She finds herself surprised by what she learns, realizing that other factors related to how the data were collected are at play and that the mitigation strategies are, in fact, working. She expresses her sincere regret for the email she sent the night before and thanks her directors for their efforts to stay vigilant. She even pokes fun at herself by pointing out that her beloved Rangers have been on a losing streak and that it must be affecting her judgement. She vows that she will come speak with them personally before firing off caustic emails in the future. When she returns to her office in time for lunch, the gauge reads 84. She smiles and boots up her computer to check her emails.

The gauge Denise uses to continuously monitor her leadership performance does not exist, of course. It's a fictitious representation of indicators that instead exist in the form of team-member attitudes and feelings of engagement. Everything you do as a leader or influencer of people, whether in or outside of their presence, has a direct and lasting impact on them and their performance. Unfortunately, you don't always have the luxury of immediate feedback. Instead, you depend on your own *sense* of things, your intuition, and whatever objective measures you may employ to accurately assess how well you're doing.

Denise's employees are counting on her. They depend on her to be more than just the person *occupying* the CEO position. They count on her to execute the powers of her position in a way that optimizes the conditions in which her people are working and, therefore, enable the levels of performance that are expected. For Denise, the infection rates are a key performance indicator, or KPI, so she acts with due deliberateness when they suggest a problem is emerging.

But if these KPIs are so important to Denise, then why did she bring dishonor upon herself and her goals by resorting to a careless and undisciplined way of reacting? It seems as if the importance of the situation should have inspired a savvier approach to dealing with it. But it didn't. Denise fell back on some of the old superior tendencies that she's worked so hard to suppress and, in doing so, had a deleterious effect on her leadership team. Thank goodness for her realization of the damage she caused. It allowed her to make an immediate adjustment, and it worked.

The Art of Adjustment

You don't have a leadership gauge hanging on your wall to tell you how you're doing. In fact, if you're like some leaders, you may not even care how you're doing. You give orders, the orders are followed, and life goes on. What's there to worry about? But I suspect and hope you are more conscientious than this. Like me, you care about the impact you're having on people. You care about the impact you're having on your team. If you make a mistake, you want to fix the damage as quickly as possible. When your people make mistakes, you want to hold them accountable, but not in a way that wastes the opportunity for them to be strengthened by the experience. But as it is with all leaders, the effectiveness or ineffectiveness of your leadership is not always clear right away. The sooner you can be aware of the impact you're having, the sooner you can adjust and keep your team moving forward. But this is rather difficult for many leaders, and in the absence of a magical gauge like the one used by Denise, how can you be sure that you're giving your team and its members the leadership and management support they need?

The Gallup 10%

Contemporary research estimates that few people have what we might describe as natural leadership abilities. More specifically, a workplace report published by Gallup on April 13, 2015, summarized Gallup's work aimed at measuring how uncommon natural leadership talent is in the human population. Here's what they found:

"....great managers are scarce because the talent required to be one is rare. Gallup's research shows that about one in 10 people possess high talent to manage. Though many people have some of the necessary traits, few have the unique combination of talent needed to help a team achieve the kind of excellence that significantly improves a company's performance. When these 10% are put in manager roles, they naturally engage team members and customers, retain top performers and sustain a culture of high productivity."

Gallup's findings may strike you as troubling, especially when you consider how much our society, our economy, and our individual organizations rely on competent leadership to preserve and promote our well-being. You may wonder, as I have from time to time, if you are among the 10% of those naturally born leaders. And if you aren't, what does that mean for you and the people counting on you?

Well, I must admit that I've contemplated the implications of the Gallup study for a while now. And I've come to what I think is a counterintuitive but strangely soothing conclusion. It doesn't really matter if you fall in the Gallup 10%. Instead, it's in your best interest to think of yourself as being among the 90% of us for whom the effective execution of leadership does *not* come naturally. Think about it. Even if someone is born with natural leadership abilities, it doesn't mean that her abilities will naturally fit the demands of a specific position, such as the

Chief Technology Officer at Boeing, let's say. In fact, the demands faced by the CTO at Boeing may be very different than those faced by the CTO at Coca-Cola. It may be true, therefore, that leadership abilities are innate in some, but they must be refined in all. This requires anyone in a leadership position, whether endowed with natural leadership abilities or not, to put forth the effort required to meet the unique demands of *that* position. There is no advantage to be gained by banking on the assumption that one's natural abilities will be enough to get by. There is every advantage to be gained, however, by working hard and smart to continuously improve.

The Limits of Personality

Confidence tends to be a luxury enjoyed more by those leaders who work at their craft than by those who seem to rely on their personalities. And I think there are good reasons for this. As relevant and impactful as personality is, it's also fleeting. It ebbs and flows with changes in your environment, your moods, your sleep, and your energy levels. If your six-year-old son keeps waking in the middle of the night because of bad dreams, you will have less energy in the morning and so will your personality. Your most important leadership tool may be your morning cup of coffee. Without it, perhaps you feel grumpy, tired, and unfocused. Personality, it turns out, is not under as much control as we like to think it is. It can be unpredictable and dependent on a variety of factors.

One way to think about personality is that it's the experience we create for others when they interact with us. If you are described as having a great personality, it means that engaging with you tends to be a great experience. If your personality is described as sour or offensive, it means that the experience of engaging with you is just that, sour and offensive. Of course, the personality people will experience when engaging with you will be influenced by how you feel about yourself and your own well-being in certain situations. There may also be patterns that you and your people notice, such as becoming defensive when your motives are questioned, or appearing visibly anxious the week before your quarterly earnings report is due. All of us have personalities, and these personalities have peculiarities that can be helpful or limiting, depending on the context in which they are allowed to manifest themselves. Personalities are personal. Leadership requires something more.

As a leader, you want to be confident in what you're doing, and you want your people to be confident in you. With confidence, you are more likely to enjoy what you are doing and are therefore more likely to be good at it. Being good at what you do, of course, makes you even more confident, resulting in a buildup of professional momentum and energy that makes you feel like you are thriving. A team with a thriving leader is as team more likely to thrive itself, so you owe it to yourself and your people to lead in a way that maximizes your confidence and theirs.

But is it really true that we have such a small chance of getting it right? If you're like me, you can't help but wonder why only 10% of people have natural leadership abilities. Even as I write this, the number strikes me as troubling. Our society and our economy have become increasingly complex, so we rely more heavily on the competence of leaders and their teams for our well-being. Knowing that such a small percentage of us are naturally gifted as leaders can make the world feel like a riskier place. And there is no shortage of evidence to remind those of us who are paying attention just how dangerous incompetent leadership can be.

Death on the Set

During my initial writing of this chapter in October of 2021, a tragic story was playing out in New Mexico on the set of a movie titled *Rust*, starring Alec Baldwin, that I couldn't help but suspect was made possible, at least in part, by incompetent leadership. According to reports, Baldwin was practicing for a scene in which he was to quickly draw a revolver from a holster, aim at the camera, then pull the trigger. Behind the camera stood the film's director, Joel Souza, and cinematographer, Halyna Hutchins, as they made a final assessment of the camera angle and lighting. But as Baldwin rehearsed, a loud pop rang out, startling the cast and crew. Hutchins, 42, slumped to the floor with a gunshot wound to her chest. Souza, who was standing behind Hutchins, felt a sharp burning pain in his shoulder after being struck by the same bullet that perforated Hutchins' torso. She was pronounced dead a short time later.

As details emerged about the incident, reports indicated that members of the crew had used the gun for leisurely target shooting that morning. *Yes, the same gun that killed Hutchins.* When playtime was over, the gun was placed on a cart and later handed to Baldwin by the film's assistant director, Dave Halls, who advised Baldwin that the gun was safe. It wasn't. When Baldwin pulled the trigger, a live cartridge rotated into position and was struck by the firing pin. The burning gunpowder accelerated the bullet down the gun's barrel, exiting the muzzle above or close to the speed of sound and striking Halyna Hutchins in the chest. Baldwin was likely startled by the gun's recoil, something he wouldn't expect to feel if firing a blank round. Chaos ensued. A young woman in the prime of her life was now dead.

Days after the incident, Serge Svetnoy, the chief electrician on the set, also known as the *gaffer*, authored an emotionally charged Facebook post in which he alleged that negligence and unprofessionalism were the causes of the accident. In Svetnoy's own words, "the person who was supposed to check the weapon on the site did not do this; the person who had to announce that the loaded gun was on the site did not do this; the person who should have checked this weapon before bringing it to the set did not do it." Svetnoy also revealed that he was standing next to Hutchins when she was shot, holding her in his arms while she was dying.

In satisfying my own curiosity as to why Halyna Hutchins died, all I really needed to know was that members of the crew were playing with the gun that morning. *Playing.* Sheriff's deputies later found live ammunition comingled with the blanks that would normally be used on a movie set to create the sound of a gunshot. This would not be unlike cooking dinner for your kids and having a vial of cyanide sitting next to the table salt. The reported facts struck me as clear evidence that the leaders in charge – in this case, the leaders would be the directors, producers, and anyone else responsible for employee conduct on the set – had not created a culture in which firearms and firearm safety were treated with the utmost respect. Once it is known that filming will involve the use of a firearm, it should set into motion a series of checks and processes that ensure the safety of the cast and crew. But even that's not enough. By the sheer force of will, and through leadership that emphasizes seriousness and vigilance when it comes to firearm safety, the unintentional discharge of a bullet from a loaded gun should be rendered a practical impossibility.

What happened on the set of *Rust* was a catastrophe of the worst kind. When I first learned of it, I could appreciate how something like this might have happened, having spent so many years in the firearms units of forensic laboratories where several guns were analyzed and test-fired each day, every day. But I also felt a wash of eye-rolling cynicism course through me, suspecting that eventually the typical stories would emerge about persons in positions of leadership who didn't do their jobs or had unimpressive track records that made them undeserving to even be on the set of a major motion picture. Any guilt I may have felt for harboring such contemptuousness, however, was soon ameliorated.

A story by *CNN's* Julia Jones on October 25, 2021, revealed that Dave Hall – recall that he was the film's assistant director who handed Alec Baldwin the loaded gun – had what might be interpreted as a history of reckless disregard for the well-being of others. During the filming of two other movies in 2019, Hall was the subject of complaints alleging disregard for safety protocols for weapons and pyrotechnic use, as well as blocked fire lanes and exits. Another *CNN* report by Sandra Gonzalez and Lisa Respers France on October 15, 2021, added that the complaints from 2019 alleged that "Halls also neglected to hold safety meetings and consistently failed to announce the presence of a firearm on set to the crew, as is protocol." According to a crew member who asked *CNN* to remain anonymous for fear of retaliation, when Halls did hold safety meetings, "they were short and dismissive, saying the guns used would be the same as the production always uses, and questioning why they'd have to hold the meetings in the first place."

If this wasn't bad enough, then came allegations of inappropriate sexual conduct with members of the crew. Speaking with CNN, Maggie Goll, a prop-maker and licensed pyrotechnician working on the set of an anthology series for Hulu, shared that "on my first day back on the series, another crew member told me to watch out for Dave, saying he was too physically familiar with the crew, despite many rebuffs and complaints about unwanted and unnecessary touches. Nothing too extreme, but crew members of all genders and dispositions were being made uncomfortable by Dave's touches to their backs, waists, shoulders, etc."

As of this writing, the investigation into the death of Halyna Hutchins is underway and more information will emerge in the coming months. Alec Baldwin has claimed that he never pulled the trigger, which I know as a trained forensic firearms examiner to be an almost impossible scenario. Reports indicated the firearm was sent to the FBI Laboratory in Quantico, Virginia where a series of tests will be performed to confirm that the bullet that killed Hutchins did, in fact, come from the gun held by Baldwin, and to assess the gun's mechanical condition, which will be especially relevant in light of Baldwin's claim. But from what I can tell, Hutchins' death was not caused by a gun, a bullet, or a flawed procedure. Hutchins was killed by a toxic culture under the toxic leadership of a toxic man who, from what the available reports seem to indicate, didn't take very seriously his people, their safety, or their dignity.

To revisit a theme I presented in this book's introduction:

Effective leaders are empowered by the primordial inspirations that are reserved exclusively for people having a purpose. Leadership is the act of protecting that purpose. In the absence of purpose, there can be no leadership.

Halyna Hutchins, in my opinion, was the victim of an authority figure who should have made her well-being and the well-being of her colleagues his primary purpose. If he had, Halyna would still be alive, her husband would still have his wife, and her children would still have their mother. Leadership matters. It matters a lot.

Unlike our friend Denise whose magical leadership gauge we imagined at the start of this chapter, the directors and producers in New Mexico came to learn of their own leadership challenges with the most shocking of indicators – the death of an employee. And, too often, shocking is how it happens. People in positions of authority are just good enough at their jobs to get by when things are going reasonably well, but when presented with a clear and present danger, their lack of skill makes them insensitive to threats and unable to pivot. What comes of this fateful rendezvous of leadership incompetence with situational vulnerability is utter catastrophe.

A Preventable Accident. Effective leaders always accept responsibility for the outcomes they produce, good or bad. If someone from the Gallup 10% had been in charge of the movie set, would Halyna Hutchins still be alive? Of course, it's impossible to say for sure, but what I've come to know about cultures fueled by effective leadership is that there is no ambiguity about what's important. What effective leaders believe is important seems also to be demonstrably important to their people.

Humility

At this point in evolutionary time, nature seems only willing to endow about 10% of us with high degrees of innate leadership talents, which means that most of us are still wired for *survival*. But to *thrive* – which is to be unburdened by threats to survival and inspired by the opportunity for greater prosperity and relevance – is not a priority for nature, and so neither are the leadership traits needed to achieve it.

Your goal is to be better than what nature alone would have you be, and for that you must be humble. It's in your best interest to think of yourself as being part of Gallup's 90%, those to whom leadership skills and instincts *do not* come naturally. Even if leadership does not come naturally to you, you can design a personal approach to leadership that works for you by being intentional and deliberate. When you find success, you will take your leadership responsibilities seriously without taking yourself too seriously. You will make clear what's important to you. You will not display the childish signaling tendencies that entitled leaders do. You will inspire, not dominate; and your very presence will infuse the needed doses of energy and purpose your hierarchy will need to function as a team. You will be an entrusted leader.

Get excited, because the results you can produce are worth getting excited about.

Chapter 12

Invert Your Mindset

If you work in what might be described as the typical organization – such as an office, a laboratory, a hospital, a school, or a factory – I assume that you wear clothes when you go to work every day. When you get to work, everyone is wearing clothes too. My guess, however, is that your organization does not have an official policy that directly prohibits nudity in the workplace, nor do your job announcements to fill vacant positions alert prospective candidates that you are a *fully clothed employer*. People just seem to wear clothes. It's what they do. It's natural.

For something to be *natural* means that it occurs or exists without any artificial intervention. It lives on its own and has what it needs to keep living on its own. On the other hand, if you want to make something natural that isn't already, then you must *naturalize* it. To naturalize something means to have it live and grow in places where it is not indigenous. Like a new sapling planted in a garden, it needs suitable conditions and to be given what it needs to begin and sustain its growth.

If your goal, therefore, is to be an effective leader or to prioritize effective leadership across your team, begin by recognizing that it's not natural and must be planted in the right conditions. To create these conditions, your individual and collective understandings of leadership may require a complete inversion from what most contemporary organizations believe it to be.

The Shape of Leadership

Sheryl Sandberg is the Chief Operating Officer at Facebook and a world-renowned business executive, philanthropist, and author. She earned critical acclaim in 2013 with the publication of her first book, *Lean In,* which became an international best-seller almost overnight. According to Sandberg, her writing of *Lean In* was inspired by the overwhelming response she received after delivering a TED Talk in 2010 titled, *Why we have too few women leaders,* in which Sandberg exposes many of the barriers women face in the workplace, as well as barriers they sometimes create for themselves. The BBC reported that after just two years in publication, *Lean In* sold over 2.2 million copies worldwide, fueled by a growing movement of readers and fans who found inspiration in Sandberg's heartfelt message.

Lean In has been described by some and by Sandberg herself as a feminist manifesto of sorts, a call to action for any woman believing she is capable of more but, perhaps, finds herself limited by forces that feel both in and outside of her control. For this reason, I continue to recommend *Lean In* to many of my female clients when I sense they might benefit from the book's unique words of encouragement. Of course, this is the least I can do. As a man, I know of my limited capacity to fully empathize with the struggles that so many women have faced and continue to face in their careers. But I'm also a father, and I want my daughter to create and sustain her own personal and professional momentum, whatever she decides that should be. And I hope she will never entrust her momentum to those who haven't earned the privilege. Male dominance, without question, still pervades many workplaces and industries today, and I continue to be shocked by the number of men with high levels of organizational authority who still believe they own the playground. Even in a professional setting, I seriously believe some men would pull women's hair and sneak walk-by grabs at their private parts if the behaviors didn't stand out as such conclusive proof of sexual predacity. But the mentality is still there, and it blocks many an organization from fully accessing the talents and energies women bring to the workplace. In fact, when I think about the goals and ambitions my daughter will have in her life, I can only hope she will resist the temptation to dignify or give power to any unfair attitudes and behaviors that might place limits on her career possibilities.

A Perpetuated Myth. On one hand, the messages of *Lean In* are comforting and empowering. But on the other hand, they also bolster some of the very misconceptions that Sandberg is trying to confront. As an example, consider the following excerpt from *Lean In*:

"One stumbling block is that many people believe that the workplace is largely a meritocracy, which means we look at individuals, not groups, and determine that differences in outcomes must be based on merit, not gender. Men at the top are often unaware of the benefits they enjoy simply because they're men, and this can make them blind to the disadvantages associated with being a woman. Women lower down also believe that men at the top are entitled to be there, so they try to play by the rules and work harder to advance rather than raise questions or voice concerns about the possibility of bias. As a result, everyone becomes complicit in perpetuating an unjust system."

Notice the words Sandberg uses to describe where people are situated in an organization's hierarchy. She describes the people having greater degrees of authority as being *at the top*, while those with less, as she puts it, are *lower down*. In other words, Sandberg, like most of us, sees organizational responsibility as having a two-dimensional shape. Leaders are at the top, contributors are at the bottom. But why? When did organizations develop a top and a bottom, a left and a right? I can't hold an organization in my hand or touch it because it's not an object. If it's not an object, how can it have a shape?

You'd be correct in recognizing that organizations have *virtual* shapes because of the need to document how decision-making authority and lines of communication are arranged. It needs to be put on paper, and because there are far fewer leaders than contributors, the leaders are shown at the narrow end of the shape while the contributors are shown at the wider end. But somewhere along the line, the shape was propped into a position that placed the leaders on the top and everyone else on the bottom, as Sheryl Sandberg observes. The resulting pyramid, the shape of organizational structures with which all of us are quite familiar, is yet another example of superiority signaling. Leaders on top, contributors on the bottom. Or, as Bob Fuller might describe it for more toxic cultures, the somebodies are at the top, the nobodies are at the bottom.

My comments here may strike you as a rather cynical way to view what might be just a harmless and routine way of documenting authority in organizations. You would be correct in noting that the pyramid is a stable shape that's nearly impossible to tip over without a conscious effort. This stability represents the ideal that organizations strive to achieve, positioning themselves to withstand the turbulence and competitive forces that might otherwise topple them. Having a solid foundation, as pyramids do, is what any enduring team or organization relies upon for its strength and longevity. A pyramid can also be climbed, with people naturally aspiring to reach those upper levels where the views are more breathtaking and the effort needed to reach them brings personal satisfaction.

At *the top*, of course, there is nowhere else to go. It is the end point at which no more upward effort is required. And once you've arrived, everyone at the bottom can look up and wish they were there. Those at the top (the superiors) have achieved what the others (the inferiors) couldn't. And so those at the top may be inclined to believe that they are entitled to perks, rewards, and benefits reserved only for those who made it to the top.

Unfortunately, the pyramid as a representation of organizational responsibility is not based on reality, unless you feel that your leadership entitles you to exclusive spoils. But for those entrusted souls who know what it feels like to accept and bear the responsibilities of leadership, the pyramid should be inverted or turned upside down, because this is what trustworthy leadership feels like.

When a person is entrusted with leadership responsibility, she is not climbing anything; in fact, she is descending downward into the foundations of the organization where the gravity of decision-making and the pressures of the work are much greater. And because the upside-down pyramid is so *un*stable, it requires the leaders at the bottom to exhaust considerable energy to keep it balanced. There is no rest and there are no entitlements. If things tip in one direction or the other, it is those as the bottom who we depend on to bring it back to center. With the nonmanagerial contributors at the top, any incompetence or carelessness among them will only worsen the instability and make it harder to correct. Contributors must be thoughtful, responsible, and effective if they wish to have a stabilizing influence. Even the strongest leaders will be unable to compensate for any disorganization or substandard performance if it gets bad enough.

The upside-down pyramid requires considerable effort and know-how to keep it balanced. But it is, nonetheless, the shape of the thriving organization. It is strong, durable, and on point. Contrasted against its chaotic surroundings, when it *is* balanced, it stands with majestic symmetry and elegance, withstanding the variety of forces and pressures that conspire to bring it down. The people who comprise the thriving organization are well-positioned, well-supported, and capable of meeting their responsibilities. Their work ensures that the organization remains upright and prepared to react to the next opportunity or threat that shows itself.

As we look and listen a bit closer, we will find team members who are focused on their responsibilities and each other. They are not distracted by personal insecurities or toxic attitudes. If they were, it would compromise the internal collaboration and communication needed to maintain organizational balance. For this reason, chronic selfishness and immaturity are not tolerated. Everyone sees to this, especially the organization's leaders. Not only do their own behaviors set an example for others, they also have the courage and mentoring skills to immediately confront and correct substandard performance through skillful applications of suggestion and encouragement. Rarely do they bark out instructions or directions. The reason they don't is because they want and need their people to develop critical thinking skills, allowing them to act, behave, and decide with ever-increasing effectiveness in the future.

And, by the way, there is something else these entrusted leaders don't tolerate: signaling. Like the splash of water that melted the Wicked Witch of the West, signaling destroys the relationships that form the organizational infrastructure. Without a strong infrastructure, the organization becomes weak and out of balance. It loses its ability to recognize and react to early warnings that something may be wrong. For this reason, signaling doesn't have the same intimidating effect that it does in so many other organizations. In thriving organizations, signaling is met with the kind of parental disapproval often reserved for a misbehaving child in a grocery store. Thriving organizations don't have time for signaling. What they expect is commitment.

This inverting of one's perspective on leadership opens the door to new opportunities. Once you can see in your mind's eye the shape, structure, and responsibilities that form a thriving organization, the problems described by Sheryl Sandberg appear less complicated and, perhaps, easier to solve. Nonmanagerial women, like my daughter, need not look upon leaders, male or female, with jealousy or bitterness. But to the extent women encounter male leaders who treat their managerial jobs like thrones to which they are exclusively entitled, women who care about competent leadership should stand resolutely as the voices of mature reason, reminding everyone that true leadership is a responsibility to be met, not a reward to be envied. Displays of male entitlement, after all, are nothing more than the childish signaling of fictitious superiority, and should be confronted with a squint of annoyance, followed by the setting of clear expectations of what consummate leadership professionalism looks like, sounds like, and acts like. Those who refuse to meet and respect those expectations need to go. It may be a long road to haul, but such is the vision of any competent leader seeking to rise above the stormy clouds of the old superior and into the sunlight of entrusted leadership.

Chapter 13

Think AC

When you plug your toaster into the outlet above your kitchen counter, you're tapping into a supply of *alternating current* (AC) that's generated by a powerplant. To create AC power, large coils of wire are spun inside a strong magnetic field, causing the electrons in the wire to flow. This moving of electrons is called electricity. But because magnets have two poles, one positive and one negative, each time the wires pass into and out of one of these polarities, the electrons reverse or alternate their direction. Alternating current, therefore, is electricity in which the electrons vibrate rapidly back and forth. *Direct current* (DC), on the other hand, is the kind of electricity created by a battery or solar panel, whereby the electrons move in one direction all the time, that is until the battery runs out of power, just as my phone has done many times while waiting for a delayed flight at the airport.

The example of AC current is a useful analogy to explain how the most influential people apply themselves, and how they leverage the power of their rank, stature, and authority in ways that create healthy engagements among people in a professional setting. They display a masterful ability to alternate back and forth between superiority and subordination. In one moment, they are doing the talking, calling the shots, running a meeting, making a decision, communicating a vision, and setting expectations. But in the very next moment, they are listening carefully, asking questions, receiving input, and considering the advice of their people. At its best, this alternation between superiority and subordination can happen instantaneously as circumstances require. Among the many things that make effective leaders *so* effective is that they spend most of their time as equals in the moment, and they reserve their organizational superiority only for those situations when they are required to make a decision or take an action. They know when to use their superiority and when to shut it off.

Alternation in Practice

The scene from *Apollo 13* that I described earlier is an example of alternating superiority. You may recall that John, our young engineer, stepped forward to challenge the director of flight operations, Gene Kranz, and his colleagues on their confusion about exactly how much power was remaining in the Lunar Excursion Module. Kranz quickly subordinates himself to make space for John's input, then reasserts his superiority when it comes time to make the fateful decision to power down the LEM. Also significant was John's willingness to alternate his own standing in the matter by assuming a position of superiority, however momentary, so he could ensure his team had the advantage of knowing what he knew about the gravity of the situation.

Organizational leaders favoring a dominant style of influence have a difficult time with alternation. The idea of subordinating themselves to someone of lower rank not only strikes them as silly but insulting as well. They may feel they've earned their superiority, and to just give it away is not only a sign of weakness, it betrays the same hierarchy that enabled their rise to power in the first place. What they don't understand, however, is that being stuck in the superiority mode is like a car being stuck in a single gear. It may work for a while, but eventually the car will either stall or rev so high that the engine will explode.

Chronic Subordination. Superiors are not the only ones who get stuck. Subordinates – those without managerial responsibilities – get stuck too, and they do so quite often. The result is an unwillingness to share opinions, challenge ideas, or raise legitimate concerns. Of course, being trapped in a state of subordination is sometimes the natural consequence of leaders who are stuck in a state of dominance, but this isn't always the case. Some team members are chronically burdened with the sense that self-assertiveness is somehow disrespectful to their leaders or peers, so they keep their mouths shut or limit their input to comments that simply validate or agree with what their leaders have already expressed. The team is worse for it because good ideas go unexpressed, and the opportunity for mutual accountability gets lost.

Catastrophe on the Horizon

Leaders and team members who have the maturity and flexibility to alternate between superiority and subordination are, in my experience, the essential foundation for risk mitigation at scale. And in making mention of risk, I'm talking about exposure to ethical risks, quality assurance risks, health and safety risks, and operational risks, to name just a few. Risk tends to dissolve in the routine bantering that takes place among leaders and followers who feel comfortable asserting themselves, asking difficult questions, and reminding each other of what's important. Team environments where the various players know when and how to step forward and then step back again are mentally and emotionally agile, creating space for ownership of the issues to be shared, regardless of individual rank, stature, or authority. Within this space, team members can recognize and deliberate on emerging risks with greater speed and confidence. This simply cannot happen when people are stuck in their hierarchical identities.

When Things Go Really Bad. If you've ever watched the evening news or read a story about a company being accused of severe wrongdoing – perhaps the CEO is even convicted and sent to prison – you've probably asked yourself, as I have, *How the heck does something like that happen? When did THAT become a good idea?* When it does happen, it seems to arise from people who are chronically stuck in their respective positions of superiority or subordination. Leaders don't listen to subordinates and subordinates don't challenge their leaders. Everyone seems to live and work within their own little bubbles. Unfortunately, risk tends to infiltrate teams and organizations *between* these bubbles, where they go unnoticed and therefore unmitigated. In the worst instances, exposure to risk will fester for so long that the eventual harm is almost unspeakable in its severity.

One such example occurred in 2008 at the Peanut Corporation of America (PCA), a food processing and distribution company with about 90 employees headquartered in Lynchburg, Virginia. Authorities backtraced a massive Salmonella outbreak to peanut meal manufactured and sold by PCA. Over 700 people were infected; nine lost their lives. Although outbreaks of this sort are never outside the realm of possibility, an especially large number of people were impacted. FBI investigators later uncovered emails demonstrating that PCA executives ordered the distribution of peanut meal they knew to be contaminated. If that wasn't bad enough, they covered-up laboratory results that confirmed it. In one instance, according to multiple sources reporting within the food safety industry, Stewart Parnell, the now defunct company's CEO, was advised by employees that the distribution of a large batch of peanut meal was being put on hold until results from laboratory contamination tests were completed. Parnell's email response, later tendered as evidence by prosecutors during his trial, was abrupt: *Just ship it.*

As part of the initial response to the Salmonella outbreak, federal investigators inspected a PCA plant located in Texas. As reported by Reuters in March of 2009, "Dead mice and rodent droppings were found." Investigators reported that "effective measures are not being taken to exclude pests from the processing areas and protect against the contamination of food on the premises by pests." It became increasingly evident that health and safety were not critical priorities for the Peanut Corporation of America.

Stewart Parnell and other executives at PCA were indicted, tried, and convicted. Among the many counts for which Parnell was found guilty included conspiracy to introduce adulterated and misbranded food into interstate commerce, mail fraud, wire fraud, and obstruction of justice. Parnell was sentenced to 28 years in prison. His brother, Michael, was also found guilty of multiple felony counts and sentenced to 20 years. The convictions sent shock waves through corporate boardrooms across America, serving as stern reminders of the potential consequences of executive misconduct.

If you're inclined to read more about what happened at PCA and the tragic deaths that resulted, you will likely find, as I did, that Stewart Parnell and his c-suite cohorts were enabled by people who were stuck in a perpetual state of subordination. Parnell's *just ship it* directive would have had no serious consequences if someone with a backbone said no. Instead, contaminated peanut meal was shipped out and found its way into food products that were purchased by innocent consumers.

Disciples of Dysfunction

So, the question remains: *How the heck does something like that happen?* Well, when scoundrels reach the executive ranks of companies, government agencies, and other kinds of institutions, they can be remarkably effective at rewarding loyalty and surrounding themselves with disciples who are unlikely to push back or get in the way. For these disciples who, for so long, found safety and solace in being compliant, it would take a herculean demonstration of self-awareness, courage, and character to stand up and resist any attempts by a corrupt leader to put innocent people in harm's way.

In my own professional life, I've worked for scoundrels, leaders who I came to know were of very weak moral fiber, and I committed myself, long ago, to never do it again. I encourage you to make the same commitment. To work for a scoundrel is to confront a painful reality: that your character and integrity will *dis*qualify you from opportunities to grow, to be entrusted with more responsibility, and to contribute to the executive decision-making process. You will be seen as a threat, and every possible effort will be made to keep you from disrupting the status quo. Scoundrels are habitual superiors. They must be, lest they be subjected to scrutiny and held accountable for the adverse outcomes they produce. So, they make it a practice to surround themselves with habitual subordinators. Then, in those unexpected moments of desperation, when crisis comes knocking and difficult decisions need to be made, this unholy alliance of scoundrels and subordinates will be quite willing to preserve its power and well-being at the expense of others, even in matters of life and death.

The Value of Alternation

In the exercise of leadership, you will find that your ability to earn and retain trust is remarkably enhanced when you can alternate quickly and seamlessly between superiority and subordination, but it's important to understand why. Leaders who've gained a mastery of this most useful of professional talents have done so because they have sufficient self-confidence to make themselves vulnerable in front of others. For a leader to be willing to momentarily subordinate herself means she has the personal strength one needs to expose herself to criticism, push-back, difficult questions, and the expressing of challenging ideas that might cause her to rethink her own. Her sense of timing must be sharp, allowing her to recognize when it's appropriate to reassert her superiority, thank everyone for their contributions, and bring the conversation to a close so that a decision can be made. Sometimes, the alternating between superiority and subordination happens quickly and among multiple individuals, depending on the circumstances. Other times it happens slowly, especially in those instances where more time is needed to deliberate on complex issues or vexing problems. Either way, the most effective leaders are masters of both alternation and facilitation, giving the members of their teams the opportunity to assert themselves without fear of reprisal. The result is a culturally reinforced expectation that everyone be willing to participate in decision-making and voice their opinions when they believe mistakes are being made or exposure to risk is unacceptable. In this kind of culture, the decisions and actions that led to the PCA Salmonella outbreak become a practical impossibility.

Trust at Scale. In some ways, this alternation that I'm describing might also be characterized as *sharing* – leaders and contributors sharing the opportunity to influence the direction their teams or organizations are going. The more people who share the responsibilities of leadership, the more perspectives will be permitted to deepen the quality of the decisions being made. This is not to suggest that some situations won't arise from time to time when leaders will have no choice but to act decisively with minimal input. But experience tells us that such situations are not very common. Most of the time, there is plenty of latitude for leaders to involve their people, seek input, and consider opposing viewpoints. In fact, the more frequently nonmanagerial employees within organizations are afforded the chance to participate in decision-making, the more incentive there is to learn and develop themselves professionally. This is how leadership is incubated.

Tangible Benefits. If we take some time to inventory all the ways in which alternation creates value for teams and organizations, we will find the list to be a long one. But there are some worth emphasizing here:

Pleasantness – Let's face it, it's exhausting trying to be the superior all the time, and even more exhausting trying to cope with the unilateralism of someone who can't or won't alternate. With more energy, there is less irritability and more kindness circulating through the work environment.

Engagement - Input is welcomed and people feel safe voicing their thoughts, even when doing so may disrupt conventional wisdom. They feel like players in the game rather than spectators, and it shows in the way they commit to the mission of the team.

Awareness – More engagement means more conversation and more sharing of information having relevance to the decisions being made. People know what's going on and what's on everyone's mind. The team is not burdened by the secrets and blind spots that come from the hoarding of information.

Diversity – Because leaders make room for all team members to lean in and contribute, there is a greater variety of backgrounds and perspectives brought to bear on the challenges and opportunities facing the team. No one is excluded from contributing for illegitimate reasons.

Confidence – Team members trust themselves to make smarter decisions because their ideas have already been shared and subjected to scrutiny. By the time those ideas are put into action, they've been refined and strengthened by a process that encourages the consideration of multiple perspectives.

Preparedness – Greater awareness means team members are more alert to threats and able to mitigate risk faster. If a crisis erupts, they've already built the foundation of mutual trust needed to engage the crisis with poise and purpose.

Learning – Because team members have a platform from which to share and contribute, they will seek to expand their capacities to utilize this platform with greater ease and effectiveness. They are more likely to invest in their own learning and take the initiative to develop relevant skills.

Vision – The team or organization can see the future with more clarity because leaders are not distracted by their impulsive need to preserve their own superiority. The viewpoints and projections of multiple people, including both leaders and contributors, are blended to form one cohesive vision over which people feel a sense of ownership.

Opportunity – Where alternation is practiced and emphasized, leadership candidates who might otherwise have been regarded as nontraditional or not fitting the typical mold are more likely to emerge and be considered. This creates new opportunities brought forth by new ways of thinking.

Relevance – Alternating leaders are exceptionally skilled at building and maintaining teamwork. The higher levels of performance observed across these teams makes them more relevant to their customers, clients, and stakeholders.

Getting Yourself Unstuck

If you happen to be one of those leaders stuck in a chronic state of superiority, you may be resistant to the principles being advocated in this chapter. Your position of superiority may give you feelings of strength, security, and control, and you might find it untenable to just give it away and expose yourself to the risks that arise when others are empowered with the opportunity to express themselves freely.

But here's something to keep in mind: Your unwillingness or inability to let go is *already* exposing you to significant risk. In fact, it's a clear and present danger to your trustworthiness and your overall effectiveness as a leader. Leaders who compulsively cling to their superiority do not appear strong or secure. They look like babies, unwilling to let go of the blanket, which makes them nearly impossible to trust. And if you happen to report to an upper-level manager or executive with higher levels of emotional intelligence, one who does, in fact, value and practice the skills of alternation, then it's likely your rigidity is already eroding your credibility and your prospects for upward mobility.

The good news is that you can pivot quickly and reposition yourself as the trustworthy, effective leader you want to be and *need* to be. Begin with internal reflection, scrutinizing your perceptions of what it means to be a leader and what it means to have power. Try to recognize the illusory nature of the power you think you have right now. With enough time and effort, you'll discover that it's not power at all. Instead, what you have is the false sense of power that comes from the assertion of dominance. But if you want *real* power, change how you perceive yourself and what you perceive to be your responsibilities as a leader.

Ask yourself the following questions which, perhaps, you've ignored in the past. Take time to reflect on each with sincerity and honesty:

- *What have I been entrusted with?*
- *Who is counting on me?*
- *How can I use my position to strengthen others?*
- *How can I allow others to strengthen me?*
- *How can I access the insights of my people more often?*
- *In what situations can I make room for others to be leaders?*
- *How can I make my people feel safe expressing themselves?*
- *How can I make my people feel safe making honest mistakes?*
- *How should I speak, act, and behave if I want to earn trust?*
- *How can I make myself more approachable and accessible?*

Notice the above questions don't require you to waste energy looking backwards. They're intended to help you look forward and facilitate whatever changes in thinking will allow you to relax your grip. Like anything new, you'll need *practice, practice, practice.* If you've never experienced what it's like to alternate fluidly between states of superiority and subordination, get ready, because you may discover sources and degrees of power that startle you. Just keep practicing, and when you've practiced enough that alternation comes naturally to you, it is then that being an effective leader will become naturalized with you. You might just become part of Gallup's exclusive 10% club.

Chapter 14

Prioritize Your Principles

Well, I've never been to Spain
But I kinda like the music

Three Dog Night
Never Been to Spain, 1971

As of this writing, I've never been to Spain, and it's a country I hope to visit very soon. I've heard only great things about it – the friendly people, the beautiful landscape, the delicious food, the vibrant culture. If you've been there, you may recall that Spain is all of that land and water that falls inside of Spain's borders. Whether by air, land, or sea, it was the crossing of Spain's border that was the final critical step in your effort to get to Spain. If there was no border, there would be no Spain.

One can make the argument that even without a border there would still be the people, the landscape, and the culture, but what you'd be left with is only the *idea* of Spain rather than an actual place having a defined set of boundaries that establish exactly where Spain begins and where it ends. In the absence of those boundaries, Spain would simply blur itself into geographical ambiguity, and with it, its customs, traditions, and culture – everything we love about Spain. Without anything to define its place, without anything to defend, Spain as we know it would not exist, and the world would be worse for it.

Boundaries vs. Barriers

Boundaries are a funny thing. For some people or in some situations, boundaries feel like the limits of human possibility, that which keeps our hopes out of reach. As such, when those boundaries are crossed, such as when Roger Bannister eclipsed the 4-minute mile, or when Thurgood Marshall became the first black justice of the U.S. Supreme Court, it is with much enthusiasm that they are celebrated as evidence of progress. This, however, confuses *boundaries* with *barriers*, which are two very different things. Barriers, we break; boundaries, we protect.

Boundaries, in fact, are what define us. When a parent teaches a child not to steal candy from a convenience store, the parent is setting a boundary that protects the child and her sense of moral and ethical integrity. Within that boundary, the child will be safe and secure. Outside of that boundary, the child will expose herself to harm.

We tend to be at our best when we stay inside of our protective boundaries. Now, this may strike some as overly conservative, but it's not; and even the appointment of Thurgood Marshall applies to this reasoning. This is to say that, despite the progress it represented, Marshall's rise to the Supreme Court was not the breaking of a boundary, it was the breaking of a *barrier*. In fact, Marshall's appointment was a hard yank of the Supreme Court into the protective confines of our American constitutional boundaries, wherein all people are created equal, and wherein the color of a person's skin does not disqualify him from being entrusted with such a momentous responsibility. Marshall's appointment honored and strengthened those boundaries, which happen to define what it means to be an American. To deprive someone of Marshall's intellect and good standing from reaching the Supreme Court simply because of his skin color lies *outside* of our American boundaries and, therefore, is un-American.

The civil rights movement has been as much about protecting boundaries as it has been about breaking barriers, which is why we should hold its leaders, such as Thurgood Marshall and so many others, in such high regard. At times, our social obsession with breaking barriers leaves us ignorant of the important work being done to reinforce boundaries, which is deserving of equal respect, if not more. It is much easier to destroy things than to build and protect them. To destroy something is to absolve oneself of the responsibility to care for it. Indeed, leadership sometimes inspires us to break down barriers. But it also builds, protects, and reinforces boundaries, and it's in our best interest to know the difference. To appreciate how people perform, and to understand the quality of the contributions they make, it's incumbent upon leaders to eliminate unnecessary barriers to progress, while encouraging awareness of and respect for those boundaries in which everyone's best work and best behavior are most likely to occur.

Principles

The critical distinction between a boundary and a barrier is that boundaries protect and empower, while barriers limit and demoralize. In the exercise of leadership, we describe boundaries of thought and behavior as *principles*. Principles are fundamental truths that, if accepted and honored, empower people to make certain outcomes likely to occur. If surgeons in an operating room, for example, accept and honor the principle that a full five-minute scrubbing of the hands with an antimicrobial soap, according to an established procedure, will significantly reduce or eliminate the presence of bacteria, then they will follow the procedure and the outcome of surgeries uncomplicated by infections are more likely to happen. To *not* scrub according to the established procedure falls far outside of the boundary set by the principle. Principles govern behaviors; behaviors produce outcomes. To create the desired outcomes, one must adhere to the principles that maximize the likelihood of those outcomes.

Stay in Your Lane. I'm reminded of the importance of principles and how they regulate behavior when I'm at a bowling alley where families are gathered. Parents with small children often request that bumpers be placed along the sides of the lanes so their kids won't repeatedly roll balls into the gutters. If a ball is released at a bad angle, the bumpers will redirect the ball down the lane until it strikes the pins. The bumpers establish boundaries beyond which the ball will not travel, making contact with the pins much more likely. It's a simple way to visualize how principles regulate behavior. They keep us from wandering. They keep us on target.

Of course, this doesn't mean that conflict won't arise from time to time when there's disagreement about what principles matter and which ones don't. Continuing with our bowling analogy, highly competitive parents might balk at the idea of using bumpers, taking the position that gutters are a part of bowling. If you block the gutters, you take away the primary incentive for children to become better bowlers, resulting in future bowlers who will throw gutter balls more often. This is a principle that's easy to argue and, on its face, is a reasonable one. But there's another way to look at it. Without the bumpers, young children won't have as much fun. In fact, they will throw so many gutter balls that they will be at risk of disliking the game so much, they won't want to play. So, it won't matter how good they become at bowling because they'll hate it.

Conflict is okay and should be expected. But to debate the utility of certain principles when compared to others requires what will sometimes be very feisty conversations about what outcomes are trying to be achieved. The principles most likely to produce the desired outcomes are the ones to which everyone must agree. But first, everyone with a stake in which principles are judged to be best must be willing to engage in these conversations.

A Principle in Action. Back in 2003, I met a gentleman named Joe Bonacci while vacationing down in Marco Island, Florida with family and friends. Joe was the owner and CEO of a sandwich shop called Rudy's House of Submarines – Rudy's Subs, for short – which are popular in Pennsylvania. Joe purchased several stores in the 1950s and built the brand into a successful franchise by the time he sold it.

Our paths crossed at a school playground where I was letting my 3-year-old son, Kevin, burn off some energy before we headed back for lunch at the condo we rented for the week. Joe was with his grandkids, doing the same thing, as it turned out. In passing, we said hello, introduced ourselves, and struck up a conversation. He was a good bit older than me, but we were fascinated by each other. I admired the success he had as a businessman and he enjoyed speaking with a real-life forensic expert. But Joe was also a natural coach, very curious and inquisitive. He wanted to know what plans I had for my career and shook his head in amusement when I told him about my interest in pursuing a master's degree.

"I didn't need a master's degree to build my business, John." He smiled as he said it, but I could tell he was serious. "I wish you luck in whatever you do, but do you wanna know what worked for me? Wanna know why my business did so well?"

"Yes, I do," I replied, curious to know any secrets he'd be willing to share about his path to success.

He was happy to oblige. "I believe 100% in a fundamental principle that determines whether a customer will come back to a restaurant or not," he said. "And that principle is this: the food tastes better when the service is good."

I paused for a moment to take in what he said, but the message wasn't hitting me right away.

Sensing I was confused, he elaborated. "John, I believe that the food we serve in my stores actually tastes better to my customers when they experience good service. When the cashier smiles and welcomes them, the food tastes better. When the chairs are pushed in, when the tables are wiped down, and when the floors are kept clean, the food really tastes better. I know it. Don't get me wrong, our food tastes great, but it tastes *really* great when the *service* is really great. So, I've made it a practice to reinforce this principle with every single person I hire, and it works. It affects how they conduct themselves and the experience they create for my customers. And the customers keep coming back, and they're happy to do so."

Joe Bonacci, who passed away in 2011 at the age of 79, built a successful business around one simple principle, one that had a deep and lasting impact on the members of his team and, therefore, the likelihood that customers would come back again and again. *The food tastes better when the service is good.*

The One True Boss

One of the most important roles that principles play in organizational leadership is that *they* are superior. No individual is more important than the principles of the team, not even its highest ranking or most senior members. Principles come first. When principles come first, and when those principles are well-considered and fairly administered, everyone thrives. If failure is to be eliminated as an option, to call on the words of Gene Kranz, principles will have to be put into practice at all times. Not just some of the time, all the time.

As I mentioned earlier, the defending of principles, will inevitably precipitate conflict and the need to make difficult decisions. In leadership, this requires not only courage, but also a firm belief in the principles themselves and a clear understanding of why they are important. Leaders who don't *really* believe, in their heart of hearts, that certain principles are worth defending, or who can't explain how and why those principles increase the likelihood of certain outcomes, will be stunningly ineffective in resolving conflict or making critical decisions. Worse, they may betray those principles out of fear of looking bad or having to engage in conflict that might be uncomfortable.

The Courage to Be Principled

My own guts and resolve were put to the test several years ago in what became one of the most frightening decisions I ever made. The rape kit crisis in Detroit prompted a statewide rethinking about how the crime of criminal sexual conduct was investigated. On the average day, as the director of Michigan's forensic laboratories, I expected complicated issues to arise and was always prepared to deal with them. What I did not expect, however, was to be confronted by a problem of such a personal and emotionally charged nature that I would lose sleep for days. The solution became clear only when I subordinated myself to what I believed were fundamental principles in the investigation and prevention of sex crimes – that a survivor of sexual assault is less likely to participate willingly in an investigation if doing so causes her physical or emotional pain. And if she does not participate willingly, both the investigation and the prevention of future assaults will be compromised. Unfortunately, that's exactly what was happening.

After a sexual assault occurs, the survivor is asked by investigators if she would be willing to subject herself to a Sexual Assault Nurse Examination, or SANE. During a SANE examination, a specially trained medical practitioner interviews the survivor, examines her body for evidence of trauma, and collects any physical evidence that might later help to confirm the identity of the perpetrator. For some survivors, and depending on the extent of their injuries, the SANE examination can feel like being victimized all over again, with their bodies being probed and penetrated with swabs, which are used to collect cellular material containing DNA that may have been deposited during the attack.

The worst part of this experience, however, was having to endure the physical plucking of several pubic hairs directly from the survivor's body. This was done for a specific reason. If a hair possibly belonging to the perpetrator was found at the crime scene or on the survivor's body, there was always a chance that it could be confirmed that the hair does or does not belong to the survivor. If it doesn't belong to the survivor, then it likely belongs to the perpetrator. And the reason for plucking or pulling the hairs from the survivor, rather than cutting them with scissors, was to ensure that the roots of the hairs, which contain DNA, were collected and preserved.

It was my team in the Michigan forensic laboratories who were responsible for the design, purchasing, and distribution of these rape kits used to package evidence during SANE examinations. And, as it turned out, the opportunity presented itself for us to reconsider the design, and possibly eliminate, as a matter of practice, the plucking of hairs from the bodies of survivors. The decision would be mine to make, and it would not be an easy one.

A basic tenet of complex decision-making is *do no harm*. You won't get every decision right and you'll make mistakes of varying seriousness but at least you should endeavor to not cause damage. In those moments where a decision needs to be made but the right decision is less than obvious, going with the option that avoids making unnecessary changes and gives you some degree of control over the outcomes is probably the best way to go. But in this instance, I was contemplating a decision that would change how sexual assaults were investigated and potentially interfere with critical forensic evidence being collected and used to identify a perpetrator – a perpetrator who might then go on to rape again. *And what if the next victim is a child?* I thought. *What if that child dies? What if the rape and death of that child might have been prevented if I hadn't decided to end the practice of pulling control hairs from survivors? Could I live with that?*

Making matters worse, the decision I was considering was not yet fully established in other states, so I couldn't use the *emerging best-practices* argument in the event I was challenged. So, after many conversations and phone calls with my team, subject-matter experts, and relevant stakeholders, and after having reflected on the many implications of changing the rape kit design or *not* changing the design, I made my decision. We would end the practice of pulling hairs from the bodies of survivors, and I would accept whatever responsibility might be heaped on my shoulders in the event that an unforeseen catastrophe results from my actions. In my judgement, the chance we would prevent future victimizations by making it easier for survivors to participate in their investigations was greater than the chance we would *cause* future victimizations due to the loss of the hair controls.

Over the course of your own career, you may have been involved in the making of decisions that were complex or difficult. If you haven't, you will. And if you aren't careful, you can feel sorry for yourself for being the one and only individual who will be held accountable if things go wrong. But this is, in fact, the nature of leadership. And although leadership does not require leaders to be perfect, it does require leaders to be principled and to make decisions based on those principles, whether proven or not, that offer the greatest likelihood for successful outcomes. Especially when leaders in positions of public trust make decisions that turn out sideways, citizens are remarkably forgiving when those leaders make their decisions on what a reasonable person would believe were sound principles.

The Risk of Being Principled

I'd be remiss if I didn't mention what I've personally witnessed to be the dark side of being principled: self-righteousness. Self-righteousness is a manifestation of superiority signaling in which the principled person uses her principles to dominate others; and she views herself as being better than everyone else *because* she is principled. She feels so strongly about her beliefs that she can't fathom any reasonable person having an opposing position or a different way of seeing things. But even if her principles are, in fact, sound, her attitude and behaviors are so off-putting that others may oppose her simply out of protest. This is why the self-righteous are such poor ambassadors for the principles they hold dear, and why they are so damaging to teams. Their principles become guilty by association and are therefore less likely to guide decision-making in the future.

To be a principled and purposeful leader is not only a good thing, it's the only thing. Without principles, leaders are not really leaders; they're simply decision-makers whose overall impact will be left more to chance than to purposeful intention. But being principled and having strong belief systems are not substitutes for alternation. Holding on to a set of principles should never alienate others and should never stand in the way of healthy conversation and debate, assuming circumstances don't require a decision to be made right away. This means that even when armed with sound principles, being fluid in your transitions between superiority and subordination – again, we call this being an equal in the moment – will continue to be among your most valuable leadership skills. As enduring and timeless as your principles may be, their successful application will always require some thoughtfulness, caution, and the input of others. Self-righteousness will prevent you from accessing the support and insights of your people, both of which are necessary for even the most principled leaders to succeed.

Subject to Reconsideration. It's easier for some to believe they never have to reevaluate or reconsider their principles after they've already adopted or bought into them. Reality, of course, requires more honesty with self. Principles do require revisitation and reconsideration from time to time, not necessarily because they're wrong, but because they don't afford the same protection from bad decision-making as they once did. Recall that principles are boundaries that keep you and your team as safe and effective as possible. They keep you from encroaching on territory where you're more likely to be met with trouble. But as all structures do, they develop holes and cracks that require attention before you can trust them again.

Think back for a moment on the Peanut Corporation of America and the catastrophic decisions made by its leaders. Recall the set of *Rust* where Halyna Hutchins died of a gunshot wound. In both instances, fundamental principles of safety were violated, and the result was death. But these principles were violated not from a lack of awareness, but a lack of interest. So, if we could go back in time to a point before death occurred, we would likely discover something important. The earliest evidence that leaders lacked sincere interest in the basic principles of safety was their penchant for not talking about them.

When principles are truly important to leaders, those leaders talk about them and do so regularly with anyone and everyone. It is through conversation and communication that principles are reinforced within a culture. Policies and procedures are rarely good enough. That which predicts success or failure is how frequently or infrequently leaders discuss principles in conversation. When they are talked about often, they are honored often, and the desired outcomes are likely to occur. When they're not talked about, well, you know what happens then.

Principles and You. When entrusted with the responsibilities of leadership, think about and talk about core principles often. *What are they? What do they mean? What outcomes are they most likely to produce? In what situations is it most important for us to apply them?* Chances are that your work environment requires, from time to time, difficult or weighty decisions to be made. These decisions must be made on principles most likely to ensure the outcomes you want. This of course requires you to *know* what outcomes you want, something that too many leaders struggle with. If you don't have a clear sense of what outcomes you and your team are trying to achieve, then it will be difficult to identify a set of foundational principles to which you can adhere. As a result, your future is more likely to happen by accident than by design.

Imagine an alternative reality in which CEO Stewart Parnell envisions, with great clarity, a healthy and safe community of customers consuming peanut-based products manufactured and distributed by his company. Or imagine the directors and producers of *Rust* envisioning with equal clarity a healthy and safe cast and crew. What outcomes are likely to occur then? How many people die then? The answer, most likely, is none.

Chapter 15

Testify

Leadership is like time travel in that it requires you to place yourself at various points in the future and observe what's happening. You look around, you watch people, listen to people, and evaluate. On a dime, you can pivot, shift your perspective, and see a completely different set of conditions and circumstances. The more time you spend in the future and the more you observe while you're there, the more you will be able to see and experience with greater clarity a specific future that you judge to be optimal for you and your team. It makes you happy. In fact, you notice how much happier your team is also. They seem energized and driven by purpose. They have access to resources that allow them to do more than they could before. They don't seem to be reacting to circumstances as much as they are acting on intention. They are players, not spectators. Your team is thriving and succeeding. It's fantastic! You only wish they could be there with you to see what you see.

Your journey to the future, of course, is a mental exercise but it's real, nonetheless. And when you have a clear picture in your mind of the future most pleasing to you, you will come back to the present moment to tell your team about it, hoping they'll want to join you for a return trip so they can experience it for themselves. But you wonder if you have the skills to adequately convey the beauty of what you saw and felt during your trip. You wonder if you can convince your team to leave the comforts of the status quo and join you for this trek to a place they've never been and may not necessarily enjoy as much as you did.

Bear Witness to Your Vision

The act of truthfully describing what you personally witness is called *testimony*. Witnesses testify every day in courts of law, for example, where they explain to a jury what they saw, heard, or felt. During my forensic career, I testified in many criminal and civil trials, sometimes death-penalty cases; and when you do it often enough, you get pretty used to walking into a courtroom and realizing that not a single member of the jury is going to believe a thing you say until you establish your credibility and earn their trust. And part of earning that trust is communicating facts and opinions in a way they will find both understandable and meaningful to them.

On my best days, I enjoyed seeing jurors nod their heads in comprehension of what I was saying. It always felt good to make that connection and know that my words were making an impact. But on my bad days, one or two jurors might tilt their heads and flash me a *watchoo-talkin-about* glace at something I said, sending me the clear message that I wasn't making any sense. But in every trial or hearing in which I appeared as an expert witness, my goal was to make the jury feel like they were right there with me in the laboratory, watching me fire the gun into the water tank, disinfect the bullet that came from the autopsy, and compare the bullets under the microscope to see if the autopsy bullet was or was not fired from the suspect firearm. Nothing theatrical of course, but I really wanted the jury to understand exactly what I did, why I did it, and what it all meant. I wanted them to *see what I saw*.

To be a leader, without question, is to be an expert witness. This is to say that you must be an expert in the future you envision and the path you will take to get there. Then, you must have the skills to describe this vision in its totality so your people can see it as clearly as you do. As a leader, your vision and your interpretation of what it means are always key evidence. Your people are the jury. They are counting on you, your expertise, and your honesty. The verdict they will render is whether or not they should exhaust their precious time and energy to go where you want them to go. If your vision is unclear or not believable, they may wallow in a chronic state of deliberation, putting forth just enough effort to keep the team functional. They may humor you, go through the motions, and meet the most basic of their responsibilities, doing so quite well, perhaps, and with much enthusiasm. But if they decide conclusively that your testimony lacks credibility or relevance, this jury of your peers will officially rule in favor of the status quo, electing to keep things as they are. And your punishment, of course, is solitary confinement. There, you will endure the pain of both isolation and stagnation, subjected to the cruelty of having to languish alone with your vision of what was possible, watching helplessly as your dreams of the future fade into obscurity.

On the other hand, by giving clear and compelling testimony of what you see and experience when you visit the future, and what you see as being your team's potential, you can get your people to rule in your favor and commit to making this important trip with you. But remember, your people may have their own testimony to give. They may have their own vision, having also visited the future and perhaps seeing things a bit differently than you do. The more you can incorporate multiple visions into a single, unified vision, the more commitment you will achieve. At that point, your people will do what everyone does before embarking on a long journey; they will pack their bags. Not real bags, of course. What I mean is they will take time to identify what skills, knowledge, and abilities they will need along the way. They will anticipate the new burdens they will have to shoulder, the new expectations they will have to satisfy, and the new challenges they are likely to encounter. They will take inventory of their strengths, looking for opportunities to better leverage their existing talents while building talents in areas where they may be lacking. Once the bags are packed and the course is charted, the journey can begin.

A Valuable Skill

Bearing witness to what's possible in the future and giving subsequent testimony that's sufficiently clear and convincing are abilities that fall somewhere along a lengthy and sometimes foggy spectrum. As an executive coach, I've come to appreciate that this ability is not commonplace and may help to explain why such a small percentage of people have natural leadership abilities. Transporting oneself into the future is difficult. During coaching sessions, I've asked many clients over the years, clients who were otherwise quite intelligent and articulate, to paint a picture for me of the future as they would like to see it play out. For some, the question is answered with ease, but for others, the question is met with blank stares, fumbled words, and incoherent logic. They just can't seem to do it. I know they have sufficient oratory skills and may even be quite flowery in their overall use of language, but questions about the future seem to stump them. This suggests that the disconnect comes not from an inability to testify but from difficulties in forming a vision. And for those who really struggle with this, they may cope with their innocent myopia by just staying put and not venturing too far from home base. They may elect to never wander into the future. They might never imagine.

Visualizing the future is an artform, perhaps not unlike how a painter can visualize an image before putting it to canvas. Part of my own development and maturity as a coach has been my realization that clients who struggle with visualization have nothing wrong with them but can benefit from some help. This may come in the form of coaching, consulting, or facilitated conversations in which questions about the future can be posed and considered. It might also come from team members who are, in fact, able to envision the future with clarity.

Like the principles we discussed in the previous chapter, a vision of the future also takes a position of superiority when it's articulated with the requisite detail, clarity, and credibility. Members of a team will choose to volunteer their best efforts in pursuit of this vision when they not only see the vision for themselves but crave it, developing an emotional attachment to the possibilities before them. They envision the future state like the climbers of a mountain envision what it will be like to stand at the summit. The vision is inspiring, energizing, and compelling, enabling the members of a team to willingly subordinate themselves, their personal interests, and their personal ambitions to the vision itself. It is the vision and its enabling principles that dominate, not people. The most effective leaders are skilled at testifying to both.

It's doubtful if the Apollo 13 mission or any of the NASA missions to the moon would have occurred if President John F. Kennedy did not articulate the vision with such clarity. Many critics thought he lost his marbles, including experts in the aerospace fields, the very experts who would go on to make the moon landing possible. But Kennedy, still shaken by the Soviet achievement of putting a satellite into orbit, was looking to wake up his country. He knew that putting a man on the moon and returning him safely to earth was not possible in 1962, the year he delivered the famous *Moonshot Speech* at Rice University. But he understood the power of testimony and its potential to spark the learning and innovation that could make a trip to the moon possible by the end of the decade.

The United States reached the moon because an entire nation and its leaders subordinated themselves to a grand vision. No personality, no individual, no government agency, and no corporation was superior to the vision. The vision ruled, and the result was a collaborative effort of historic proportions. Some historians argue that President Kennedy's murder added a necessary emotional jolt to the space program, which then stood as a living tribute to his memory and his vision. Without this emotional jolt, perhaps America's race to the moon might have been delayed or even failed.

I beg to differ. It was more likely that Kennedy's death would derail the space program. The growing intensity and costs of the conflict in Vietnam, exacerbated by the societal turbulence arising from the civil rights movement, were good reasons to rethink federal priorities and expenditures. With Kennedy and his leadership removed from the picture so soon, the conditions were right for cynics to rise up, as they often do, and put a stop to what they might have argued was a wasteful, unnecessary endeavor. The presidential elections of 1964 and 1968 were suitable backdrops for this cynicism to take center stage. But it didn't. Instead, the mission carried on, fueled by the compelling and credible testimony that allowed an entire nation to see what President Kennedy saw. His vision was superior, and it lived on long after he was gone.

Compelling Possibilities

Chances are pretty good that your team is not one that seeks to achieve such a historic goal as putting people on the moon. You may be a leader or manager at an accounting firm, an airport, an engineering firm, a bank, or a hospital. And among the many challenges confronting your team on a regular basis are the hypnotic effects of routine and monotony. Sure, your team works hard and delivers great value to its stakeholders, but each day is pretty much the same, and everyone in your environment has settled into ways of meeting their responsibilities with minimal thought. In fact, they're so good at what they do that it comes as second nature to them. You may find it nearly impossible, as it is for many leaders, to conjure up a vision of the future that anyone on your team would find even remotely inspiring. Perhaps inspiration is not part of your work or your culture, at least not as much as persistence, focus, and discipline are. So, for you, effective leadership is more about keeping things rolling along with minimal disruption or distraction.

If this describes you and your team, you have nothing to feel bad about. In fact, I offer my sincere congratulations on your ability to remain steady and consistent. This is an achievement of its own sort in these turbulent and ever-changing times in which we live. But I wish to encourage you to give serious thought to the potential benefits of envisioning a major goal or collection of goals toward which you and your team can strive over the next 2 to 3 years, something you can celebrate when you've checked all the boxes and turned the entirety of your vision into a reality.

It is certainly okay for your team to strive for steadiness and consistency, but without a critical victory in its sights, your team is exposed to risk. When there is no vision to put on a pedestal, the empty pedestal becomes the aspiration of dominant personalities hungry to draw attention to themselves. Internally, you may feel that your team is operating with sufficient effectiveness, but externally across the larger strategic environment or relevant marketplace, your team will meander, reacting to circumstances as they play out. Over time, these reactions will occupy space best reserved for your intentions, forcing you to accept a future that happens by accident rather than by design.

As I mentioned earlier, the best way to spark your imagination about what's possible in the future is to ask the right questions. Here's a few to get you started:

What is my team capable of accomplishing?

In what ways are we underperforming?

What are the topics we are going to be talking about most?

If we do nothing differently, what can we expect to happen?

If we could have any future we wanted, what would it be?

If each member of my team could improve, how would they?

What factors or conditions are getting in our way?

What opportunities do we have to optimize our conditions?

In what ways are we coping with barriers to greatness?

Upon whom do we rely for support and how can they help?

Who is slowing us down and how can we deal with them?

What decisions or changes could significantly energize us?

Spark the Conversation

If the questions are not difficult to answer, then the answers are not likely to precipitate compelling opportunities for change. Keep in mind that you are seeking to establish a vision that is more powerful than personalities. You want your vision to be superior while the members of your team, including yourself, subordinate themselves to both the vision and the fundamental principles that will bring it to fruition. If President Kennedy had said, *before the decade is out, we will send a Golden Retriever to Moscow in a hot-air balloon and return him safely to Washington DC*, this might have presented a challenge, but not one sufficiently compelling to inspire a national movement. The vision has to be exciting, meaningful, and worth the effort for everyone involved.

Convey Your Intent. Let's say, for example, that you are the branch manager of a large retail store in the suburbs of a major metropolitan city. You've experienced high employee turnover in recent years and sales have slipped, despite strong performances from your competitors. In the seven years you've been managing the store, you've never held a strategic visioning session with your employees, but you decide that you'd like to try. One evening after the store closes, you gather your team together in a large conference room. They take a seat, while you remain standing. With a serious but resolute tone, you ask for their attention and begin speaking. Here's what you say:

Look everyone, I know I don't say this enough, but all of you are important to me. This store is important to me. We are important to each other. And when I think about my own responsibilities and what you need from me as your manager, I can't help but feel that I'm not doing my job as well as I should be. I've made the decision that I want to be a better manager, I want this to be a better store with a better reputation in our community, and I want each of you to feel like you're doing something more than just stocking shelves and making sales. I want you to feel like you're making a difference in people's lives, and I want you to feel like you are a part of something special. So, I want to let you know that I'm going to be doing some soul-searching and deep thinking over the next few weeks. And my intent is to develop a comprehensive strategy for our store that focuses on 3 things:

You pause for a moment and turn to a large dry-erase board where a blue marker is waiting. You write as you speak:

First, we are going to produce historic increases in sales – not just slight increases, historic increases. Second, we are going to create a revenue-sharing incentive plan for all our employees that rewards both high performance and strong customer service practices. I want to make sure that your contributions to our store are rewarded, and I don't feel like that's happening right now. Third, we're going to remodel the entire store, inside and out, to improve the experience for both customers and employees. But here's the deal: I need your input. I want your thoughts and opinions for what these goals should look like, how specific they should be, and how lofty we can make them. So, what I'm asking you to do is think about these 3 things over the next month or so. Write down your ideas, talk with each other, talk with me – and then I will pay you double your current hourly wage to attend three consecutive evening sessions in which we will hammer out a specific plan that we will seek to achieve within three years. If we work together, we can start a new chapter in the life of our store and have a lot of fun doing it.

Notice what you did by communicating with your team in this way. You signaled your intent to make major changes, but you invited your team to be a part of the process. You didn't dump a personal vision onto their laps, however impressive or creative it may have been, expecting them to just buy it. You certainly communicated a vision, but your speech was an invitation to become involved, and you made it clear that you too have an opportunity to improve. This, in fact, may have been the most important part of your message because you affirmed your intent to subordinate yourself to whatever vision you and your team decide to pursue. You positioned yourself as an equal in the moment, and by doing so, you made it more likely that your team members will do the same.

Self-Sabotage. A sure-fire way for a leader to compromise even the most well-crafted vision is to brandish the vision like a weapon with which she will threaten or force her team into submission. A vision only has credibility when the leader herself willingly and enthusiastically subordinates herself to it. If she doesn't, her team won't either. Unfortunately, there are leaders out there who love to strategize, love to develop plans, and may be quite effective at articulating a compelling vision, but they refuse to step down from their pedestals. They can't bring themselves to put the vision before themselves, which sends the message to every team member that the vision isn't quite as important as the leader's own ego. The result is a vision that's not worth embracing.

The old superior has a remarkable capacity to prevent the formulating or following of a strategic path that leads teams in the right direction. But it's not always the sole fault of the old superior. Sometimes there are deep psychological factors at play that weaken the ability of leaders to establish a compelling vision. By understanding how to overcome them, leaders can inspire commitment with greater ease and clarity.

Change Management

There is not an executive coach in practice today who hasn't or won't be asked by a client, at some point, why the client's team is so resistant to change. "It just doesn't make any sense," the client laments. "What's being proposed will make everyone's life easier, will make our team stronger, and will relieve us of some of the burdens that we've been carrying on our shoulders for years. But all I get are employees who drag their feet or complain. I feel like I'm beating my head against a wall."

Change management has emerged as an industry in itself, with even professional certifications offered in this area of expertise. The underlying hypothesis is that resistance to change can be quite natural, and it requires a special set of skills to imagine, design, and implement change in the right way so that the members of a team can embrace it without hesitation or suspicion. This, of course, is certainly true, but only to a point. The manner in which change is conceived and executed does, in fact, influence the degree to which its beneficiaries will buy into it. At the heart of effective change management is affording those most likely to be impacted by the change an opportunity to lead the change effort.

This instills a sense of ownership and stewardship that help to accelerate the pace at which the change will eventually be adopted.

By the same token, however, people crave novelty and variety. We are wired for change. It wakes us up and creates what is often a much appreciated contrast from that which we find boring or monotonous. This means that something else is lurking in the background that sabotages even the most well-executed attempts at change, a challenge that only attentive and empathetic leaders can overcome with any effectiveness. And that something else is *grief*.

It's Hard to Say Goodbye. Imagine a man named Paul who strolls into a funeral home where his golfing buddy, Eddie, is standing beside the casket of his beloved wife, who at the young age of 48, lost her long battle with breast cancer. Paul walks confidently to up to the casket, then turns to Eddie with a smile. "Well, Eddie," he chimes. "Life is for the living, buddy; you have to move on."

Paul, of course, is right. Life is for the living and Eddie does need to move on. But the accuracy of Paul's message does nothing to ameliorate its offensiveness. His poor timing fails to accommodate Eddie's grief. Eddie will be unable to process Paul's message until enough time and reflection have passed for Eddie to peak through the clearing fog of his sadness toward a new life without his wife.

The problem with change is that it represents the loss of something that people value. Anytime the members of a team are asked to step through a door that leads them into the future, they have no choice but to say goodbye to some things that are important to them. Leaders who push their people with poorly timed vigor, just as Paul did to Eddie, may discover that the emotional portfolios of their people are heavily invested in the past. Until those investments are liquidated, the stakeholders can't bring themselves to flow in the direction that their leaders want to go.

Among the emotional investments causing team members to struggle with change, there are two deserving of your deepest consideration.

Unpunished Mistreatment. *Unpunished mistreatment* is a perceived injustice that one believes to have gone without an appropriate response. In other words, somebody got away with it. It could be an injustice that someone experienced himself or one he witnessed being inflicted on a colleague. Either way, the notion that perpetrators will not be held accountable for their behaviors, and that the victims will not be compensated for their losses, is a difficult pill to swallow and often quite painful to accept.

In those instances where a team member feels that the employer is culpable in the infliction of injustice, it can be nearly impossible to move forward, especially when moving forward will render justice less likely to be administered. The employee may protest by resisting any strategic priorities that seek to put the past *in the past*. Some common examples of injustices that get people stuck include:

- Harassment
- Hostile behavior
- Unfair discrimination
- Chronic rudeness or discourtesy
- Abusive management practices
- Incompetent management
- Failure or catastrophe
- Refusal to redress a grievance
- Being unfairly denied a promotion
- Being unfairly disciplined for misconduct

We must acknowledge that the examples on this list may be perceived as injustices even when they are not. What matters, however, is that they are injustices in the opinion of particular employees or team members, injustices about which something should have been done – perhaps the righting of a wrong, an apology, or a punishment of some sort would have sufficed. Somebody should have been held accountable. Somebody should have paid a price.

Unrecognized Contributions. Just like mistreatments that went unpunished, contributions that went unrecognized are perceived as injustices of their own sort. *Unrecognized contributions* are acts of professional excellence for which gratitude or recognition were never expressed with adequacy. A fundamental part of being a professional is the need or desire to earn esteem. Esteem is recognition for being effective. For many professionals, when they demonstrate their effectiveness and find that it goes unrewarded or unnoticed, it can leave an emotional wound, however minor it may seem at the time. If it happens over and over again, small wounds become big wounds and big wounds become deep wounds. With enough time, the accumulation of emotional pain can destroy one's sense of commitment to a team's priorities, especially when change is in the air.

This lack of commitment can be quite remarkable when change threatens to undo what a team member created himself. For example, the head nurse at a trauma-care unit, Madison, develops an innovative way to make it easier for physicians to categorize the types and severity of injuries observed among patients, data to be used for an ongoing study. Using tablets mounted to walls in the unit, she develops a macro-enabled spreadsheet that can be easily accessed by the doctors, with the data being automatically sent to a nearby medical school for analysis. Although the doctors are thrilled with the development, Madison's work goes almost entirely unrecognized by the hospital's administration. Later that year, when word comes down that the hospital is looking to implement a new software platform to better manage patient care, one that will also replace the system Madison developed, Madison is hurt and her mood turns toxic, refusing to participate in the implementation meetings scheduled by the administration. Eventually, her reputation suffers.

Be Real About the Past

As important as it is for leaders to be effective in giving testimony about what they envision for the future, it is equally important to testify accurately about what happened in the past. When it is known that a team member suffered mistreatment, it needs to be discussed. If serious enough, a leader may even elect to offer a sincere apology on behalf of the organization, a gesture that will be appreciated if the guilty parties are no longer employed. If a work culture has a history of ignoring the contributions of its people, those contributions need to be acknowledged and rewarded in some way. Not only does this help with the change process, it's also the right thing to do.

As a coach, I spend a lot of time encouraging clients to not obsess on disappointments or injustices from the past. There's just very little value in being emotionally stuck, and it tends to hurt the aggrieved far more than the perpetrators. But I also encourage leaders to never let something that warrants discussion go undiscussed. To do so is a dereliction of duty. If people have suffered in the past, that suffering needs to be acknowledged and, to the extent possible, those people should be made whole. If people achieved in the past, those achievements need to be recognized, even if doing so is simply a sincere expression of gratitude. Effective leaders never waste an opportunity to comfort the suffering or reward the contributions of achievers.

Commemoration. Any time a person, a team, or an organization embarks on a journey requiring significant change, the enormity of the moment must be commemorated. Our most noteworthy transitions into the newest chapters of our lives are made smoother by taking sufficient time to reflect on what was. In these reflections, we express our gratitude for all that was good, and we forgive others and ourselves for what was bad. Life is challenging, and we don't get through it without some scars or sometimes feeling like we weren't appreciated or respected. But when leaders are willing to do the emotional work that's needed to help teams put the past in its proper place, the members of those teams will give themselves permission to step through that magical door that leads them to a new and exciting future.

Chapter 16

Be Generous

The morning I arrived at the offices of an executive leadership team, I was feeling a bit pensive. About a month had passed since I had begun working with this team and, although I'd spent a good bit of time with the CEO, the CFO, and the HR director, I had yet to sit down with the COO. His name was Wes, and although he came up in numerous conversations, circumstances seemed to point me away from his direction. This was far from usual as I generally make a point to meet and interact with all executive decision-makers early in my engagements, but this time was different. I could tell that Wes was a source of frustration for the other members of the team, and he had yet to be invited to a meeting in which I consulted with the other executives. But what I found even odder was that Wes never seemed to take it upon himself to come say hello to me when I was in the office. Eventually, I voiced my insistence that I meet Wes as soon as possible. A meeting was scheduled.

When I arrived, I made my way to the office of the HR director, Kaitlyn, who was waiting for me. With a couple taps of my knuckles on her door, I announced my arrival. She looked up, smiled, and greeted me warmly. I set my briefcase on the floor, removed my black trench coat, and draped it along the back of a chair next to a small conference table across from her desk. I glanced at my briefcase to grab a pen and notebook but stopped myself. *Nope*, I thought. *Not taking notes for this one. Just going to ask questions and listen.*

I was escorted to an office flanking a large open administrative area sectioned into individual workspaces for the executive assistants. I followed Kaitlyn into an office where she introduced me to a slightly rotund man with thinning brown hair who was working intently on his computer. If we hadn't previously scheduled the appointment, I might have felt we were interrupting him.

"Wes," Kaitlyn chimed with an obligatory tone, "this is our executive coach, John Collins. John, this is Wes, our Chief Operations Officer. I'll leave you two alone to get acquainted."

Kaitlyn stepped out of the office and closed the door behind her. I offered a hello and stood facing him, waiting for him to greet me and offer me a seat. He didn't. Instead, he continued working on his computer as if I wasn't there. After about 10 seconds, I took it upon myself to sit down in one of the two guest chairs on the opposite side of the desk, staring at Wes with a polite expression of amusement on my face.

Another 15 seconds or so passed before Wes finally acknowledged my presence. Without turning away from his computer, he mumbled, "give me one second, I'm trying to finish something up." *Sure you are*, I thought. *I've seen my share of superiority signals, but this one is for the books.*

"No problem, take your time," I replied in a clear, authoritative voice. I sensed that he took notice of my tone, after which he sat back in his chair, looked at me, and said "hi."

Wes and I chatted for the remainder of the hour. I asked him questions and he answered them. He was pleasant enough, but many of his answers were adorned with self-congratulatory embellishments, as if to convince me that he was good at his job, experienced, and deserving of the rank he held in the organization. I responded in kind, voicing my. admiration for his expertise and my respect for his many responsibilities.

But when I asked Wes about any frustrations he experiences in his work, he shifted in his chair, paused, then turned his attention to the CEO and his other colleagues on the leadership team, including Kaitlyn, complaining about decisions made recently to scale down the extent of his authority. He'd been relieved of several responsibilities and his bitterness was evident.

I admitted to being aware of the decisions to which he was referring. Kaitlyn had explained to me how the CEO asked her to design and implement a partial reorganization that would pull several employees out from under Wes's span of control. Reasons for doing so included poor communication skills, a tendency to antagonize employees, and other counterproductive managerial tendencies that put him at odds with his direct reports. When I asked Kaitlyn why Wes's conduct was being accommodated in this way, she said it wasn't; and while they hoped executive coaching might help Wes, she was in the process of drafting a severance agreement in preparation for his possible termination if things didn't improve.

When I asked Wes about the limiting of his authority, he seemed nothing short of incredulous. "It makes absolutely no sense to me," he lamented as he glanced back at his computer screen, perhaps checking if something more interesting might be happening there. "I think some of the decisions being made around here are going to hurt us in the long run."

I listened carefully to Wes and tried to put myself in his shoes, but our allotted time was running out. So, I asked if he had any questions for me, about me, or about the work I was doing with his organization. As it so often happens with superiority signalers, he had none, at least none that would indicate the kind of deep professional curiosity I've come to expect from competent executive leaders.

"Well, I'd love to meet with you again sometime soon, if that's okay with you, Wes." I was hoping to get another meeting with him on our calendars before too much time passed.

"Sure, sounds good," he agreed.

Kaitlyn was not in her office when I parted company with Wes, so I grabbed my things and left. On the way back to my office, I reflected on my conversation with Wes and the poor manners he showed when Kaitlyn announced me. I remember thinking to myself, *Wes just seems like a guy who has absolutely nothing to give.* That morning as I stood before him waiting to be greeted, not even a quick hello or glance of the eyes could be mustered by this high-ranking officer with a six-figure salary. All this rank, all this responsibility, yet he couldn't even bring himself to welcome a guest. No wonder he was stripped of so much authority. I can only imagine what else he wasn't willing to do.

Wes was eventually terminated, but not before I had the chance to meet with him a few more times. During one of these meetings, I challenged him with razor-sharp pointedness on the way he behaved when we were first introduced. "Wes," I began, holding my gaze with his to make clear my seriousness. "You gave up the opportunity to make an immediate connection with me, a fellow professional. What do you think was going through my mind while I sat there and watched you ignore me?" I asked. "How do you think my opinion of you was affected by how you were acting?"

He looked down at his lap and then back at me. "It couldn't have been very good, I suppose." He seemed defeated, as if I learned a secret he'd been keeping; but he never expressed remorse and never apologized. The old superior had been called to the carpet and, by being exposed, had the wind taken out of its sails.

After a couple of coaching sessions, Wes seemed to respond. At one point, Kaitlyn asked me what the heck I did to Wes because he was in such a good mood and had become much more pleasant to work with. "It's too soon to get excited," I warned. And I was right. Although Wes seemed to be making improvements in his relationships with the other executives, he was continuing to make his employees miserable. The grip that the old superior had on his management style was simply too strong. Wes had to go.

I want to be clear about something, here. Wes did not lack ability. He didn't lack knowledge or skill. He was qualified for his position; and as I got to know him better, I found him to be a rather pleasant guy who was easy to talk with. Like you and me, he had his own set of strengths and redeeming qualities. But something was terribly wrong. He lacked something else, the absence of which impaired his ability to manage his team and make sincere, lasting connections with his people. What Wes lacked was *generosity*.

The Gift of Effort

Generosity is the emotional fuel that motivates a person to take an interest in others, to be gracious with others, and to exhaust one's own precious energy for the good of others. Generosity is what prompts you to smile and say hello to a stranger you pass in the hallway, even though you're not really in the mood for it. It's the voice on your shoulder that whispers a reminder to check on a colleague who's been having a rough day, even as your own day has been filled with its own challenges and frustrations. Generosity is what sparks your curiosity about how your employee's softball game went the night before, even though you're distracted by a deadline looming for your annual report to your company's board of directors. And, yes, generosity is what nudges a busy executive like Wes to stop what he is doing, stand up, and greet a visitor with a warm smile. To do so is to give a gift, the giving of an effort in service to someone else.

As an ingredient of effective leadership, generosity is indispensable because the act of leading is a form of self-sacrifice. To lead others is to make others your priority and expose yourself to judgement or blame when things don't seem to be going very well. Selfish is not a word used to describe effective leaders. In those moments when effective leaders choose to be selfish, it's usually to recover or tend to their own personal needs. In fact, followers often wish their leaders would take more time for themselves, recognizing and appreciating the toll that leadership can take. These loyal followers know that just a bit of selfishness, from time to time, is necessary for leaders to maintain their strength and refresh their engines, and they are happy to accommodate it.

The work of Kathryn Cronin and her colleagues gave us a scientific basis from which to better understand how the energies of inferiors are dimmed by dominance behaviors that are excessive in their heavy-handedness. Although I have no specific evidence for the following assertion, both experience and intuition tell me that it's the selfishness inherent to dominance behaviors that shuts people down, more so than the dominance itself. People in positions of inferiority can sense the self-interest and personal ambitions that dominators are trying to protect, and they are not for long willing to belie their own sense of personal dignity and self-worth in the cause of the dominator's gratification. Just as selfishness undermines leadership credibility, it also inflames the protests of those who refuse to be a party to it. The result is a team whose collective energy is wasted on coping with the emotional burdens that precipitate from having to answer to a selfish dominator.

Generosity, therefore, is what transforms dominators into leaders, workers into professionals, and hierarchies into teams. Where there is excellence, there is generosity. So, setting a good example for what it means and how it looks to be generous must be a top priority for anyone striving to be an effective leader or influencer of people. Generosity begets generosity, just as selfishness begets selfishness. By being generous yourself, you naturally inspire acts of generosity among those around you, many of whom may be hesitant to extend their own generosity until they see others doing it first. This, of course, is a sign of immaturity but is common, nonetheless. Given enough time, however, chronic generosity can spread like a virus throughout even the largest organizations, encouraging and reinforcing a culture that makes future acts of generosity increasingly probable.

The Science of Empathy

In the early 1990s, researchers identified what became known as *mirror neurons*, which are brain cells that respond equally to the performing of a task, regardless of whether the person is performing the task himself or watching someone else do it. The discovery helped explain why humans have such a high capacity for empathy. We have the neurological tools needed to literally experience life from another's vantage point. If we observe someone being treated fairly and generously, we feel it as if it were happening to us. Therefore, one simple act of generosity can have a positive impact on a large number of people.

No matter who you are or what you do, you have a great capacity for generosity. But being generous is not always extravagant or complicated. Simply making an effort to smile when you greet people, for example, or asking about what's new in someone's life or career is an act of generosity. But there's reasons to fear that this is becoming harder and harder for people to pull off. Many of us are exhausted. Technology allows encroachments on our time and attention that didn't exist before. Many of us are overinformed, overstimulated, and overworked. The lines that used to separate work from home have become either blurred or eliminated, making us feel like each wakeful hour is spent working in some form or fashion. And for those of us raising young children or caring for aging parents, the opportunities we have to rest and refresh ourselves are few and far between. As our energies become depleted, so too does our interest in others and, therefore, our generosity.

The impact of this situation on leaders and their teams cannot be overemphasized. The perception that a leader lacks generosity is quickly interpreted as a lack of competence. If we think about this for a moment, it makes complete sense. Incompetence, after all, is exhausting. Much energy is spent trying to compensate for any lack of necessary knowledge, skill, or ability. So, when a leader is perceived as lacking generosity, there is often the assumption that she must be exhausted and therefore not very good at her job. It is here that the relationship between generosity and credibility comes into sharper focus. Generous leaders are perceived as credible leaders. Selfish leaders, on the other hand, are impossible to trust.

The Lessons of COVID

In 2020, during the first wave of the COVID-19 pandemic, organizations were forced to do what many had always been reluctant to do, which is allow their employees to work from home. To the old superior, this was especially unwelcomed as remote work gave employees more freedom and autonomy. The new trend collided with conventional wisdom that an employee unseen is an employee who must not be working. This, of course, is how the old superior thinks – that no reasonable person works when they aren't being watched. But as time went on, many businesses and their executive leaders realized that productivity either remained the same or increased with this newly forced flexibility.

According to the Society for Human Resource Management, a study by Mercer, a workplace consulting firm, confirmed what was happening.

Employees *can* be trusted to work remotely, and productivity *can* increase because of it. According to Mercer, "60 percent of employers said they're letting parents adjust their schedules, with 22 percent saying they're letting parents temporarily shift to part-time status if needed. Another 37 percent are letting parents choose when they do those parts of their job that don't need to be done at any particular time or place, in order to better accommodate their caregiving responsibilities during the day."

What the pandemic really seemed to do, however, was force employers to be generous in ways they weren't willing to before. They had no choice but to be flexible, accommodating, and creative in how they aligned their talent with the work to be done. It also seems this generosity was mirrored by employees in the workforce who responded by giving an effort that kept productivity at an acceptable level or better. But I believe caution is warranted here. A strong case can be made that teams that are together are more productive and more competitive than teams that are dispersed, assuming all other variables are kept the same. Moreover, it is quite possible – even likely – that many organizations benefited from remote work because the pandemic allowed previously demoralized employees to separate themselves from the sources of their pain, those being toxic coworkers, dysfunctional managers, and oppressive cultures. It only makes sense that this separation would create degrees of productivity and innovation where before they were lacking.

The Burdens of Bureaucracy

Bureaucracy has a long and deserved reputation for draining the energy of teams and suppressing the urge of individuals to be generous with each other. Anyone who's worked in a large corporation, a government agency, or a major university might know exactly what this feels like. So much energy is exhausted on satisfying the demands of the bureaucracy and complying with its many inefficiencies that its members come to feel suffocated. Whatever energy remains is spent on emotional recovery, with almost nothing left over to give to anyone else.

As organizations grow, the hierarchical distance between executive decision-makers and the people doing the work becomes an operational and psychological disadvantage. Those in whose hands the future of the organization rests become less and less familiar to those who are actually engaged with customers, clients, and stakeholders on a daily basis. Trust in executive leaders, as it turns out, is remarkably inelastic, meaning that it does not stretch with organizational growth. Creative methods must be designed and implemented to keep decision-makers relevant to those on the ground. But because this is so hard to do, especially for the soldiers of the old superior, many businesses don't survive their own success.

Writing for *Forbes* in April 2017, Terry Howerton presented some sobering statistics about the challenges faced by the largest companies in the world. According to Howerton, "nearly three out of four of the Fortune 1000 companies have been replaced in the last 10 years. In the next decade, over half of the Fortune 500 will no longer exist."

Executives who deal intensively in corporate strategy often speak of the importance of being able to *see around corners*. This has much to do with the rapidity and unpredictability of social and technological change, necessitating an almost clairvoyant ability to pivot in the right direction with minimal information. But the ability to see around corners is not nearly as important to organizational survival as being able to *see each other*. As organizations grow, the people doing the work and the customers they serve seem to fade from the view of executives who become separated from the action – both literally and figuratively. To assuage their anxieties, these executives may succumb to the temptation of creating unwieldy bureaucratic systems of checks and balances that choke off the creative and productive energies that made growth possible in the first place. The more that people are forced to cope with the resulting inefficiencies, the more limited is their capacity for mutual curiosity and generosity. In the worst instances, the members of a team become but mere objects to each other, ravaging the collaboration needed for teamwork. The culture might become almost sociopathic in its disregard for the people upon which it depends for its competitiveness, stability, and longevity. What once was a growing and thriving team is now paralyzed.

Take the Initiative. Even if you are part of a growing company or find yourself in the thick of a heavy and cumbersome bureaucracy, you can still have a positive impact. Generosity begins with you. Take a sincere interest in the people with whom you interact on a regular basis, especially if you are somehow responsible for their well-being and professional effectiveness. Without question, they will sense your goodwill and it will make them feel good about themselves and you. The positive energy you create will be reflected back to you.

To be candid, our world needs a lot more generosity in just about every context and domain. We need it at our places of work. We need it in our schools. We need it in our communities and our gathering places. We need it in our families and our circles of friends. Generosity sends two critically important messages, one to the giver and one to the receiver. To the receiver, it says *you are important; you matter.* To the giver it says *I have the power to brighten the world around me by being a source of light.* Because there are so many social pressures and trends that seem to encourage selfishness, selfishness has become the bane of our existence. And when we take it upon ourselves to become prolific givers of sincere generosity, the world changes for the better.

In a professional or team context, generosity doesn't need to be extravagant or complicated; just the simplest of gestures can make a positive difference. Here are just a few:

- Smile and greet people you know by name when your path crosses with theirs
- Smile and say hello to those you don't know; perhaps introduce yourself and see if there are any mutual interests
- Listen carefully when people speak and signal your comprehension of what they are saying
- Thank colleagues for making good points during meetings
- Talk nice about people behind their backs
- Draw attention to the ideas and accomplishments of others
- Be supportive of what your upper managers are trying to accomplish, even when it doesn't make sense right away
- Be willing to give encouragement to upper managers; they are people like you and have hopes and fears like everyone else
- Give people the benefit of the doubt
- Trust people even before they've earned it
- Keep a list of key points of contact and reach out to them on a regular basis, even if just to let them know you're thinking about them
- Know what's going on in the lives of your colleagues, within reason, and take a sincere interest in their well-being
- For colleagues with children, make a point to ask how their kids are doing and what they're up to

For all that is written and spoken about leadership and the ability of leaders to maximize the contributions of their people, it's actually not that complicated. I want to reemphasize some words of encouragement I expressed in Chapter 10, because it just may be the most important act of generosity you could ever extend to the members of your team. Simply put, *enjoy them.* Few things will ever have more of a positive impact on the members of a team than a leader who genuinely enjoys their company. In fact, this rule applies to any relationship, including the relationships that parents have with their children and couples have with each other. When people enjoy each other, their capacity for mutual collaboration and communication are amplified exponentially. So too is their coachability and receptiveness to being influenced. When you sense that someone enjoys your company or enjoys collaborating with you, you will tend to trust them because you know intuitively that their enjoyment of you is based on an appreciation for who *you* are and what *you're* trying to accomplish.

As we'll discuss in the next chapter, our personal and professional lives have become so inundated with noise, information, responsibilities, and competing priorities that not only do we turn our backs on the people most important to us, we sometimes even reject them as nuisances, failing to enjoy the wonderful qualities they bring into the world in their own unique way. If we could just find a way to unclog the mental and emotional conduits through which people can access each other, we could find ourselves energized and inspired in ways that accelerate our growth, not only as professionals, but as human beings.

Chapter 17

Create Your Process

Sometime around 2006, I received a call from one of our crime scene technicians that a fired bullet was found by students and teachers in a school corridor in DuPage County. Above the location where the bullet came to rest was a window cracked by what appeared to be a bullet hole. No one heard a gunshot or saw anyone firing a gun at the school. Police were called and a forensic crime scene technician was dispatched to the scene in keeping with normal protocol.

I always enjoyed receiving calls from crime scene technicians who were looking to connect with someone at the laboratory because it gave me the feeling of being helpful and doing what I got into forensics to do, which was to help solve crimes using science. But when I became a laboratory director, the rigors and challenges of management cut short the time I could spend on casework. Because my forensic expertise was in firearms, I often took calls from the members of our crime scene team when they had questions about something strange they encountered at a shooting scene.

When I answered the phone, the voice at the other end of the call was familiar. It was Kevin, one of our crime scene technicians. He told me about the bullet and asked if I'd be willing to take a quick look at it if he brought it directly to the laboratory within the next 30 minutes.

Perhaps more important was what he didn't say – that he wanted some answers right now and didn't want to be delayed by the cumbersome evidence-intake process, which meant completing paperwork, submitting the evidence to our laboratory through the proper channels, having the bullet sit in the vault before it came up in the queue to be worked by a scientist, and then waiting for the required quality-assurance checks to be completed before a report could be issued.

Having spent the first years of my forensic career in Atlanta at a time when it was ranked the most dangerous city in America, I was trained and conditioned to make sure investigators of shootings had forensic results as quickly as possible. We weren't accredited yet, so we weren't affected by many of the quality-assurance checks that make today's laboratories more reliable but also less responsive to on-the-fly investigative inquiries. And although our laboratory in DuPage County was accredited, I was still keen on helping to expedite the issuing of forensic results when they could potentially nudge an unsolved case in the right direction. I was troubled by a fired bullet being discovered in a school, and I wanted to help figure out how it got there.

When the bullet arrived at the front desk of our laboratory, our receptionist called to alert me. By now, I was immersed in one of the many administrative responsibilities that consume the time and energy of a contemporary forensic administrator. Since I first became a laboratory director in August of 2000, our growing dependence on federal grants and the ever-increasing complexity of our quality assurance systems made my job and the jobs of my peers more demanding and more time consuming than ever. So, it was difficult, under any circumstance, to break away to the workbench to conduct a forensic analysis. *But this was a bullet found in a school*, I reminded myself, so I stopped what I was doing, threw on my lab coat, and made my way to the front desk.

There I found Kevin standing to the side of the reception area holding a small paper bag in his hand. I escorted him to the firearms room where I opened the bag and found a small white box containing an intact copper-jacketed bullet with observable gun-barrel impressions that confirmed it had indeed been fired. Right away I recognized the tell-tale features of a 44 Magnum bullet – a jacketed hollow point, a long bearing surface, and a knurled groove around the circumference of the bullet called a *cannelure*. Hoping to have Kevin on his way (and me back to my office) as quickly as possible, I affixed the bullet to a mounting stub on our comparison microscope and used a special eyepiece to measure the widths of the grooves left on the bullet by the gun that fired it. I then referred to a database maintained by the FBI and gave Kevin a short list of the most likely 44 Magnum revolvers that he could use to help track down the suspect weapon. Kevin jotted down a few notes and thanked me as I resealed the evidence bag. Within moments he returned to the front desk to formally release the bullet to the custody of the laboratory for a full analysis. *Zip, bam, boom.* Another happy customer and hopefully a case to be solved using the information I provided.

When I got back to my office, all I can say is I felt like something was wrong. I wasn't sure what it was, but the more I thought about it the more I realized that in my zeal to be of help to Kevin and the investigation team, I had completely bypassed all our technical and administrative checks that were in place to prevent error. Of course, I hadn't issued a formal report yet because the official analysis still had to be completed and Kevin knew that. But I had sent him back out into the field with information that I provided based on an abbreviated protocol that was inspired more by a desire to help than a desire to confirm accuracy. Worse, I relied almost entirely on my own personal familiarity with bullets – much like someone can quickly recognize dimes, nickels, and pennies in a handful of change – to determine the bullet's caliber. I used my instincts, which had always served me well. After all, the features of a 44 Magnum bullet were all there, but my gut reminded me that I hadn't taken the time to actually measure the diameter of the bullet or weigh it, both of which are part of the routine protocol for determining bullet caliber.

So, in a huff, I threw my lab coat back on and went to the vault where the bullet had been stored to await its official and final analysis. I brought it to the firearms room where I set it on a digital scale. A cold sweat seeped from my pores as the scale read 230 grains, not 240 grains as I would expect for a 44 Magnum bullet (three U.S. quarters weigh about 260 grains). I opened a small drawer beneath the scale and removed a handheld measuring caliper. With a gentle touch, I closed the jaws of the caliper onto the sides of the bullet and measured a diameter of .45 inches. That which I feared was now true. The bullet found on the floor of the school was not fired from a 44 Magnum revolver; it was fired from a 45 Auto semiautomatic pistol. I had been wrong about the caliber *and* the type of weapon.

Kevin was gracious when I gave him the news. It didn't really matter to him because he had yet to act on the information, but I was mortified. I had made a mistake and I knew darn well why it happened. I was in a hurry, and my hurriedness conspired with other factors that prevented me from recognizing what was an unusual configuration for a 45 Auto bullet. Nobody knew better than me why and when errors tend to occur. They occur when *confusion collides with confidence in a commotion.* It was the shooting of a school. I wanted to help an investigator. He was in a hurry. I was in a hurry. I had other priorities competing for my time and attention. As a result, I found myself unable to meet the demands of a situation that required my best. The result was a mistake, something that forensic science culture doesn't much care to tolerate.

Human Fallibility. In their 2007 book *Mistakes Were Made (but not by me)*, Carol Tavris and Elliot Aronson explain the importance of mitigating our natural human fallibilities by designing and committing ourselves to *processes* that help regulate the adverse impact of our *personalities*. "Because most of us are not self-correcting and because our blind spots keep us from knowing that we need to be, external procedures must be in place to correct the errors that human beings will inevitably make and to reduce the chances of future ones."

The mystery of the lone school bullet was never solved, but the error I made was a watershed moment for me for several reasons. My responsibilities as a laboratory director placed demands on me that made it difficult to bring my undivided attention to my technical casework. There were just too many distractions and too many temptations to rush. But even more important was my ongoing struggle to follow a reliable process that allowed me to do both. It simply wasn't as manageable a challenge as it had been in the early years of my directorial career. So over time, I had no choice but to distance myself from casework and leave it to those who weren't burdened by the same managerial demands as me. Although this was a difficult thing for me to do, it reduced my exposure to risk and, to be candid, made space for me to become a better laboratory director.

The Error of Disconnectedness

Everyone makes mistakes, and those mistakes are made more likely by distractions. In a position of leadership, among the most devastating mistakes *you* can make is failing to invest your time and energy in the nurturing of your key relationships, which includes relationships with family, friends, colleagues, employees, mentors, and upper managers. The sources of your distraction could be the competing priorities that demand so much of your energy, or they could originate from any loyalties you have to the old superior, which cause you to prioritize your own individual power and prominence over the quality of the connections you keep with people in your sphere of influence. Often, it is a combination of the two.

Process Over Personality. A phrase I often hear from my coaching clients is *well, that's just my personality*, which is code for, *it's behavior that's out of my control*. Personality, of course, is a very important predictor of how people speak, act, and make decisions. It has its roots not only in our cellular biology but also in our past experiences and how those experiences affected our development. Personality can, in fact, be a very powerful source for good, and many great leaders have personalities that naturally suit them to oversee a team, an organization, or an entire government. Personality matters, and to the extent that we can deliberately regulate our personalities to achieve specific results, the better off we will be for it.

But we must also recognize that personality – even that which might be described as a *great* personality – is unpredictable and subject to swings that can result in inconsistencies, distractions, and mistakes in judgement. Even our recollection of past events can be impaired by any stress or trauma we experienced while they were happening. For these reasons, it is best to use our personalities as tools with which to create positive experiences for the people who interact with us, but not for detecting when it is or isn't time to meet a particular responsibility. For the latter, *process* will always be more reliable than *personality*. You can better sustain high levels of effectiveness in everything you do by designing and committing to a trustworthy process.

The Big Blue Mistake

Before I walk you through some basics for developing your own leadership process, let's first plug this principle into a real-life organizational scenario to see how it stands under pressure. During the late 1990s, the venerable IBM was on the verge of bankruptcy. Described as *the big blue dinosaur* by market analysts, IBM had become big and clumsy, unable to reach beyond the shadows cast by its own inefficiencies. It was known mostly as a hardware company, but other high-profile competitors such as Gateway, Dell, Hewlett-Packard, and Compaq were passing by at an alarming pace. IBM seemed to be stuck and almost entirely unable to innovate or grow itself into a more competitive position. Its troubles would later be blamed, in part, on an army of sales representatives (personalities, we might say) who were no longer communicating with the mothership, aggregated into smaller kingdoms ruled by leaders who weren't being held accountable for their decisions and contributions. The result was a corporate disconnect from the marketplace and a chronic inability to *see around the corners*. Without a team of sales representatives keeping executives informed, strategic decision-making tended to reinforce the existing business models rather than disrupt the status quo. IBM had become one...big...mistake.

This all changed, however, with a dramatic shift in corporate philosophy, espoused by a new team of corporate executives who sought to uncouple their future from the cult of personality, establishing a disciplined, process-oriented approach to conducting business. Self-promoters were pulled out of the shadows and held accountable for their performance, while clear expectations and processes for delivering value to clients became a cultural imperative. Within a short period of time, IBM shocked the business world by regaining its footing in the marketplace and repositioning itself as a *service* provider rather than a *hardware* vendor. Leveraging its decades of accumulated knowledge of hardware and mainframe systems, IBM became a trusted consultant for companies wanting to evaluate, select, and implement hardware solutions best suited for their operational needs.

As it turned out, IBM not only became a corporate success-story of historic significance, it also had a new story to tell, one that could help other sales-intensive companies rethink how they do business and find new ways to regain their competitiveness just as IBM did.

A Story to Share. The principles underlying IBM's rejuvenation were published in a white paper titled *Chaos to Cadence: Transforming Sales Organizations to Win in the Global Economy*. Rather than criticizing the splintering effects of rogue personalities who can easily undermined the cohesiveness of a corporate culture, the report pays homage to them, recognizing the importance of their bold and assertive nature. "Sales is often the untamed 'wild west' in many organizations, especially in those organizations with intensive sales cycles and diverse, multidisciplinary, expert sales teams. Sales organizations thrive in chaos, relying on the energy, heroism and savvy of independent-minded sales professionals."

What allowed IBM to make its dramatic shift in organizational effectiveness was its ability to harness the power of its 'heroes' to design and implement processes that could amplify IBM's capacity to deliver new kinds of value to prospective clients in the marketplace. The following is an extended excerpt from *Chaos to Cadence* that explains this effort:

"Like other large firms with long histories of traditional sales and big-company behavior, IBM knew this environment intimately. But as IBM strove to become more agile in response to market demands, IBM discovered that sales processes needed to be refocused, sales intelligence

leveraged, and teams orchestrated across clients, product lines, roles, geographies and function. More so, Sales needed to be a leader of integration – alignment of people and technology - within the enterprise, forging unexpected partnerships with the likes of Finance and other strategic functions. Chaos needed to be managed with Cadence, providing the organization with a tightly measured and rhythmic harmony that would drive more sales and improve overall business efficiency, all while providing more value to our clients."

IBM, you might say, eliminated its vulnerability to the ebbs, flows, and ambitions of personalities and instead built its future on firmer ground: *processes* that could be trusted to maximize the positive impact IBM would have on its now-growing base of clientele. IBM, the mistake, was now IBM, the miracle.

History All Over Again. Now, you might wonder if IBM's success continued into the new century. The answer to your question is yet another lesson to be learned about the importance of putting process over personality. IBM, once again, found itself in trouble, not because it abandoned the processes it had created, but because it didn't. According to *Forbes*, executives at IBM became stuck on their existing business model of "stacking," a term used to describe the sale of packages that included hardware, software, consulting, and financing. It was a fantastic model in its day, but as clients began to migrate toward the flexibility and customization afforded by cloud computing, IBM's stack-worshipping executives wouldn't budge, resulting in profit slumps that continued over a decade. According to *Forbes*, in the 10 years ending on March 12, 2021, the NASDAQ climbed an impressive 450%, while IBM shares fell over 21%. While IBM's processes had once allowed for the building of something very special, those same processes became obsolete when IBM's executive personalities refused to destroy what they had created. Sound familiar? It sure does to me. It's the old superior rising up in a valiant stand to preserve its honor and pride, grasping at anything that will prevent it from being washed away in the rush toward the future, where the ways of the past just don't matter anymore – and neither does the old superior.

Design *Your* Process

So, what about you? What's *your* process? If you don't have one and don't feel like you need one, I think it's probably accurate to assume that you aren't much different from most people. You do what you do and work how you work because it doesn't feel like it's broken. Things are going fine and nothing is falling through the cracks. You're meeting your responsibilities, keeping up with your deadlines and workloads, and people know they can count on you to do whatever it is you do. Even in your personal life, you still make time for hobbies, and you exercise to stay in shape. You meditate and reflect. You get enough sleep. The people closest to you appreciate you and feel like you make time for them. And above all that, you have energy left over to think about what might be next for you – the opportunities waiting in the wings that may lead to more responsibility, more career growth, and higher pay. You've got ambitions, and the many possibilities that lie before you are exciting. All is well.

It would be nice if you could remain in this state of bliss forever, but that's not how it works. Your affinity for shouldering more and more responsibility gives you a sense of progress and purpose, that is until the approach taken to meet these responsibilities is no longer cutting it, which is when things take a turn for the worse. You make mistakes, your relationships suffer, your confidence declines, deadlines are missed, appointments are forgotten, your sleep becomes restless, and the feeling of being utterly overwhelmed clamps down on you like an Olympic wrestler in a bad mood.

Oh, and if you just so happen to be an entitled disciple of the old superior, you are quite vulnerable to having your pride hurt, becoming chronically irritable, and blaming others for your troubles. So, not only do you struggle to meet *your* responsibilities, you now make it harder for others to meet *theirs*. Your incompetence goes viral.

Hopefully, this isn't you. But if it is, feeling overwhelmed is the primary indicator that something needs to change. You're like a ship that's taking on water and the pumps aren't keeping up with the flood. Systems and solutions need to be engineered to help you meet your responsibilities with more ease and confidence. You need to create your *process;* and as much as I wish I could just tell you what that process is, I can't. Your process will be yours, unique to you and your responsibilities. It will be a plan with a schedule that guides you in the management of your time, energy, and focus. So, although it's up to you to design and implement the right process for you, there are seven elements of a good leadership process that I encourage you to consider as you get started:

1. Annual Goals. New Year's resolutions of the garden variety are fine, but annual goals of professional significance require a careful and honest assessment of your current state, current abilities, current weaknesses, challenges you face, and opportunities that may be available to you in the future. All must then be integrated into a single strategic vision that you commit to making a reality. This is what it means to make progress, to convert possibilities into achievements; but it requires something foundational that no coach, supervisor, or mentor can teach you: desire. You have to *want* things. You have to want things for your team, for your organization, for yourself, and for your friends and family. You have to want to be better next year than you are today. Ineffective people are more likely to allow each year to come and go. They see it as something to *get through* rather than an opportunity to advance. They're spectators and they watch the game of life play out, waiting anxiously to see how it all ends before sulking over how disappointing it all turned out to be. Winners like you, however, are different. They see each year as a competitive season and themselves as players. They strive to win those critical victories that mark the many segments of what will someday become a comprehensive timeline of growth, accomplishment, and contribution.

Because there is such value in starting each new year with focus and momentum, consider making the first two weeks of December your time to reflect on the year about to end, and use this time to make some thoughtful decisions about what you can do to make next year a special one. Consult with the people in your personal and professional life for help. They will often have insights and ideas that might otherwise escape you. Your progress matters to them, so ask for their input and advice. Review as many indicators of your current state as possible, for the more data you consider, the more informed your goals will be. Then, when you are ready, take time to write out a list of goals. They may be personal or professional, but keep them all together because, in real life, they are just that, together.

To ensure the maximum utility of your goals, refer to the SMART model described by Doran, Miller, and Cunningham in 1981, or any of its adaptations. Generally speaking, SMART is an acronym that stands for *Specific, Measurable, Attainable, Realistic*, and *Timely*. Put more simply, a SMART goal is one for which there will be no ambiguity in whether or not it was accomplished. Once your goals are documented, keep them accessible at all times and monitor your progress throughout the year. And, if you wish, establish goal-setting deadlines on a monthly or quarterly basis, anything that helps you maintain your focus throughout the year.

2. Weekly Planning. For this one, I need to be direct; plan each week before it begins. Period. There is no better piece of advice that could ever be given to you, and no bigger opportunity that you could ever put to waste. The workweek is the interval of time in which you engage in the effort to meet the many responsibilities and expectations to which you are held accountable. If you liken each year to a competitive season, each week is a game, the moment when you show up to participate in the contest that rages between your intentions and your circumstances. As you know, so much of what we encounter in life is unexpected. Priorities collide with distractions, surprises interrupt routines, and the time available for what you *want* to do is quickly devoured by what you *have* to do. When the week is over, it's rather common for many of us to realize that we lost the game, that our circumstances overpowered our intentions. All we really did was survive to play another game, which is hardly sufficient to inspire. When this happens to you, you probably feel the bitterness that's common to losing. And when you get into the habit of losing, you are vulnerable to becoming cynical and frustrated by what feels like your inability to put your many skills and abilities to use in a cause that matters.

Those, however, who take time to plan each week before it begins afford themselves a tremendous advantage. They have a game plan, a document to which they can refer during the week to remind themselves of what they intended to do when the week began. And as all good game plans do, they account for inclement weather. So, when the storm of unexpected circumstances rains down on them, they have a light to guide them. They can react to the surprises of life and then quickly refocus on executing their plans. When each week draws to a close, even though circumstances will conspire against them, they are able to get done what they set out to do. They win each week and, as a result, the chance of winning the entire year – perhaps even having a *championship* year – remains strong.

Exactly how you plan each week depends on you, your intentions, and your circumstances. For some, their responsibilities are important but don't necessarily overwhelm them. So, the planning process may be quite simple. But for those with a very complicated set of responsibilities and a wide range of distractions to which they are exposed, weekly planning will require more thought, time, and deliberation. If this describes you, each weekly planning session may feel like a major project. And that's ok, because it simply means the effort needed to create the plan has already been made necessary by reality.

Just to give you an example, my own weekly planning takes about 30-45 minutes, sometimes an hour, depending on the week. Every Sunday evening, I have time carved out to sit down and create my plan, which I document in a spreadsheet that's always kept running on my laptop computer so I can refer to it quickly over the course of each week. When doing my planning, I have a process – there's that word again – that I follow to make sure that my plan is accounting for all of the relevant things going on in my life, which, of course, includes my professional goals and responsibilities. Although yours may be different, the following is a quick list of things I do to create my own weekly plan:

- Review my previous week's plan
- Review my notes from the previous week, which I keep in a separate spreadsheet tab
- Review my calendar for the previous 4 to 6 weeks
- Review my calendar for the coming 3 to 4 months, with an emphasis on the next 3 weeks

- Review emails sent and received during the previous week, paying closer attention to any emails I flagged for follow-up.
- Review my text messages from the previous week
- Sketch a rough plan on paper
- Finalize my plan in my spreadsheet
- Begin executing my plan on Monday morning

It's very important that you not add to your plan once the week has begun because, if you do, you're simply allowing circumstances to encroach on your intentions. For any tasks that might arise during the week that require your attention, keep those in a separate list so they don't blur what you set out to do when the week began. As you execute your weekly plan, check the items off your list. This gives you the satisfaction that comes with winning your week. It will also inspire you to keep weekly planning as an important part of your process.

For a weekly planning template you can use to help you get started, please visit www.thenewsuperior.com and download the planning tool that I've created for you. Once you open it, you will discover that it includes features that will help you implement more elaborate plans over the course of the year, should you choose to use them. At a minimum, however, create an annual plan to establish your season of play and the critical victories that will make the season worth your effort. Then, establish your weekly plans to help you compete more effectively against the many circumstances waiting to keep you from realizing your intentions.

3. Rounding. Hospital physicians are known for a practice called *rounding*, which is a walk they take through certain floors each morning (or other time of day) to visit with patients, discuss their care, and monitor their progress. Often, rounds are done with other team members responsible for patient care, including residents, who are medical school graduates in training, as well as nurses, therapists, nutritionists, social workers, and other professionals whose expertise is relevant to the team. Rounding, therefore, is the economizing of multiple patient consultations into a single task, providing some economies of scale that could not be achieved if each patient visit was scheduled and performed as its own individual event.

Rounding is something you can do also, and it can have a positive impact on your overall productivity and professional effectiveness. If you are leader, your rounds may be similar to those at a hospital, where you take time each day to visit with the members of your team. Or, perhaps you have some clients that you typically contact once a month by phone or email; you may opt to schedule a 3-hour recurring block of time on your calendar each month to make all of these contacts on the same day at roughly the same time. Any time you can consolidate multiple routine tasks into a single event or *round*, it prevents the spotting of your available time with randomly distributed tasks that otherwise make it harder to accommodate more significant priorities.

To economize your time through the practice of rounding, pay close attention to the many tasks you complete over the course of a day, a week, a month, or an entire year. See if you can group common or routine tasks into recurring rounds. For example, if you are a small business owner, you might choose to pay your bills and reconcile your books every Friday from 2pm to 3pm. So, you set a recurring appointment on your calendar for this time block. And because you do it each week, you establish a rhythmic effect called *cadence* that conditions your brain to know that at 2pm each Friday, it's time to do your bookkeeping.

I especially urge you to apply rounding in your effort to keep connected with the people who are most important to you in your life. In your personal life, this might mean blocking off some recurring time to catch up with family and friends. Professionally, it might mean consolidating your communications with a group of contractors or project managers with whom you and your team must keep in touch. Use rounding to offset the adverse impact that stress and pressure have on your most important relationships. The antidote to *chaos* is *cadence*. More on cadence in a moment.

4. Organization. To organize is to arrange multiple disparate parts into a single, functioning whole. When you are organized, everything *has* its proper place and is *in* its proper place. Organized people have a distinct advantage over those who aren't because they don't waste time and energy having to cope with the burdens of inefficiency. They have a system for keeping everything where it needs to be, and that system allows them to orient themselves in their world and meet their responsibilities with minimal effort. They operate like a well-oiled machine, and they rarely find themselves delayed or frustrated by an inability to react to a situation simply because they didn't have their act together.

The cost of *dis*organization is what's called *decision fatigue*. Scientific research has confirmed that humans can only make so many decisions within a given period of time before they run out of gas. The more decisions you make, the more you drain your capacity to make them. Former President of the United States, Barrack Obama, once explained in a *Vanity Fair* article that "You'll see I wear only gray or blue suits. I'm trying to pare down decisions. I don't want to make decisions about what I'm eating or wearing, because I have too many other decisions to make."

Being organized affords you a similar advantage. It cuts back on the number of decisions you must make. When you need something but can't find it, for example, you are forced to make decisions about where you should look, and depending on how important it is, you may have to make a lot of decisions before you find what you're looking for. Similarly, if a colleague sends you an email with an interesting article attached, one that you'd like to reference later in the year, not having a way to store and retrieve it will tempt you to just let it sit in your inbox. Then, every time you access your inbox, the waiting email will ever-so-slightly complicate your decision about what emails you should or should not read in that moment.

Clutter, therefore, is the primary symptom of fatigue, damage to your personal space left in the wake of unmade decisions. The professional journals piled on your desk, for example, comprise a stack of unmade decisions. Each time a new journal arrives, you have neither a place to put them nor a system for archiving them in a retrievable way, so you take a pass – you throw each journal on your desk or credenza with the others, convincing yourself that you will either read them later or make a decision about what to do with them at some point in time when you have the energy and motivation for it.

Perhaps even more frustrating are the ideas that creative people keep in their heads because they have no place to put them. This was a challenge for me over most of my professional career until I came up with a system for dealing with the mental clutter produced by my active imagination. In fact, much of this book is based on ideas and concepts that, at one point or another, I dictated into a digital recorder and then transcribed into a spreadsheet. Doing so is part of my process, which is the documenting of random thoughts and ideas that I capture the moment I conceive them. I use an Olympus VN-7200 digital voice recorder that I purchased online. With two clicks of a button, I can start recording whenever something of value comes to mind. Then, once each week, I make a habit of documenting my recordings and erasing them from the recorder. With my thoughts safely stored in my spreadsheet, I can release them from my mind, confident they will be available when I need them.

There's one final point I'd like to make about the importance of organization. An organized leader is easier to trust. He is perceived as having his act together, free of the inherent frustrations and inefficiencies of clutter. This gives the organized leader the appearance of having a high capacity for engagement, making him more approachable and attractive to team members wanting to keep him informed and involved. By being organized, leaders convey the unspoken message that they are open for business – competent, alert, and always ready to contribute to the effectiveness of their teams. So, just as clutter is a trail of unmade decisions, being organized is proof of decision-making excellence. Being organized boosts your confidence and the confidence others have in you.

For more information on getting organized, I highly recommend the following books:

- *The Five Choices: The Path to Extraordinary Productivity*, by Kory Kogon, Adam Merrill, and Leena Rinne
- *The Effective Executive*, by Peter F. Drucker
- *It's All Too Much*, by Peter Walsh
- *Organized for Success*, by Stephanie Winston
- *The Checklist Manifesto*, by Atul Gwande

5. Coordinated Cadence. Imagine, for a moment, the executive leadership team of a mid-sized company that has an established practice of meeting once each month for about three hours to discuss a variety of issues relevant to their business. Usually around the end of each month, the CEO sends out an email with a call for discussion topics and a suggested date and time that works best for her schedule. The other members of the team respond to indicate their availability and to suggest topics, if any, that warrant conversation among the members of the team.

If most or all of the team members are available, and if there are items to be discussed, the meeting will be held as scheduled. But if availability is limited, or if there isn't sufficient business to justify the time commitment, the meeting will not be held.

On one hand, this approach may seem reasonable, and we might be inclined to credit the CEO and the rest of the team for prioritizing communication while also respecting each other's time. But on the other hand, it is inherently chaotic because it's uncertain exactly when meetings will be held, if they will be held at all, and what exactly will be discussed. Anyone who's counting on these meetings to occur because she values the opportunity to connect with her colleagues will find herself frequently disappointed. There is no *cadence* to the process and, therefore, the process can't be trusted.

Cadence is uninterrupted rhythm, like a drumbeat that keeps a steady, reliable tempo throughout a song. And like songs having a nice, infectious rhythm, they make it easy and enjoyable to dance. In an organization, a lack of cadence makes everyone vulnerable to decision fatigue because each occurrence of an important task or event is handled as if it stands alone in time, requiring choices to be made about when, where, and how they are scheduled. But an organization in cadence simply dances to its own rhythm without having to think about it.

If the CEO I described a moment ago wanted to harness the full power of cadence, she would schedule the executive meetings on, for example, the fourth Thursday of every month at 1pm in the main conference room. Meetings would never be canceled or rescheduled unless an emergency or conflicting holiday requires it. The agenda for each meeting would be the same, including brief updates from each of the executives, a review of key performance indicators, progress updates on the company's strategic priorities, an update from the CEO, and time carved out for the discussion of new business and old business, both of which would be solicited by the CEO's administrative assistant exactly 10 business days prior to each meeting. At the end of each meeting, once the necessary business has been conducted, time would be included for casual conversation. And, as an added benefit, because the meetings are so much more efficient and well-prepared, what used to take 3 hours can now be completed in 90 minutes.

This is what it means to be in cadence. There are no decisions to be made regarding when or if each meeting takes place, or what will be the primary categories of topics discussed. Those decisions have already been made. The team simply follows the *process*.

Cadence, however, can be taken one step further, which is when it transforms entire teams or organizations. This is to say that the cadence of seemingly disparate teams or units can be coordinated with each other to produce cross-functional cooperation that amplifies their mutual effectiveness and efficiency.

Continuing with our example, let's say the executive team maintains its cadence for a full year without interruption. With a set rhythm firmly in place, the CEO hopes to get the company's major divisions to dance. Because the executive meeting occurs on the *fourth* Thursday of every month, she suggests that the VPs in charge of sales, marketing, HR, and IT hold a joint meeting sometime during the *third* week of each month – one week earlier – so that major issues and needs at the division level can be pulled up for consideration during the executive meeting. It works; in fact, it works so well that the VPs ask that their own senior team-members have brief operational huddles sometime during the *second* week of each month, from which the most important discussion items, if any, are pulled up to their respective VPs for review in their third-Thursday meeting.

Now realizing that they've created a machine that seems to be running on its own, the CEO and her executive team decide that their cadence should include an official response to any and all items that make their way to the executive meeting for consideration. They don't want to leave people hanging. So, they decide to add one more item to the executive meeting agenda, which comes to be known as *Pull and Push*. During pull and push, the executives deliberate on all items they *pulled* from the VP meeting, document any decisions or actions taken, then *push* the official disposition of those items back to the VPs for their attention, completing an important feedback loop that gives everyone throughout the organization confidence that the executive team is engaged and responsive. Recognizing the importance of closing this loop in a timely and consistent fashion, the executives decide to set a deadline for completing their push of deliberated items back to the VPs, which they set for the *first* Thursday of each month. This, they decide, will give the VPs time with their teams to act on any urgent priorities before the next cadence cycle starts.

Coordinated cadence is how multiple people and multiple teams, even those having very different functional responsibilities, stay synchronized with each other. It systematizes and schedules the execution of key responsibilities and tasks upon which organizations depend for their agility and competitiveness. If it's deemed to be vital to the success of the team, then it's worthy of being set to a schedule and holding everyone accountable for following the schedule. But unlike what less-effective teams are willing to do, coordinated cadence also ensures the disciplined and generous sharing of critical information and ideas as they arise during a cadence cycle. Nothing is wasted.

6. Feedback Loops. A *feedback loop* is a reliable and self-sustaining cycle of soliciting, receiving, considering, and acting on the ideas and advice of others. These may originate from employees, colleagues, fellow managers, customers, stakeholders, and others whose opinions are deemed to be relevant and useful. What is meant by *self-sustaining* is that there is a triggering event that causes feedback to be shared with a leader, usually a request or invitation of some sort. By *loop*, I mean that the people who are sharing their individual perspectives receive some confirmation that their input was received, considered, possibly acted upon, but most certainly appreciated. This confirmation has the effect of incentivizing the future sharing of feedback the next time around.

Leaders can solicit feedback through formal means, such as an annual employee-engagement survey or a periodic customer-satisfaction questionnaire, or through informal means such as simply asking an employee or customer for her opinion during a casual conversation. The only thing more valuable than the feedback itself is having a way to let the giver know how and why his feedback was useful. After all, the sharing of honest and candid feedback is an act of generosity, which deserves reciprocation through an expression of genuine gratitude.

In my coaching practice, I make a habit of asking my clients for a shortlist of people, or categories of people, whose opinions are most relevant to them and their respective teams. Invariably, my clients will identify their employees, a direct supervisor, customers, professional peers, and other key stakeholders. But when I push further for an explanation about the processes followed to access these perspectives, I usually come to learn that no such processes exist.

Not only should you have clearly defined and repeatable processes in place to access the perspectives and opinions that are relevant to the decisions you make, these processes should be set to a coordinated cadence that produces an infectious rhythm. All information you gather should be given thoughtful consideration and acted upon in some way. It is then that the individuals who shared their input should receive confirmation about how their feedback was used and why it mattered.

The goal of reliable feedback loops is to get personal observations and perspectives having operational and cultural relevance out of the shadows and into the light. It also makes bureaucracies more human and, therefore, more capable of enabling teamwork. Granted, the old superior doesn't much care about soliciting feedback because the opportunity to share feedback tends to empower those they'd prefer to remain *out of the loop* and, therefore, inferior. Entrusted leaders, on the other hand, regard personal perspectives as fuel for team propulsion, creating opportunities to see things differently, do things better, and identify opportunities that might otherwise have been missed.

As you develop your own personal leadership process, include ways of gathering feedback, remembering that how you access this information can be formal, informal, or both. At a minimum, establish a cadence for soliciting feedback from the following individuals, if applicable to you:

- Your direct employees
- Your direct manager or supervisor
- The peers with whom you work most often
- Your customers, clients, or stakeholders
- Any coaches or mentors with whom you work
- Your spouse, partner, or significant-other

7. Celebration of Victories. Celebrating individual and team victories when they occur is crucial to maintaining momentum. When victories aren't celebrated or not given their due recognition, it sends the conflicting message that progress isn't as important as it's made out to be. As a leader, when you expect and encourage your team to make progress, whatever that may look like, ignoring it when it happens is destructive. Worse, the members of your team may question if you're even smart enough to recognize progress at all. Or, perhaps, they may sense that you feel entitled to whatever progress occurs, which would officially confirm your allegiance to the old superior.

The bigger the victory, the greater the celebration should be. Never waste an opportunity to bring attention to progress made by your people, your team, or your entire organization. Call it out. Express genuine gratitude and admiration for what occurred and the people who made it happen. And if you find it difficult to do this, you may need to explore your own motives and emotions; they may signal some leadership immaturity that you'd be wise to address through reflection, coaching, or even therapy. The good news, however, is it doesn't take much for a leader to extend the celebratory recognition that high-performing professionals crave. Sometimes just a knowing nod of the head or a wink of the eye lets someone know that what they accomplished was noticed and appreciated. But if it warrants something more, then give something more. Be generous but sincere in heaping praise on people who deserve it. And if you find that your people are willing to heap praise on *you* as their leader (one of the most gratifying things a leader can ever experience), don't be coy. Smile and say thank you. By doing so you reinforce praise as a cultural priority.

It's worth noting that there's a subtle nuance to praise that we need to acknowledge lest we mistakenly portray ourselves as arrogant or condescending. The best praise is given as an *equal in the moment*, without the appearance of being expressed from a position of superiority. Praise can inadvertently make the receiver feel like an inferior if the praise tends to reassert the giver's dominance. Of course, some receivers of praise may be more sensitive to this than others. But as a rule, I encourage you to focus on celebrating *what* happened rather than *who* did it.

The following is a list of examples of praise that can be misconstrued as condescending, accompanied by alternative expressions that can signal the giver's position as an equal in the moment:

Condescending: *You did a good job*
Alternative: *That was a job well-done*

Condescending: *I'm proud of you*
Alternative: *You should be proud of yourself*

Condescending: *You really impressed me*
Alternative: *That was really impressive*

Condescending: *I was pleased by the skill and ability you showed*
Alternative: *Your skills and abilities were very evident*

Condescending: *I liked the comments you made at today's meeting*
Alternative: *Your comments at the meeting had a positive impact*

Condescending: *I think you've got some great potential*
Alternative: *Your potential is something to be excited about*

As you probably noticed, in each of the condescending statements, the person giving the praise positioned himself as a judge of the person being praised. In the alternative expressions, it is the outcomes produced by the person being praised that are being recognized. The differences are obviously subtle but can have a tremendous influence on how the praise is received and how the motives of the praise are interpreted.

To make praise and the celebration of victories more consistent, establish cadence in what activities you monitor and what indicators of progress you measure. Consider giving annual or quarterly awards and hold social gatherings to commemorate them. Don't wait for formal performance appraisals as these are stuffy and mechanical. Get your praise and celebrations out in the open for everyone to share. By being smart and generous with your praise, you will create more reasons to give it in the future.

Make It Count

Establishing a process for how you conduct your business, which includes how you lead your team, elevates your effectiveness and gives people more reasons to trust you. A good process will expand your capacity to be productive, approachable, responsive, engaging, and consistent. Through your consistency, the members of your team will dance to the beat of your rhythm. You won't need to direct or instruct them; they will just dance, and dancing makes people happy.

Chapter 18

Unify the Committed

I've spent a lot of time in my career wrapped up in chains. No, not that kind of chain. I'm talking about the virtual chains that keep people in compliance with established ways of doing things. These include the chains of command in the many law enforcement agencies in which and with which I've worked over the last 30+ years, and chains of custody, the documented accounting of all the people and places to which criminal evidence was entrusted prior to court. When there is a break in the chain of custody, for example, it's a very serious matter, as the integrity of the evidence comes into question and may render the evidence inadmissible in court.

Strength and Loyalty

Chains are a symbol of uncompromised strength and durability. In a chain, each link falls in line and is equally responsible for keeping the chain together, even when exposed to forces that try to break it. In a chain of command, each person is like a link, and failing to meet one's responsibility for maintaining the strength of the chain is like an act of treason. Because rank, superiority, and order of decision-making are so culturally ingrained in the guardian professions – recall that these include police, fire, and the military – when chain of command is broken, or when communication fails to pass through the proper links in the chain, it is the organizational integrity that comes into question. Chain of command, at least within organizations that depend on it, is what keeps everyone on the same page. As such, remaining loyal to the chain of command is among the most important conditions of employment.

But what we know about the best teams is that they are loyal to something else. The best teams are those loyal to a core set of *principles,* boundaries in which words, actions, and decisions are known to catalyze team effectiveness. As we discussed in Chapter 14, when teams stay within the boundaries they've set for themselves – in other words, they are loyal to their principles – they outperform and outlast those where loyalty to *personalities* and subservience to rank govern individual behavior. Principled teams are more focused, more reliable, more productive, more competitive, more agile, and more enduring. When people are united by principles, they are not distracted or demoralized by the chaos that's inherent to the ebbs and flows of personality. Principles enable high-impact teamwork. Personalities invite hierarchy.

Commitment to a team's principles has a propulsive effect. But we must also acknowledge that among the most important principles of sustained teamwork is that members of a team must feel safe and secure in challenging the status quo and advocating for change when there is evidence that change may be necessary. Being principled is not the same as being rigid, stubborn, or righteous, and some principles may require tweaking or refinement as conditions in the strategic environment change. Being stuck in an outdated pattern of thinking will set into motion a cascading sequence of almost imperceptible mistakes that, one day, will become obvious failures. When a team is stuck for too long, catastrophe becomes a distinct possibility. The *right* way to be principled, therefore, is to encourage creative and critical thought about what those principles are, what they mean, and what is the most responsible way to apply them. The principles of a healthy team are often the subject of feisty conversation.

Everybody On Board. You will know your team's principles are dialed-in when the degree of commitment is so strong that it regulates behavior at all levels of rank or authority within an organization. When this happens, the loyalty to your team's principles is voluntary, not compelled; and team members are confident in holding themselves and each other accountable for conducting themselves in alignment with those principles. They become *conformers to* and *champions of* their principles.

What results from this institutionalized alignment is as fascinating as it is transformative. A *chain of commitment* forms that becomes stronger and more enduring than the *chain of command*. Within the chain of commitment is a network of believers who find energy and inspiration in each other. Dominance gives way to mentorship, hierarchy facilitates teamwork, and selfishness succumbs to generosity. The chain of commitment is held together by the loyalty of its members to principles, and the strength of each link is reinforced by the willingness of individuals to function as equals in the moment. Chains of commitment rely far less on rank, stature, and authority because open communication and the sharing of ideas ensure that what *needs* to get done, *does* get done. Respect and deference are therefore granted to those who empower others, those who are the embodiment of the principles to which everyone is committed. Because dominance and hierarchical behaviors have a disturbing effect on the group's efficiency and effectiveness, they are shunned, dismissed as primitive artifacts of the old superior. A chain of commitment thrives on the generosity of its members and the ability of those members to support and encourage each other. It is nothing short of professional nirvana.

I had the opportunity to experience the chain of commitment that formed among the forensic experts in the investigation of the Atlanta bombings. We held ourselves accountable to a fundamental principle of investigative science – that expertise and ideas rule the day. If you have them, then you have something to offer. Of little concern to the team was your age or rank, and certainly not your sex, skin color, religion, or other personal attributes that were immaterial to our decisions. Within a chain of commitment, only your contributions and your *potential to contribute* matter. If, for some reason, circumstances limit the contributions you can make at any one moment, simply paying attention, encouraging your team members, and scrutinizing the team's thought patterns are all that the team may need or expect of you. As long as you are committed to the team and the principles that are holding it together, then you have something to offer and will be appreciated for it.

It is utterly remarkable how the bonds of even the strongest chain of command will weaken and break when exposed to the force of commitment. I've seen it happen over and over again in major criminal investigations. High-ranking egos we expected to suck the air out of the room sat quietly and respectfully, surrounded by a team of committed investigators, forensic experts, and prosecuting attorneys who were driven by the urgency reflex, and who didn't give a damn about ranks and egos. Which reminds me of something else that's fascinating about chains of commitment. Individuals who might otherwise be intimidated by rank, stature, and authority will suddenly find themselves supplied with a reserve of courage and assertiveness that amplifies their willingness to engage and spar. In a chain of command, they are quiet and consenting. In a chain of commitment, they are open and bold. Chains of commitment are a force of human nature to be reckoned with.

Start Small

Like the proverbial butterfly that flaps its wings to form a hurricane, urgency is the spark that ignites collective commitment. All it takes for a chain of commitment to form is one or two individuals who see value in focusing on something transcendent. At that moment, the principles that will eventually grow the chain of commitment may not be clear, and this is okay. What *is* clear, however, is the opportunity to apply talents and energies in a new and more focused way, one that is likely to produce more good for more people than how things are done right now. With enough time, and with others on board who are willing to collaborate and commit to this *new way*, empowerment principles will emerge and solidify their bond. A chain of commitment will form on its own.

This phenomenon we call the chain of commitment has considerable implications for you as a leader, suggesting an approach you can take to best influence and enable your people. To be a champion of the old superior is to expect that your people be loyal to *you*. But to get out of the way and allow your people to thrive requires you to relax this egotistical expectation and instead facilitate the creation of a chain of commitment, one based on a core set of principles that your team – not just you – determine are more important than any single individual. And it all begins with you being an equal in the moment, positioning yourself as a participant in a grand conversation about what's possible. And to initiate this conversation, assuming it hasn't started already, you can ask some probing, thought-provoking questions that force you and your team to think differently. Here are some examples:

- What are the barriers that keep us from being the very best we can be?

- What are we coping with, and how does this coping impair our effectiveness?

- In what ways do dominance behaviors or superiority-signaling cause a reduction in motivation?

- In what ways do we function like a hierarchy?

- In what ways do we function like a team?

- In what ways might our potential be limited by unnecessary rules or bureaucracy?

- In the last 12 months, what frustrations have you experienced and what caused them?

- If our team was forced to go without a leader for a few months, what would change? How would it be worse or better?

- In what ways do we have the opportunity to change how we think and work so that we have a greater impact?

- If we could start doing our very best work and function as the best possible team we can be, what would that look like and feel like?

- If we were functioning at our very best, how would we be different than we are today?

- What must we *start* wanting or expecting?

- What must we *stop* wanting or expecting?

- What must we *start* believing?

- What must we *stop* believing?

- What must we *start* doing or do more of?

- What must we *stop* doing or do less of?

Each of these questions, in their own way, have the potential to expose the things that may be wrong with your team. And because you, as a leader, are responsible for what's wrong, asking these questions will make you vulnerable to criticism or having your effectiveness questioned in the presence of others. This can be painful, and I know this from

268 THE NEW SUPERIOR

experience. But there is a way that you can initiate transformative conversations and ask revealing questions in a way that won't feel awkward or grating to your emotional well-being.

When there is the opportunity or desire for transformation, leaders should position themselves as wanting to be a part of that transformation – and it must be genuine. The members of the team must know, with certainty, that they and their leader are at a precipice – a moment in time when they can change the game that is being played. They can unite in a collective effort to do things in a different way and, as a result, change the outcomes they experience. But for this to happen, those with the most power and influence must be the first to admit both their fallibility and their desire to become better themselves.

Here's how the conversation can start. The transformative leader can begin by saying: *In my opinion, I am not as effective a leader as I could be, should be, and want to be. I think we have a lot of untapped potential as a team, and I think I have a lot of untapped potential as a leader, but we have to have some very honest and open conversations about how all of us, including me, can change how we do things as individuals and as a team. I want us to start having those conversations right now, and I want every voice to be heard and understood.*

A leader who is willing to make himself vulnerable in this way will have the necessary effect of helping individual team members bring down their emotional walls and be a part of the change effort. It may take some time, of course, for the team to be convinced of the leader's sincerity, depending on things that have happened in the past. Patience may be needed for the leader to demonstrate his genuine desire to change. But if he is truly willing to be vulnerable and subject himself to scrutiny, which he should be, then the leader who once may have been a mere personality can soon become the facilitator of principle. Those principles will arise organically within the team once the leader steps to the side and allows the natural energies of the team to go to work.

To put a fine point on it, leaders who influence their people through chain of *commitment* are more trustworthy and more effective than those who do so through chain of *command*. The kinds of professionals you want on your team are too skilled and too well-informed to be insulted by the indignities of command. They want to commit to something meaningful and to collaborate with others who are committed to the same things. For many, they've invested too much time, money, and effort in developing themselves into reasonably competent professionals to then relegate themselves to nothing more than mindless minions in a hierarchy. They want purpose, and they want to honor principles that bring this purpose to life. They want to solve problems and test their abilities. They want to learn and grow. They want to influence, in their own way, how work is done and how decisions are made. The moment they feel stuck or unappreciated is the moment you've lost them.

The good news is that chains of commitment will form naturally among capable, generous individuals in the presence of urgency. And these chains can achieve scale when hierarchical behaviors, including runaway bureaucracy, don't deprive people of their personal and professional autonomy.

Designing Your Urgency

To get a feel for what a chain of commitment would be like within your own team or organization, imagine all of your people being in a room together, however large that may be, with people of all different ranks, all levels of experience and education, and all levels of job complexity. The highest-level decision-makers are there. So are the custodians who clean the washrooms. Now, imagine everyone in the room thinking of themselves as being equal to everyone else – and when I say equal, I mean *really* equal. Although each person in the room is keenly aware of her or his own knowledge, skills, and abilities, not a single person in the room views herself or himself as a superior, only an equal, a collaborator. And not a single person in the room thinks of herself or himself as an inferior. Only equal.

If you find this to be an almost impossible scenario to contemplate, you are not alone. The extent to which this thought-exercise may extend beyond the limits of your imagination may be due to your belief that there are people on your team or within your organization who would be incapable of such a feat. Those with rank are perhaps too conditioned in the ways of hierarchy to give up that which they believe they have earned. Those without rank are too conditioned to subordinate themselves. The result would be a room full of hierarchy, exactly what you have now. Nothing would be different. The elements of hierarchy, you correctly recognize, live within people, so they cannot be escaped.

But the truth is they can. And it happens when the members of the group sense an urgency in which anything but their full commitment and willingness to engage strikes them as ridiculous or offensive. They rise and engage because no other alternative seems reasonable. Domineering personalities relent because they know they have an oppressive and stifling impact on team members. Subordinators step forward to offer their talents and insights, propelled by newfound feelings of courage and purpose that become more compelling than the fears they had for the dominators. In the presence of this urgency, the personality-based frameworks of hierarchy – the chains of command – come crashing down in the gale-force winds of commitment.

Professional facilitators and leadership coaches are skilled at using a variety of creative games and team-building exercises to replicate these conditions. When conducted properly, they synthesize an urgency reflex that causes individuals to dissolve out of their hierarchical identities and into participative collaborators, eager to do anything to help meet the demands of the urgency, including – and pay close attention to this one, please – getting out of people's way when they have something valuable to offer. This is what collaborators do in a chain of commitment, and it's what dominators often *fail to do* in chains of command.

Get to Work. Among the most innovative and eye-opening team-building games is the *marshmallow challenge,* developed by creative-design expert, Peter Skillman, who introduced the challenge in a 2006 TED Talk. As Skillman explained, to play the game, small teams compete for exactly 18 minutes in a contest to build the tallest structure out of a basic allotment of raw materials: 20 strands of dry spaghetti, one meter of tape, one piece of string, and one marshmallow. The structure must be strong enough to support the marshmallow, which at the end of 18 minutes must be intact and positioned at the highest point of the structure.

As one might imagine, this exercise inspires a wide variety of structures of varying size, shape, and complexity. Some are impressive; some are not. But it's not the structures that make this all so intriguing. Skillman reported that, by every objective measure, kindergarten-aged children outperform all other groups in creating the tallest towers within the 18-minute time constraint, even beating out engineers.

According to Skillman, the reason children are so much more effective is because they don't waste time on planning and posturing in the way adults do. They just get to work. They set their ideas into motion, experimenting with what works and what doesn't. As the clock ticks, they react to whatever circumstances or new possibilities they encounter along the way. Adults, on the other hand, engage in a sort of pregame ritual in which there is competition for dominance. Once dominance is established, the team defers to those they've identified as the superiors and the building begins.

The inefficiency encountered by the adults is a *coping* problem. The time used for deliberation and power-sorting is time used by the children to build. This gives the children more opportunities to experiment, fail, and then make the necessary adjustments. As I've witnessed in my own facilitation of the marshmallow challenge, when adults encounter a structural flaw or failure, the subsequent adjustment comes rather slow as the team exhausts precious time and energy on giving dominators a chance to assess the situation and formulate their opinions about what the new strategy should be. But it gets worse. Dominating behaviors shut down subordinators who become reticent to share or test their own ideas. So, not only does this cause the team to be limited by the ideas to which it does *not* have access, it has less time to act on the ones it does.

As Skillman explains, "Multiple iterations almost always beat the single-minded commitment to building your first idea." This suggests that any factor tending to limit the number of iterations that a team can attempt will come at the expense of its competitiveness. In a manner similar to what Kathryn Cronin and her colleagues found, dominators in the marshmallow challenge will limit the effectiveness of subordinators and, therefore, the entire team. Energy that should be applied to innovation and experimentation is wasted on the formalities of hierarchy. Children, unburdened by these conditioned patterns of hierarchical thinking, are able to perform as equals in the moment. And when confronted by the challenge of building a crude structure out of spaghetti noodles, tape, and string, they become a chain of commitment, entirely focused on meeting the demands of the urgency before them.

Toleration of Risk. The team *you* lead is more likely to be successful and competitive if it is allowed to be more childlike. This is not to suggest that carelessness or immaturity are somehow advantageous; they are not. But there must be freedom to play and to experiment. Your team must talk about emerging opportunities, hear and consider strange ideas, try things that haven't been attempted before, and learn through experience what works and what doesn't. Risk-takers must be given the latitude to be the pioneers they are wired to be, pushing against the limits of what is currently thought possible. Of course, there will be mistakes and there will be surprises. But if you succumb to the temptation to assert control over your team, giving in to your fear of the unexpected, the long-term damage you cause will likely be much greater than anything you might suffer as the result of people being bold and creative. Like the many springs that keep the fabric of a trampoline secured to its frame, the individual commitment of your team's members will help you withstand the rough and tumble that comes *when*ever and *where*ver ideas are put to action.

Oh, and by the way, if you were wondering what group performs the worst on the marshmallow challenge; according to Peter Skillman, it is business school students. They spend so much time *talking* about the perfect structure that a *good enough* structure never has the chance to be built.

Chapter 19

Sit Gently on the Trampoline

On July 2, 2019, at the age of 94, a leader died. He was born in Allentown, Pennsylvania to Italian-immigrant parents who called him Lido Anthony. Lido became an American original, an automotive manufacturing innovator celebrated for his vision, criticized for his brashness, but always respected for his willingness to be bold and back it up with confident decision-making. He helped invent the Ford Mustang and is credited with pulling Chrysler out of bankruptcy by adopting innovative production methods that allowed multiple vehicle models to be built from a single platform. Some of his critics argue that Chrysler's survival was really the result of a government bailout, but it was Lido Anthony Iacocca, or Lee, as he was known, who convinced the federal government that not only would his plan to revive the sputtering manufacturer work, but that all taxpayer money would be paid back with interest, which it was. Because of his persuade-and-execute reputation, Iacocca was later tapped to spearhead the fundraising for the 1986 restoration of the Statue of Liberty. He also gave serious consideration to running for President of the United States in 1988 until his old friend and Speaker of the House, Tip O'Neil, talked him out of it.

Perhaps it is because of recency-bias that so many contemporary visionaries like Elon Musk, Jeffrey Bezos, Bill Gates, and Steve Jobs are set as the standards for how to grow companies into juggernauts. But as CNN Business reported on the announcement of his death, "there was only one Lee Iacocca."

In his 2007 book, *Where Have All the Leaders Gone?* Iacocca rages about what he saw as a stunning lack of national leadership among America's political elites. In his view, decisions of grave importance were being made without the backbone or thoughtfulness needed to ensure if they should be made at all. Worse, Iacocca blamed America's leaders for being professional pugilists, focused more on trying to out-dominate each other (to use my own terminology) than to inspire widespread commitment toward a common set of goals and values.

To his credit, however, Iacocca didn't resort to the same political mindlessness he sought to expose. Instead, the problem of weak leadership, as he saw it, transcends political parties. He wrote, "And don't tell me it's the fault of right-wing Republicans or liberal Democrats. That's an intellectually lazy argument, and it's part of the reason we're in this stew. We're not just a nation of factions. We're a people. We share common principles and ideals. And we rise and fall together. Where are the voices of leaders who can inspire us to action and make us stand taller?"

A Bit of Signaling. As much respect and admiration as I have for this giant of a business leader and thinker, I would be remiss if I didn't point out that on the cover of *Where Have All the Leaders Gone?* Lee Iacocca is pictured smiling with a cigar in his right hand. If you read his book, you will likely find, as I did, that the cigar has absolutely no relevance to the messages he conveys. In my observation, the cigar is used often to signal superiority, an irreverent celebration of status and its achievement. In fact, according to JR Cigars, the cigar became a symbol of prosperity and celebrity in the early 20th century as the world was gripped in war, controversy, and economic hardship:

"Sports stars such as Babe Ruth were famous for smoking cigars. The Great Bambino was the biggest star in the world, and pictures of him smoking a cigar became iconic. During the Great Depression, another enterprise began to emerge that would further enhance the image of cigar smoking. The American Mafia made millions of dollars during prohibition. For the first time, a criminal enterprise was not just a gang of thugs, but a collection of wealthy, proactive businessmen. Gangsters like Al Capone and Lucky Luciano fancied themselves as CEO's rather than criminals. They took up cigar smoking to further enhance their image of men of wealth, power, and influence."

Even the revered Winston Churchill chewed on cigars as a way to signal British resolve in the face of Adolph Hitler's aggression. As explained by Danor Aliz, writing for Upscale Living Magazine in 2020, "During the Second World War, it's almost impossible to find footage of Churchill without a fine cigar in his mouth. For him, it symbolized more than just wealth and power. It was a symbol of defiance for everything he was fighting against. He puffed the cigar as a way to metaphorize the British strength against Nazi Germany, blowing the smoke into the air, just like how the British would blow the Nazis out of water."

None of this, of course, is to suggest that cigar smokers don't genuinely enjoy their sticks or that every cigar is enjoyed only because of the statement it makes. But a better image for his book would have been a photograph of Lee Iacocca being an equal in the moment, perhaps mingling with line workers at one of Chrysler's manufacturing plants. Any signaling of superiority suggests that some of what Iacocca's critics argue about him might be true, that he enjoyed being the center of attention. As CNN Business reported in its eulogy, "Iacocca's leadership style left a trail of bruised and battered egos and careers — including his own. Many of the automotive industry's great leaders of the last half of the 20th century worked with or for Iacocca and often clashed with him over differing strategies.... Iacocca was willing to take a stand for what he thought was the right way." Lee Iacocca was certainly a handful, but he should be given his due credit as a worthy facilitator of corporate America's exit from the equip-it-and-rip-it industrial age to that of the emerging knowledge-based worker, who would eventually require a corresponding change to how leadership is envisioned and executed. Lee Iacocca's legacy is that of the watchman who stood guard through this transition.

Cut Yourself Some Slack

My purpose for sharing some of the complexities of Lee Iacocca and his approach to leadership is to emphasize something important about dominant leadership styles that you would be wise to recognize in yourself and put to rest as quickly as possible. Dominant leaders see themselves as *the cause*. If there is success to be had, they believe they must be the ones to cause it. If there are results needed, outcomes to create, changes to occur, threats to mitigate, customers to satisfy, or problems to fix, dominant leaders take the position that each of these are effects that must have a cause before they will occur. That cause, of course, must be them. Dominant leaders see themselves as being in the business of causing all of the good things that a team or organization is striving to create. And because the carrying of this burden is so taxing and lonely, dominators enjoy having their *sacrifices* rewarded with appropriate degrees of respect and gratitude. So, they resort to superiority signaling in a variety of forms to let everyone know who's responsible for their teams' success and well-being.

But here's the problem. As the world becomes more complex, and as team members have more access to knowledge and opportunities for personal and professional growth, there is less tolerance for leaders who monopolize the success-building enterprise. High performers want and need to be part of the process of creating positive outcomes, solving difficult problems, and leveraging emerging opportunities. These special individuals are offended and disengaged by dominators who deprive people of the chance to be players in the game. In this new era in which we find ourselves, the most successful leaders will be those who can enable individual and collective greatness through *facilitation* rather than *dominance*.

The Facilitative Leader

As we explored in Chapter 10, a facilitating style of leadership tends to spark and fuel the kinds of conversations from which innovation and problem-solving are born. But it's not easy, and some leaders develop this skill more readily than others. This is because facilitation requires that elusive ability to alternate seamlessly and strategically between positions of dominance and subordination – in one moment being able to control the tone and direction of a conversation and, in the next, allowing others to assert themselves and exact some degree of influence over the direction the team decides to go. Getting in the way of this alternation, or this sharing of superiority, is being chronically stuck in a dominant or subordinate orientation. As we've already discussed, this clogs the interpersonal pipelines through which collaboration receives its most vital nutrient: communication.

Facilitation, therefore, is now the key leadership competency of our time, while coaching has become its most ardent champion. Coaching is a form of facilitated learning in which coaches act as accountability partners to their clients, setting an example for how to facilitate meaningful conversation. It also exposes clients to a way of influencing people through such conversation. This may explain why coaching has become such a useful and popular tool in the development of effective leaders. According to the International Coaching Federation in 2019, coaching was estimated to be a $15 billion industry, with the potential to grow to $20 billion by 2022. During that same year, TrainingIndustry.com estimated that another $3.5 billion was spent specifically on leadership development programs and the acquisition of other products and services from vendors identified as offering leadership development solutions.

Turning Things Around. One of the many reasons why a leader seeks the assistance of a professional coach is to get help correcting what she might describe as a culture that's broken. It often happens that the leader is new to her position and has inherited a hornet's nest. Her people don't get along or are resistant to change – so, turnover is high, productivity is low, attitudes are toxic, and the reputation of the team is about to flame out like a meteorite in the evening sky. She tries to *lean in*, as Cheryl Sandberg encourages her to do, but the more she does, the more she exposes herself to the group's poison. Her upper managers seem to be of no help and, at times, seem to exacerbate the problem by simply avoiding it. But it doesn't matter. She owns it now, and her future will come into question if she doesn't get things turned around. She envisions a stronger and healthier team, and she's put it on herself to be the *cause* that produces the *effect* she is looking for.

I've been there and perhaps you have too. It's a tough place to be. If you serve in positions of leadership long enough, you will find yourself coping with a similar problem, convinced that your team needs to be fixed and that it's your job to fix it. It feels like you're paddling upstream with a gorilla jumping up and down in your canoe. The energy you exhaust to keep things afloat and moving in the right direction leaves you very little in reserve to put toward other critical leadership priorities, such as – *God forbid* – preparing for the future.

The first steps you will take in confronting this kind of a problem begin with acknowledging that it is not a problem for *you alone* to confront. Think not of yourself as the sole cause of the desired outcome but rather the facilitator of the many individual contributions it will take to right the ship. Putting it all on your shoulders, however honorable your intentions may be, is likely to be perceived by a struggling team as superiority signaling, which will intensify any toxicity that already exists. The vestiges of the old superior live within all of us, and as leaders we are easily lured into believing that our so-called superiority bestows upon us the unilateral responsibility of correcting what we, in our infinite wisdom, judge to be the misbehaviors or substandard contributions of inferior performers. But this is the opposite of what it means to be an equal in the moment. By resorting to hierarchical maneuvers in situations that are already inflamed, the flames will burn further out of control, like throwing water on a kitchen grease-fire. The ways of the old superior are likely what caused the toxicity you face, and they will only make problems worse. So, it is best to resist the temptation to follow them.

The key to correcting and preventing any kind of organizational decay, therefore, is giving people ownership of their teams and then facilitating their transition from spectators to players. But before they accept the responsibilities of ownership, something of existential importance must occur first; they must trust that you've truly let go of any emotional attachments you might have to being the one who calls all or most of the shots. They must have confidence that you will be able to hold up your end of the bargain and not step in to dominate the moment something troubles you. It is here that your own credibility is on the line.

Do you want your team to be the best it can be, or don't you? Are you willing to rethink what it means to be a superior entrusted with facilitating the talents of a high-performing team or not? As a leader, your team does not belong to you. You belong to your team. Your people must know that you are committed to empowering *them* with autonomy and self-determination. If they don't, they will abstain from your grand visions and you will have lost a precious opportunity to change things for the better.

So how do you do this? How do you approach your leadership responsibilities in a way that incorporates principles that may seem wildly disjointed from what you're used to? Well, I'd like to have you indulge me for a moment as I walk you through what, for our purposes, we'll call a thought-experiment that helps recognize the right way and wrong way to lead and influence people through times of change.

Attraction and Repulsion. Imagine that in your hands you are holding a bowling ball, one with a bright, glossy, colorful finish that seems to glisten when it's held in the sunlight. It's beautiful; and as far as bowling balls go, it's about as beautiful as it gets. In front of you is a large trampoline, the kind on which children might play in the backyard. But you're not here to play; you're here to conduct an experiment. You begin by gently rolling the bowling ball onto the trampoline where it eventually comes to a stop within a depression created by its own weight. Next, you reach into your pocket and remove a handful of marbles. You roll the marbles onto the trampoline and, as you expect, the marbles find their way to the bowling ball, falling into the same depression where the bowling ball rests.

In conducting this first half of the experiment, you notice that the marbles roll straight toward the bowling ball, and so it might seem as if the marbles are somehow attracted to the bowling ball. But, of course, they are not. Instead, it is the trampoline that guides the marbles toward the bowling ball. This happens because the bowling ball changes the shape of the trampoline's fabric, and it does so not because the ball is bigger, prettier, or shinier than the marbles, but because it has considerably more weight. Any other ball or sphere that comes along, assuming its weight is less than that of the bowling ball, will be guided toward the bowling ball just as the marbles were.

Okay. Next, you decide to make a change to how the experiment is conducted. With the trampoline cleared of all objects, you begin by first rolling the marbles onto the trampoline where they scatter and come to a stop at various random points. Now with your bowling ball, you crawl *underneath* the trampoline and, with both hands, press the bowling ball upward against its underside. Just as before, the bowling ball changes the shape of the trampoline's fabric and, as a result, causes the marbles to move. Only this time, it appears that the marbles are repelled by the bowling ball as they are driven outward toward the edges of the trampoline. Similar to the first phase of your experiment, the bowling ball influences the marbles by changing the shape of the trampoline's fabric. What's different, however, is that when the bowling ball works *against* the existing force of gravity from the *opposite* side of the fabric, it drives the marbles away.

This thought experiment helps us visualize how effective leaders draw people in and how dominators push people away. In so many professional environments today, chain of command is used as the channels through which the work and energies of people are thought to keep people under control. What is often mistaken for leadership is really nothing more than the superficial signaling of superiority. This of course may be sufficient to shape the strategic environment in a way that moves people to action, but not in a way that brings people together into a self-amplifying cauldron of collaborative genius. Too often, chain of command has itself as its top priority and therefore ignores or fights against the collective interests of the team. Without trust, chain of command fails to gain the inspirational heft it takes to bring people inward into a chain of commitment in which there is unified engagement and a mutual effort to advance mutual priorities.

The good news is that sometimes chain of command *does* work. When it does, it's usually because its leaders are effective at facilitating rather than obstructing the growing and sustained commitment of their people. When a chain of command is also a chain of commitment, it is positioned to accomplish amazing things over a long period of time.

For my leadership clients who are trying to facilitate positive organizational change, there is a phrase I use to encourage them, and will use to encourage you: *Sit gently on the trampoline.* Don't be a disturbing or upsetting influence to the members of your team. Direct your energy and focus on trying to be a confident, supportive, and welcoming presence. Draw them in. Be calm and graceful, and give people the space they need to learn, make mistakes, and reconsider old thinking habits. Help them to see a better future made possible by better ways of doing things, and facilitate the conversations and innovations needed for those better ways to reveal themselves. Only give direction when direction is needed and get practiced at asking questions that create opportunities to learn and discuss topics of relevance to your team. The more your presence has an empowering or enabling effect on the people around you, the more they will *fall in* to your space and become committed to opportunities and principles that you all decide, together, provide a reliable pathway to success.

Establish Your Position.   If you want to sit gently but confidently on the trampoline, and if you want to be a facilitative leader who attracts people to the things most important to you, give them good reasons to think and say the following about you:

Her intentions are the same as our intentions

He lives and works on the same side of reality as us

She genuinely cares about the same issues, problems, and opportunities that we do

He is effective, while elevating our effectiveness

She has the integrity to do the right thing, even when it's hard

He is a player, not a spectator; and he has influence over people and circumstances in our strategic environment

You may have personally witnessed or experienced what happens when a manager or decision-maker is perceived to be living in a different reality. It is offensive and demoralizing to be stuck exhausting your energy, time, and talents in the service of a person whose intentions are not aligned with yours. The old superior pushes from underneath the trampoline, content in the knowledge that it has the power to compel people into motion but ignorant of the repulsive and counterproductive impact it has on the commitments people are otherwise willing to make.

People are drawn to leaders they trust, leaders who they sense live on the same side of reality, reacting to the same circumstances, trying to solve the same problems, and working to accomplish the same goals. *She challenges us but she's one of us* is something we might hear about a trustworthy leader who is *in it* with her people and who gives those around her a feeling of relevance and belonging.

A Crisis of Confidence

Like Lee Iacocca, I too sometimes wonder where all the leaders have gone. Something is wrong and it's not just about the old superior holding on for dear life. What's missing is *confidence*. That's right. *Where did all the confidence go?* This is the question we should be asking in this new age of big ideas, big technology, and big possibilities. Particularly in government and elective office, there seems to be a plague of uncertainty and an unwillingness to stand confidently in defense of tightly held principles. So, they learn how to toe a party line or regurgitate talking points. But in the long run, it doesn't project any degree of intellectual or moral self-confidence. And because people are drawn to confidence, today's public leaders have struggled in recent decades to facilitate agreement on the most important issues of the day.

So, what happened? Well, I think at some point confidence became a casualty of the open-mindedness revolution, a revolution that was entirely needed and justified, by the way. After all, history is replete with leaders of limited knowledge, questionable character, and disturbing myopia who nonetheless seemed quite confident in what they were saying and doing. Remember, catastrophe arises when *confusion collides with confidence in a commotion.* And with so many instances of horror in even our recent memories to prove this theorem, confident leaders, for many, have become associated with impending doom. Many public leaders today therefore speak boldly but with an apologetic undertone that implies a lack of confidence or certainty in the messages being conveyed. Without that confidence, it becomes nearly impossible to inspire people.

Confidence is vital to the effort of earning and retaining trust, and only trusting people can be inspired into a consensus or into a chain of commitment. But the *right* kind of confidence is that based on actual knowledge, experience, and the positioning of oneself as an equal in the moment. The old superior struggles in this arena because it likes to project confidence in its signaling of superiority. Chronic dominators push people away and therefore make it harder to access the wide variety of perspectives and ideas that the members of a team could otherwise afford them. The *show* of confidence never has a chance to become *actual* confidence, and everyone but the old superior seems to know it.

CONCLUSION

Begin Again

Each and every one of us is a product of the compiled experiences and exposures we've encountered over the course of our lives, regulating how we conduct ourselves in a variety of situations. Like me, you can probably feel when your reaction to a challenging person or situation seems to originate from deep within you, taking on a life of its own without you being able to control it. It's as if there's a child inside you who's seizing control of your faculties, manipulating you like a puppet. You know it's bad but you can't stop it. All you're capable of doing is hearing the crazy words that fly out of your mouth, sensing the aloof expressions that distort your face, and feeling the sudden stiffness of your body as you react to whatever happened.

As a leader and influencer of people, nothing will erode your confidence faster than having this child take over your reactions in a way that makes you look immature or lacking in confidence. And, make no mistake, leadership requires confidence. If you don't have confidence in yourself, you can't expect that anyone else will. But your confidence must originate from your skills and abilities, not from your institutional powers. And be warned, when you lack confidence you will be tempted to draw energy from the lower branches of your power tree – your rank, stature, and authority – which in turn limits the willingness of your people to draw energy from you.

If this rambunctious child inside of you seems to be out of your control, how do you take back your control so that you can be more intentional and less reactive in how you engage the world and the people in it? After all, your ability to do so will be necessary for you to maximize the amount of self-confidence you will have as a leader. No matter where you are in your career, if you can permanently pacify your inner child – that youngster who feels his needs are being ignored – then you will liberate yourself from his grip and expand your capacity to lead and influence people as an equal in the moment. Your people expect *you* to lead them, not your inner child, and they will be able to tell the difference, I assure you.

Don't feel bad if you're already a high-level executive having years of management experience behind you but find that your inner child comes forth at times to express her discontents. Even if you have an extensive leadership resumé with tons of experience, at any moment you can find yourself in a new situation or confronted by a new personality for which you don't have the skills to properly adapt. Both will require *new* tendencies and *new* thinking habits that help you regain your effectiveness and therefore your confidence. Old dogs *can* learn new tricks, and often do, but only when it becomes clear that the old tricks don't work anymore.

Personal Transformation

If you find the demands of personal change to be intimidating, you have every right to feel this way. Beginning again is tough, but it's something all of us must do at different points in our lives, even when we least expect it. The prospect of confronting and taming a lifetime full of memories and experiences is daunting. But you can be confident that even the most volatile tendencies can be neutralized. That so many people fail to do so over the course of their lives and careers is not because there aren't ways to do it, but because they refuse to spend the time needed to do it. If you are willing to make it a priority and spend the time required, you can transform even the most deeply ingrained parts of your personality without doing harm to the person you really are.

I'm reminded of the impact that time has on our self-improvement when I think back to a sports-related accident I suffered in 2001. With my track & field career far behind me, I was looking for ways to stay in shape, so I started playing tennis with my neighbor, Doug, across the street. Doug was a much better player than me, and one day during a game, I ran for a ball he hit deep into the backcourt. Just as I was about to take a swing at the ball, everything went black. I woke up on the ground with Doug standing over me. Unbeknownst to me, a light breeze had blown open a gate that swung into my path. I ran straight into it at full speed. The direction that my body was moving aligned perfectly with an imaginary straight line running through the gate to the hinges, so it didn't budge when I collided with it. The result was two broken ribs and a massively herniated L1/L2 spinal disc that required surgery. My recovery took several weeks of physical therapy and a variety of prescribed exercises that I did at home each morning and night. Considerable time was invested to accommodate the healing that needed to be done.

One could argue that some of the mental and emotional *accidents* we experience in life are far more traumatic than those we typically experience of a physical nature. But, for some reason, we don't feel it necessary to invest the time that's needed to accommodate the healing. Instead, we plow through it with the force of will, expecting our hurts to heal on their own. But it doesn't work that way. The unique challenge presented by your mental and emotional scars is that they adversely impact the very instrument you use to detect them, which is your brain. You think you're aware of your maladaptive tendencies but, in fact, you may not be. So, you continue to press forward, creating problems for yourself and others that also escape your detection. If the cycle plays out long enough, and if the necessary healing doesn't occur to prevent further damage, your life and career can be forever harmed.

Just as you might do with treating a physical injury, you must invest time and effort to heal the mental and emotional ones. Your intentions *can* overpower your circumstances. You *can* initiate a new beginning. Your future doesn't need to be compromised by your scars. Your personal and professional relationships don't need to be marred by signaling behaviors that you rely upon for temporary relief of your insecurities. By seizing control of your tendencies and reprogramming your reflexive responses to troubling stimuli, you can lessen your dependence on the old superior and clear the path that will lead you and your team to the future of your choosing.

Step 1: Examine Both Sides of Your Strengths

Your strengths are your advantages, those aspects of your physical, mental, and emotional being that give you the upper hand in some way or in certain situations. They make you effective, and you habitually draw on your strengths to deliver value to yourself and others with the most efficiency. You are an old hat at tapping into your strengths because you've had a lifetime of practice. You are hardwired and thoroughly conditioned to leverage your strengths, and so you do it without even thinking about it. It just happens and it works for you. Your strengths give you genuine confidence and it's a great feeling.

It may seem that the opposite of strength is weakness, but this is not the case. Just as there is no such thing as the opposite of a bucket, there is no such thing as the opposite of a strength. To the extent there are certain strengths that are less developed in you, then you can fill them like buckets by working to improve yourself through reflection, practice, and experience. In fact, I encourage you not to burden yourself with thoughts of weakness. Each strength you are naturally wired to exert comes with its own blind spots, sticking points, and temptations. When your strengths are undeveloped or immature, they are raw. When you work to develop and practice them, they become refined. To become overly focused on weakness ignores the valuable opportunity you have to refine and leverage your existing strengths for greater effectiveness. All that matters are your strengths. The ones you have now will be the ones you have in the future. It is best to make them work for you in as many situations as possible.

Now for the hard part. Your strengths are your power. Power can build and power can destroy. Those moments in your life when you find yourself succumbing to your destructive impulses are often the result of your strengths being stuck in the ON position. This would be like an Olympic powerlifter picking up a pencil off the floor using the same effort he would use to clean a stacked bar in competition. Certain people or situations may trigger responses from you that are disproportionate in their intensity. In some instances, you may act out these responses in which case you embarrass yourself, worsen a delicate situation, or compromise a relationship of strategic importance. In other instances, you may hold it all in, causing toxic emotions to fester and eat you up inside, making it more likely that a damaging overreaction will happen at some point in the future.

Changing your reactions to triggers is vital to your professional success, especially if you are in a position of leadership. But it's important to begin simply by understanding your strengths and recognizing the potential they have to serve you or cause you damage, depending on the situation.

As a way to evaluate yourself against an inventory of 34 known strengths identified by the famed positive-psychologist, Don Clifton, I'd like to recommend the book *Strengths Finder 2.0* by Tom Rath. Consider taking the Gallup CliftonStrengths® Assessment to identify your unique pattern of strengths. I then recommend that you work with a Gallup Certified Strengths Coach to refine the strengths you have while taming the naturally occurring blind spots, sticking points, and temptations that might be expected for someone with your particular pattern of strengths.

Step 2: Scan Your History

Your direct experiences and observations have trained you how to protect yourself from harm. If you were ignored, you learned how to get attention. If you were disrespected, you learned how to show your worth. If you were criticized, you learned how to defend yourself. The more you were chronically exposed to the same unpleasant experience, whether it was happening to *you* or you observed it happening to *someone else*, the more efficient and well-trained your reaction to it became. Each subsequent experience *triggers* your reaction, which is now so finely tuned and well-rehearsed that it's reflexive – you can react without even having to think about it.

Hockey goalies are a great example of what it looks like when a reaction becomes a reflex. They've experienced so many shots-on-goal, and they've trained themselves to react so quickly, that when a shot is taken during a game, their bodies seem to know instinctively how to contort into a position necessary to block it. The circuitry of their brains has become optimized to perform this task with maximum efficiency and in minimal time. Even when they are asleep at night or pouring their morning cup of coffee, the circuitry is still there. This circuitry is a strength.

So, what reactions or ways of thinking have *you* developed over the course of your life to execute with lightning speed or unwavering consistency? It's difficult, or perhaps impossible, to get through life without some hardwired tendencies that begin to cause you problems when you reach points in your personal or professional life where you're expected to interact or collaborate with a wide variety of people having their own habits and tendencies. Eventually, you encounter people or situations that seem to trigger reactions that feel out of your control. And when those reactions are perceived as offensive to people whose opinion of you matters, you've got a problem on your hands.

In my experience as a former executive and as a leadership coach, the following are the reflexive reactions that most often seem to get in the way of even the most respected and accomplished professionals:

- Getting defensive when feeling criticized or accused
- Becoming emotional when challenged or questioned
- Controlling others when sensing they are confident
- Controlling others when fearing failure
- Resorting to dominance when becoming a manager
- Being subordinate in the presence of authority
- Misbehaving or acting-out when feeling ignored
- Becoming angry when feeling disrespected
- Procrastinating when feeling obligated
- Being critical of people you trust with your well-being
- Going silent when others are talking
- Compulsively talking when others are silent
- Dragging your feet when a decision must be made
- Becoming animated or explosive when frustrated

My guess is that you can add any number of reflexes to this list, some or all of which may be ones that haunt you on a regular basis. Whatever they may be, they do not change what must be your two primary goals. The first is to stop misinterpreting situations as being dangerous when, in fact, they are no threat to you. The second is to recondition yourself to react to challenging situations without reflex, becoming more deliberate and intentional in how you respond, if you choose to respond at all.

To achieve these goals, you must set the conditions for change to occur, which requires an understanding of how your reflexes developed in the first place. Growth in these areas requires you to distinguish situations that are actually harmful to you from those that aren't. So, taking some time to reflect on the past is a necessary part of shaping your future. Below are some questions you can ponder to help you:

- Since childhood, who were the people in your life in whom you entrusted your physical, mental, and emotional well-being, whether you were aware of it or not?

- In what ways were these people effective in meeting your needs or expectations?

- In what ways were these people ineffective in meeting your needs or expectations?

- At what moments in your life did you feel that your physical, mental, or emotional well-being were being harmed or threatened?

- Whose approval meant the most to you, and what did they do with this trust you placed in them?

- What *people* trigger your reflexive reactions?

- What *situations* trigger your reflexive reactions?

- In what ways do your strengths appear in these reactions?

- What expectations do you place on people that you often perceive are not being met?

- In what ways are these expectations reasonable and in what ways are they not?

- What situations do you encounter that feel threatening to you but, most likely, are not?

- What patterns are repeating in your life and career?

- What do you wish you could do more of or more easily?

- What do you wish you could do less of or with less difficulty?

- In what ways do you seek comfort from the old superior?

- In what ways can you think and behave with more intention, awareness, and collaboration?

Step 3: Become Aware of Triggers as They Happen

Psychological reflexes are intimidating because they hold so much power over us. Among these reactions are dominance, micromanagement, and other forms of control to which you may resort when you feel threatened or insecure. Becoming aware of your triggers exactly when they are happening is a key to releasing their grip on you. Until that time comes, you may find yourself frustrated after the fact, believing that hindsight is too late to the party, but it isn't. Recognizing you've been triggered, even after it happens, is still a good habit to get into because the time that lapses between the trigger and your acknowledgment of it will become shorter and shorter with experience and practice. With even more experience and practice, you will see the trigger coming *before* it happens, allowing you to avert what might've become an unpleasant or volatile situation. This puts you in control, allowing you to *choose* your response rather than your inner child doing it for you.

Step 4: Create Therapeutic Repetitions

In the average week, month, or year, your triggers may not occur often enough for you to get the amount of practice or experience needed for reconditioning to take place. This leaves lots of time between each occurrence for you to think about your triggers and imagine your reflexive responses. All this does is reinforce your existing brain circuitry by replaying, over and over again, the same cause-and-effect association that you're trying to eliminate. *Trigger, reflex. Trigger, reflex.* Again and again, becoming more and more ingrained in your psyche and, therefore, harder and harder to reprogram.

The good news is that you can use these same mental processes to your advantage. You can replay, in your mind, a trigger followed by a thoughtful and responsible reaction, one that does no harm and may even reinforce your effectiveness and credibility. *Trigger, choice. Trigger, choice.* Again and again, becoming more and more ingrained in your psyche and, therefore, destined to replace the reflex that's caused you so many problems in the past. But for this to work, you have to imagine it over and over again. Look, you've likely spent years reinforcing your reflexes and they won't go away on their own. You have to work at it. You have to work *hard* at it. Think of it as a form of meditation. If you really want to get rid of a reflex, sit down, close your eyes, and spend 20 minutes every day imagining yourself in a triggering situation, but choosing your preferred response instead of your typical reflex. Over and over again. With enough of these therapeutic repetitions, you will train yourself to react to what once were troubling situations but are now entirely under your control. The only thing that is preventing the reprogramming of your circuitry is failing to invest the necessary time to do the work and therefore not getting the necessary number of repetitions.

Patience is a Virtue

Keep in mind that it could take you weeks or months – in the worst cases, even years – to completely eliminate your reflexive responses. It's critically important that you take whatever time is required. The very act of subjecting yourself to this exercise will begin to change your behaviors without you even realizing it. Especially if you are leader, your team is counting on you to free yourself of your reflexes. Let me take a moment to elaborate on this a bit further.

Everyone has tendencies that cause problems in certain situations. But most people aren't in the position of having to lead a team, so they simply navigate the turbulence caused by their tendencies without any incentive to actually eliminate them. They say the wrong things at the wrong times, they annoy or offend people, or perhaps they're just selfish and everyone knows it. If engineering a change to one's personality isn't perceived as delivering a potential benefit, she won't be inspired to attempt it. She'll be happy to just get on with life and accept the awkward moments as they come.

But when you're a leader and people are counting you, opportunities to improve can never be ignored. Discovering that certain people or situations awaken your inner child is a call to action. Most likely, your continued effectiveness (not to mention your reputation and confidence) will count on it.

You can't just wish your dysfunctional tendencies away, nor can you wish your *desired* tendencies into existence. When you reflexively react to situations in which you feel like you momentarily lose control, you do so because you are protecting a wound. You're flinching. Somewhere in your consciousness is an open emotional sore that gets inflamed in specific kinds of circumstances. This keeps you on alert so that you can quickly marshal your energies to protect the sore. The result is a peculiar behavior of some sort that may seem excessively defensive for the situation, making you appear dysregulated to observers. The only way to relieve the defensiveness is to do the work necessary to find and heal the emotional sore. The steps I've outlined above will help you heal as a person and as a leader.

Trust Extended is Trust Earned

In their 2010 bestseller, *Rework*, Jason Fried and David Heinemeier Hansson of Basecamp explain how internal bureaucratic controls arise from assumptions about people that they need to be controlled if they are to perform at their best. Control, such as that exerted by organizational policies, becomes the institutionalized manifestation of distrust. "Policies are organizational scar tissue. They are codified overreactions to situations that are unlikely to happen again."

Fear is the underlying emotion of control and the many reflexive behaviors that come with it. It is also the underlying emotion of the old superior – fear of losing rank, fear of losing market share, fear of people making mistakes, fear of having one's rank, stature, and authority disrespected, fear of moving backwards in the organizational hierarchy, and fear of employees taking advantage of any freedoms or autonomy they are granted by their leaders. The hierarchical behaviors that are so common to the old superior are reflexes that have been conditioned over generations and generations of experience and observation. Too often it is believed that through dominance and control, leaders give their people the best chance to succeed. People, they think, are their own worst enemies, and *policies* are their savior.

Our current understanding of the enormous costs associated with distrust is relatively new and was likely accelerated by personal computers and the internet, both of which were paradigmatic revolutions that gave people historic power and control over their own lives and careers. The workforce is now saturated with professionals who work not simply because they have to but because they want to. They have the ability and willingness to volunteer their best efforts in a cause that means something to them. Direct orders, bullying, overreaching policies, and other forms of hierarchical gamesmanship do little but to suppress these energies. More than ever before, business and government must have reliable systems and practices in place to ensure the recruitment, selection, and hiring of people who can be *and will be* trusted to do their best.

In *The Speed of Trust: The One Thing That Changes Everything*, author Stephen M.R. Covey defines trust as confidence born of character and competence. That it takes competence to be an effective leader is not exactly rocket science. But to fully appreciate the amount of character it takes to resist the temptations of the old superior, you must be willing to stare it down and have the courage to champion a different and better way of influencing people. You must become a facilitator of excellence, a motivator of commitment, and a witness to what you see is possible. All the while, you must be willing and able to allow *yourself* to be facilitated, to have *your* own intentions challenged, and to listen carefully to the testimony of your people. As good as you may be and as much experience and skill as you may have, you will never be better or stronger than a team of committed professionals working together toward a common cause.

Those who insist on the ways of the old superior will continue to feel threatened by the prospect of a thriving team and will do everything possible to keep that team under some form of control. But if you are willing to sit gently and confidently on the trampoline, and if you are willing to let go and take your place as an equal in the moment, you will find that your ability to influence and connect with your people will grow in ways you might never have imagined. Safe and secure in the chain of commitment that surrounds you, no unexpected circumstance will be able to get in the way of your intentions.

You, my friend, are the *new superior*.

EPILOGUE

Strength and Sweetness

During the writing of this book, my childhood idol died after a short and painful bout of pancreatic cancer. His name was Kevin Collins, and I named my son after him. He was only 64, leaving behind his wife and two grown children. Kevin was a special man for many reasons, not the least of which was his rare combination of enormous physical strength, wicked athleticism, and a gentle sweetness that was as disarming as it was welcoming. On the football field he was an animal, playing on the defensive side of the ball for Central Michigan University. He went on to practice briefly with the Miami Dolphins before an injury ended his career. He then became a deputy for the Los Angeles County Sheriff's Office before another injury forced him to take disability, bringing his brief career in law enforcement to a close. Even in the photograph I included in the dedication of this book, you see Kevin with a bright smile on his face, an expression of warmth and joy that's often lacking in the grumpy scowls that are so common in uniformed police portraits, even today.

Growing up, my parents made a point to emphasize what they seemed to love most about Kevin, which was how he blended his strength with his sweetness. They wanted me to be the same way. I doubt very much that I've met the standard that Kevin set but I feel pretty confident that striving for it has served me well in both my personal and professional pursuits. It is why I make such an effort to remind my clients of the importance of not getting stuck in their strengths and tendencies.

By recognizing the value of being fluid and flexible in our relationships, we can also gain insight into why romantic relationships, marriages, or other kinds of life partnerships are so challenging. It is because within each of us there is both a superior and an inferior. Within every woman is a little girl, just as there is a little boy within every man. Within every mother is a daughter and within every daughter, a mother. Within every father is a son, and within every son, a father. One of the greatest challenges that exists in this life is to be and remain in supportive, loving, life-long relationships with those we can trust to be our equals in the moment.

Although I have no training or education in child psychology, my practice as a coach, in tandem with some personal experience, has taught me how damaging it is when parents get stuck in positions of superiority or subordination while raising their children. Their children may never have an opportunity to learn, through direct observation, how to alternate effectively between the two. I have observed the effects of this in my expert witnessing classes where I've encountered students who seem unable to express themselves in an audible voice. As we simulate courtroom testimony, I find myself having to remind them, *use your voice*, but to no avail. One memorable student shared with me that her father was a very dominant personality in her household when she was a child. She was conditioned over many years to speak softly and to not challenge her father's position as the superior personality in the home, which was also how her mother coped with his dominance. She experienced the same feelings when testifying in court in front of intimidating, high-powered attorneys, unwilling to assert herself as an authority. She expressed genuine gratitude for my bringing to her attention her whispering voice, making a remarkable effort to speak louder as the class went on, even though I knew it was hard for her to do.

Before I close, I want to share with you that I am a recovering, amiable, low-voltage disciple of the old superior, to steal a few words from my favorite essayist, George Will. I was never a bully or anything like that, but up to the point when I became a forensic laboratory director at the young age of 30, my notions of leadership were rather self-absorbed. I interpreted my promotion as a reward, and I felt just the slightest tinge of desire to have my newfound superiority admired and celebrated. *Kiss my ring, please.*

But then came the day in January 2002 when my wife and I brought home our newborn daughter, Karen, from the hospital. She was perfect, but as all babies do, she cried incessantly and was impressively loud in doing so. One evening while I was changing Karen's diaper, my 2½ year-old son, Kevin, was sitting on a rocking chair we'd recently purchased for Karen's feedings. Once again, Karen started wailing. In the corner of my eye, I could see Kevin beating himself in the head, as if Karen's crying was causing him physical pain. I turned and watched with horror. It was the very first sign that something was wrong, and the beginning of my new life as the father of a son with autism.

If I could go back in time to the moment of Kevin's birth and somehow undo his autism, part of me would do it gladly, but another part wouldn't. I would be more than happy to trade in all of the epileptic seizures, all of the appointments with therapists and neurologists, all of the disruptions to our household, all of the worries about Kevin's future, all of the coping with Kevin being unable to fully care for himself, and finally my divorce, which no-doubt was made more likely by the stress that Kevin's disorder had on our 20-year marriage.

But I wouldn't want to undo how Kevin's disability changed me as a man and as a leader. Kevin's autism and its comorbidities broke me. There was nothing I could do to father it all away. There was nothing I could do to *cause* the disappearance of Kevin's many symptoms. I had no choice but to accept the cards as they were dealt. As a result, I became more compassionate. I learned how to accept and work with personal limitations. I became more patient, graceful, and understanding. I learned the importance of focusing on strengths to make your way in this world. And perhaps the most important lesson of all: I learned that there is no such thing as normal. Every human being is a living, breathing miracle, with unique attributes, tendencies, and capacities for contribution that are worthy of our respect and appreciation.

Which circles us all the way back to where we began on this journey of ours; there is a choice to be made. What kind of leader do you choose to be? What kind of impact will you choose to have on people? *Leadership emerges naturally when purpose is threatened by circumstance in the presence of a champion.* If a 15-year-old schoolgirl in Pakistan can defy the Taliban and risk her life championing the rights of girls to receive an education, you can overcome whatever resistance might be keeping you or your team from doing the best work of your lives. What is the purpose you should be protecting? What is the threat that lurks in the shadows to undermine it? These are two questions that I encourage you to spend much time thinking about, especially if you are entrusted with the care of a team. It is the answers to these questions that will determine the kind of leader you need to be.

Acknowledgments

Success is usually the result of a collaborative effort and the combined contributions of many people who have a positive impact on our individual journeys. This is not to suggest that I've somehow reached a point of success with which I'm satisfied. I haven't; and if you think that what I know is impressive in any way, what I *don't* know will utterly astound you. This book, however, is a success of a special sort for me, the culmination of a long personal journey that has come with many ups and downs, trials and tribulations, successes and disappointments. Along this journey there have been certain people who've been especially important to my growth as a coach, consultant, and writer.

First, I'd like to thank my friend Donna Gardner, a fellow Gallup Certified Strengths Coach for introducing me to CliftonStrengths® and the power it has to transform lives and careers. Donna, along with the other amazing researchers and coaches at Gallup have had a profound influence on how I think about coaching and the promise it holds for clients seeking to make a positive difference in their lives. I look forward to many years of collaboration and learning with the Gallup family.

I'd also like to extend my thanks to Leena Rinne and Kory Kogan for the opportunity they gave me to work with and learn from the amazing team of professionals at Franklin Covey in Salt Lake City, where some of the most impactful thinking in the areas of organizational leadership and teamwork is happening every day. Having the chance to collaborate with Franklin Covey was one of the greatest professional experiences of my life.

Other than my family, perhaps no human being has had more of an impact on my understanding of leadership and of simply how to be a good human being than Albert Fracassa, the legendary and retired head football coach at Brother Rice High School in suburban Detroit. Coach

Fracassa is one of the winningest coaches in the history of high school football in the United States, and his success was the direct result of being a master motivator and teaching his boys about leadership. *Do things right all the time* was one of the many inspirational mottos he used to commemorate each new season. It was a primary focus of his life to help and witness young men learn how to overcome adversity in the pursuit of personal greatness. Many were the early mornings when I sat with teammates in Coach Fracassa's Leadership Awareness Workshops in which we discussed leadership and listened to guest speakers share their stories and perspectives about how to influence people the right way. How many high school boys get a chance to be exposed to this kind of education so early in their lives? Not many. Not many, at all.

Michael Popson was my high school track coach and taught me about self-restraint and the importance of conducting myself with class. He died too early in a car accident that happened not far from where my office is now located. He encouraged me to throw the discus at Michigan State, where another man I want to acknowledge, Coach Jim Bibbs, was the head track & field coach. A former world-record setting sprinter, Coach Bibbs loved his boys and we always knew he was right there with us, competing, striving, and learning.

My high school education also put me in the presence of an amazing and quirky English teacher, Marcel Gagnon, who had a profound impact on my development as a writer. I was hardly the best of his students, but to this day I remember specific lessons that he taught about the art of writing, and I credit him with much of the success I've had as an author. Any evidence of poor writing in this work is my fault, not his.

More recently, I've had some high-impact professionals to thank for being sounding-boards in matters related to leadership, psychology, and coaching. Donna Sternicki, an HR leader and coach at the Taubman Company near Detroit, has been a breath of fresh air in my personal and professional life, encouraging me to question my own views and notions about leadership and expanding my appreciation for some of the unique challenges that exist in corporate America today. Joseph Bono, a former president of the American Academy of Forensic Sciences, has been a great friend and mentor over the years, demonstrating how effective leadership can, and often does, originate from very kind, unassuming individuals whose hearts are much bigger than their egos.

I also want to thank those who took the time to review my manuscript prior to publication, providing candid and creative input that allowed me to make major improvements leading to the final copy. Reading for editorial purposes is labor intensive and these individuals took time from their very busy schedules to help me complete this project. While some wished not to be mentioned, I'd like to extend my deepest thanks to Stacy Hissong and Shannon Thackray for their amazing work and attention to detail. The changes they recommended enhanced the quality of the final product to a degree that both pleased and surprised me. That's what great editors do.

I'd also like to thank my friend and fellow author, Keith Kindred, for the many interesting and enlightening conversations that we enjoy about the art of writing. I find his insights and passion for the written word to be infectious and inspiring.

Finally, I wish to extend my very personal and heartfelt thanks to Barbara and Albert Gimesky, the dearest friends of my mom and dad who became sources of unconditional love and encouragement in the years following my parents' deaths. The presence they continue to have in my life is both grounding and sustaining. I love you both.

About the Author

John Collins is a leadership and expertise coach specializing in working with clients in authoritative, high-stakes occupations. He started his private practice in 2013 after retiring his award-winning, 20-year career in forensic science, having served as the director of forensic science for the State of Michigan. He is also the  author of three books on leadership, professionalism, and public policy in forensic science. As a facilitator, John's range of experience is unmatched, having facilitated corporate strategy retreats, as well as highly sensitive domestic and international meetings on behalf of the United States Government. John's career highlights include his part in the forensic investigation of the Atlanta serial bombings, which included the bombing of the 1996 Olympics in Atlanta (for which he received a commendation from the Department of the Treasury), as well as his 2013 participation in a historic meeting with Attorney General Eric Holder and other experts to discuss solutions to gun violence following the Sandy Hook Elementary School shooting. In his practice, John combines principles of executive coaching and leadership education with forensic analytical methods that quickly and accurately identify opportunities for his clients to improve their professional effectiveness. John has a master's degree in Organizational Management and is formally certified as a senior HR professional by the Society for Human Resource Management (SHRM). In 2012, John was trained as a professional coach by the College of Executive Coaching, and he became certified as a Gallup Strengths Coach in 2022. He lives and works near Detroit.